Cultural Selection

Cultural
Selection.

GARY TAYLOR

BasicBooks
A Division of HarperCollins*Publishers*

Published by BasicBooks,
A Division of HarperCollins Publishers, Inc.

Library of Congress Cataloging-in-Publication Data
    Taylor, Gary, 1953–
        Cultural selection / Gary Taylor.
            p.   cm.
        Includes index.
        ISBN 0-465-04488-3
        1. Culture—History.   2. Social evolution.   3. Arts—History.   I. Title.
CB151.T28   1996
306.4'09—dc20   95-44536
                                                                      CIP

96 97 98 99 ❖/RRD 9 8 7 6 5 4 3 2 1

This book is dedicated to
REBECCA GERMONPREZ
who made me and let me
write it

Contents

Illustrations

Human Remains.

I will crawl through my past
Over stones, blood, and glass
In the ruins

MELISSA ETHERIDGE

P art of the meaning of Stonehenge is that we do not remember what it means. Like a string tied around a finger, the circle of stones was deliberately put there to remind us of something; the string remains, but we have forgotten exactly what it represents.

Whatever it meant, Stonehenge was meant to last. For the purposes of astronomical observation, its latitude and orientation are crucial, but the construction materials were optional. Wooden buildings served similar ritual functions elsewhere. But wood decays or burns. Stone keeps.

Whatever it meant, Stonehenge must have meant a lot. Construction of the high bank and outer ditch alone required at least thirty thousand unit hours of labor. Each of the seventy-seven sarsen stones would have taken a thousand or more people two months to drag from the Marlborough Downs.

Whatever it meant, Stonehenge meant different things to different people. Thousands built it, but the space within the sarsens could accommodate no more than twenty or thirty people. Many of the fifty-six evenly spaced chalk pits, which surround the central circle like a necklace, contain the remains of human cremations, but those burials can account for only a tiny fraction of the community that built and used Stonehenge for centuries.

Whatever it meant, Stonehenge's meanings depended upon collective memory. The astronomical patterns of sunrise, moonrise, and eclipse, which the builders recollected in the disposition of their collection of stones, could have been ascertained only through centuries of accumulated observations.

Endurance, significance, difference, remembrance—these are the constants of human culture. Stonehenge is the fossil of a community that once danced and sang and created, but is now dead. Like other fossils, it supplements our knowledge of life by pointing toward forms of being that are no longer present. Fossils, biological or cultural, enable us to link the living and the dead, the present and the absent, in patterns that become visible only across time. This book attempts to describe those patterns, which shape our own experience now as much as they shaped human experience five thousand years ago.

Why do we behave in this way? Why do people make things like Stonehenge? Why do other people make things so unlike Stonehenge? Why do we remember some of the things people have made, and not others? What are the laws of cultural selection?

The Death
of Culture.

Now I'm dead in my grave with my lips moving
and every schoolboy repeating the words by heart
OSIP MANDELSTAM

In 1934 the Russian poet Osip Mandelstam was arrested. After reciting a poem denouncing Josef Stalin ("he rolls the executions on his tongue like berries"), Mandelstam was imprisoned, then sent into internal exile. He tried to commit suicide, but he failed, survived, and continued to write verses like the one I have quoted. In 1938 he was arrested again and died soon after, perhaps of a heart attack, on his way to the labor camps. Between 1930 and 1960, none of his writing was in print in the Soviet Union; his collected works were not published in his native country until four decades after his death. During that period of persecution and neglect, his unpublished work was preserved by his widow, Nadezhda. She became a fugitive, hiding rolled-up copies of his songs in the handle of a saucepan, and memorizing everything, so that his work would survive even if the manuscripts were found and confiscated.

Nadezhda Mandelstam was, literally and figuratively, the human carrier of Osip's memory. In the 1970s, she published two memoirs and oversaw a Leningrad edition of her husband's poems. For forty-two years, Nadezhda lived for and preserved the memory of her dead poet-husband. Before she died, she had communicated that memory to millions.

Although exemplary, the story of Nadezhda Mandelstam is not unique. After the American artist George Bellows died unexpectedly in 1925 at the age of forty-two, his wife Emma organized almost immediately an exhibition of his lithographs, then invested the next thirty-five years in nurturing his reputation, supervising reproductions, and releasing his six hundred unsold paintings a few at a time in annual shows—never glutting the market, but never permitting Bellows to vanish for long from public view. The posthumous kingdom of T. S. Eliot has been ruled for more than three decades by his second wife, dowager queen Valerie. Jealously, she defends the old frontiers of copyright; periodically, she sorties out to conquer new territory (*The Waste Land Facsimile, The Letters*).

Such dedication to the dead is not limited to the twentieth century or to widows. In ancient rural societies, grandmothers were chiefly responsible for teaching the young: for most of human history, the great tradition has been, literally, an "old wives' tale." Vincent Van Gogh sold only one painting in his lifetime; the preservation of the rest we owe to his brother, as we owe the preservation of most of the work of Sir Philip Sidney to his sister, and most of John Donne to his son. Our knowledge and admiration of Socrates derives almost entirely from the work of his pupil Plato; our adoration of Jesus from the acts of his apostles, and the four conflicting biographies of him collected in the posthumous Gospels. The author of the first autobiography in English, Margery Kempe, could not write or read; her book survives only because a priest agreed to write down what she dictated. Kafka owes his reputation, and the publication of all his novels, to the devotion of his friend and executor, Max Brod. Seven years after William Shakespeare's death, his *Comedies, Histories, and Tragedies* were collected into a single large and expensive volume, where about half of them were published for the first time; the preface was signed by John Heminges and Henry Condell, two fellow actors who had worked with Shakespeare for virtually his entire professional life. In a study of etchings, the sociologists Gladys Engel Lang and Kurt Lang demonstrated that a crucial determinant of artistic reputation is the availability of *someone* who, after the artist's death, has a stake in preserving his or her memory. Husband, wife, child, parent, grandparent, brother, sister, pupil, priest, friend—there are as many kinds of survivor as there are kinds of human relationship and genres of human achievement.

Culture is the gift of the survivor. It is always bereaved, always retrospective, always at war with the present. And anecdotes like the story of Osip and Nadezhda Mandelstam are not just human-interest footnotes to literary history. They encapsulate the very mechanism by which culture is made. Such stories are all simple and similar. They have three things in common: a death, a survivor, a struggle.

STORIES
A Death

In 1968 the French intellectual Roland Barthes announced "the death of the author." This obituary has been taken as a revolutionary manifesto, typical of all that was good or bad about deconstruction or the sixties. But culture has always died. Barthes himself is now dead. So are many others—Paul de Man, Michel Foucault, Jacques Lacan, dead authors interred in the pantheon of postmodernism. As I am writing this, my radio informs me of the death of the director Federico Fellini, of his body lying in state in Film Studio Five, of his state funeral. The death of Osip Mandelstam was not announced on Soviet radio; we do not know when, exactly, he died, because the state had already rendered him invisible, dead socially before he was physically. Mandelstam died without our knowing it. As you are reading this page, other artists are dying, unattended by the mass media. Every minute, somewhere, a creator is dying.

Death is the foundation of culture. We look at images, at buildings, carvings, drawings, engravings, paintings, early advertisements, posters, photographs, and films, all of them made by people who are now dead. We listen to music composed by people who are now dead. We commune with our gods using prayers and rituals and spiritual exercises recommended by people who are now dead. We read texts by and about people who are now dead. We obey laws written by people who are now dead. Our lives are regulated by institutions founded by people who are now dead. We are here surrounded by, we are at this moment employing, objects manufactured using techniques invented and developed by people who are now dead. We speak a language taught us by people who may well already be dead; certainly, most of those who taught it to us learned it from people who are now dead. We are enveloped by the remains of people who are now dead just as surely as we are enveloped by air.

A Survivor

The environment and material of our lives, physical and intellectual, is possible only because someone survived, someone who remembered what the dead had done, someone who passed on that memory. What has been done, thought, written, or spoken is not culture; culture is only the fraction that is remembered. In Greek myth, Memory (Mnemosyne) was the mother of the Muses, the source of comedy, tragedy, history, music, astronomy, dance, sacred hymns, and heroic and erotic poetry. From Stonehenge to Hollywood, culture is born of memory.

Even death is a memory. That is the defining thing that we humans remember, that we will, at least physically, die. How do we know we will die? Because we remember the deaths of others; because we remember being told that every living thing dies; because those who told us about mortality remembered other deaths, remembered being told what they in turn told us. Every living adult is a survivor who remembers others who have not survived. The history of culture is a history of the memories of survivors.

So, to understand culture, we first have to understand memory. But what is memory?

That question continues to exercise neuroscientists, philosophers, psychologists, and sociologists, but we can begin with the simplest answer, with the single property of memory that precedes and shapes all others. Memory is an action. Memory is performed. Nadezhda Mandelstam read her husband's poems, repeated their words over and over, aloud and in her head, until she could repeat them perfectly without seeing them; she hid the texts, she hid herself, and then she came out of hiding, and brought them out of hiding; she spoke, she wrote, she published.

Memory—as Nadezhda's example reminds us—is an expenditure of powers. It would have been so much easier not to memorize the poems, not to keep track at every moment of every place where she had hidden every piece of paper, not to move so many times, not to carry those memories on her back every time she moved. Of course, most of the time memory is not so much work. But it is always work. It takes time and energy. It is always a struggle: against inertia, against indifference or hostility, against the relentless decay of things and thoughts.

A Struggle

Every survivor remembers that she is mortal. To protect the memory she carries, she must survive until she can pass it to another carrier. If memory stands still, it will die; it can survive, it can fulfill its obligation to the dead, only by communicating what it has to someone else. Memory is rabid; it is driven by a need to infect others, a compulsion to repeat itself. For a lifetime, Nadezhda Mandelstam fought to persuade others to remember her memories.

The "culture wars" of the last decade, the angry debates about "political correctness," the "scandals" provoked by the politics of Paul de Man or the sexual habits of Michel Foucault, are simply the latest skirmishes in the same interminable struggle. They are all disputes over the right to rule memory. When E. D. Hirsch laments the decline of *Cultural Literacy*, when the *Wall Street Journal* denounces changes in the curriculum at Stanford University, when Secretary of Education William Bennett urges us *To Reclaim a Legacy*, when Harold Bloom hosannas *The Western Canon* and damns "the School of Resentment," when Pat Buchanan as part of his campaign for the Republican presidential nomination gives a speech at Duke University attacking modern critics of Shakespeare, when Robert Hughes complains about a *Culture of Complaint*, they are all trying to ensure that the next generation will remember what an older generation remembers. They are fighting, like Nadezhda Mandelstam, to preserve the memory of what they love.

But the resources of the human memory, like those of even the richest human economy, are finite. If one person is relatively rich, another will be relatively poor. If one person or poem is remembered, another will be forgotten. Memory depends upon forgetting, just as the freedom of classical Rome and antebellum America depended upon slavery. Within the human brain, only a fraction of what is held temporarily in short-term memory is translated into long-term mental storage. Those who loudly enjoin us to "Remember!" are also, always, silently insisting that we forget: forget something else, which seems to them less important than what they demand that we remember. Choices must be made, and then they must be made again, and yesterday's choices are not necessarily today's. Because the dying of human carriers never ceases, the need to pass on memories to new carriers never ends, and so society never stops asking itself, "Whose memories will prevail?"

Comrade Josef Stalin answered that question by having Osip Mandelstam arrested, tortured, and exiled. Winston Churchill's widow answered it by destroying Graham Sutherland's portrait of her husband. Senator Jesse Helms answered it by demanding that the National Endowment for the Arts stop funding obscene art. The Czechoslovakian Communist Party answered it by imprisoning Václav Havel. The Ayatollah Khomeini answered it by calling upon Muslims to kill Salmon Rushdie. The undesirable memory is regarded by the guardians of the present as a communicable virus, rapidly reproducing itself, infecting society; those who are already contaminated must be destroyed, or quarantined, or cured, before they infect others.

Such loss, such repression, cannot be dismissed as an unfortunate accident or an undesirable anomaly. To select what will live requires us to select what will die. Culture is often violently made. For the Greeks, the first and greatest human poet was Orpheus—who was in the end torn to pieces (mythologically) by an angry crowd of pagan women. An angry crowd of Christian men tore to pieces (actually) the first famous woman mathematician, Hypatia, in Alexandria in A.D. 415. Sometimes the makers of culture are deliberately killed (the pagan Socrates, the Jew Jesus, the atheist Christopher Marlowe); sometimes they kill themselves (the poet Sylvia Plath, the physicist Ludwig Boltzmann); sometimes they are sent into foreign exile, where no one at home can hear what they say (the poet Ovid, the novelist Aleksandr Solzhenitsyn); sometimes they are exiled to mental asylums, where no one will care what they say (the poets John Clare, Ezra Pound, and Joseph Brodsky).

The new always threatens the old. In 1824 Sir Walter Scott, writing Lord Byron's obituary, compared the dead young poet to "the noble victim of the bull-fight . . . maddened by the squibs, darts, and petty annoyances of the unworthy crowds beyond the lists." In 1864 Victor Hugo concluded that "a genius is an accused man," and that "to throw stones at men of genius is a general law." Images of embattled creativity have appealed to creators in all media. Galileo, imprisoned by the Inquisition, still inspires scientists and playwrights. Painters and sculptors have often portrayed Marsyas, who, thinking himself a better musician than Apollo, was flayed by that god. And the most popular and potent icon in Western art for two millennia has been the image of a crucified creator.

A Death

We have returned to where we started. The struggle for cultural supremacy is a war to the death, a war fought over the dead. On the final morning of their defense of the pass at Thermopylae in 480 B.C., three hundred Spartans charged the whole Persian army; their leader, King Leonidas of Sparta, was killed early in the fighting, "and over the corpse of Leonidas, Persians and Spartans jostled and fought hard, and the Greeks heroically retrieved it, and four times drove off the enemy." All these Greeks were going to die, and they knew it; they knew that a flanking Persian battalion was about to enter the other end of the pass and attack them from the rear. Nevertheless, the doomed survivors of the initial killing fought to protect, as long as they could, the body of their dead commander. And after they had all been slaughtered, the Persian King Xerxes walked among the corpses, "and finding that of Leonidas, whom he recognized as the king and commander of the Spartans, he ordered the head to be cut off, and the trunk crucified." Xerxes defaced what the Greeks fought to preserve.

Although the Persians ruined the body, the Greeks preserved the memory. The invaders were routed at the battles of Salamis and Plataea; at Plataea, the Spartans annihilated the Persian elite corps and thereby achieved "the vengeance which was due to them for the slaughter of Leonidas." The memory of Thermopylae helped defeat the Persians at Plataea. And after the war, the Greeks erected a memorial column at Thermopylae, bearing the names of all three hundred Spartans. And the poet Simonides wrote their epitaph:

> Oh, stranger, take this last dispatch to Sparta:
> Report we did what they required, and died.

And the Greek historian Herodotus, the founder of European historiography, told the whole story in a book that can still be found in most school and town libraries in the West. Like everyone else who writes about the battle of Thermopylae, I have been quoting Herodotus. Even in Turkey, modern textbooks owe more to Herodotus than to native sources.

A Survivor

Herodotus wrote his book, as he tells us in its opening sentence, "in the hope of preserving from decay the remembrance of what men have done." The three hundred Spartans all died that morning at Thermopylae; we know what happened to them only because Herodotus interrogated witnesses on both sides, collecting and organizing and writing down everything he could discover about the Greek-Persian wars.

In the making of culture, who is more important, Leonidas or Herodotus? The hero or the historian? Osip or Nadezhda? Samuel Johnson or his biographer, James Boswell? Without the survivor, nothing would be remembered; without the maker, there would be nothing to remember. Is it the artist who matters, or the interpreter? Do we remember certain human actions because of the intrinsic "greatness" of past achievements or because they appeal to the present "ideology" of a powerful community?

But the relationship between maker and survivor is even more complicated than these questions suggest. During his exile, Osip Mandelstam was utterly dependent emotionally on Nadezhda; without her, he was simply unable to go on. This kind of dependence is not an individual aberration, but symptomatic of a cultural norm. The maker, after all, knows or hopes there will be a survivor, and his actions are motivated, at least in part, by the desire to make a particular impression on that survivor. For instance, why did Leonidas not retreat when he learned that the Persians were about to outflank him? Most of the allied Greek army chose to fall back, preserving itself for later battles, but Leonidas and his Spartans stayed. Herodotus considers several explanations. There may have been disagreements in the allied command, and it would not be surprising if some of the troops Leonidas sent away "were disheartened and unwilling to face the danger to which his own mind was made up." The Spartans' final suicidal resistance that morning allowed the main body of allied troops to retreat intact, without being routed by a triumphant Persian army chasing their heels. But Herodotus believes that Leonidas was motivated above all by the knowledge that, "if he stayed, glory awaited him," and that he wished "to secure the whole glory for the Spartans." Leonidas, that is, fully expected the sacrifice of the three hundred to be remembered by the Persians, by the Spartans, and by the Greek allies—just as Osip Mandelstam anticipated every schoolboy repeating his words by heart.

Strategically, the memory of Thermopylae helped dishearten the Persians and inspire the Greeks. Leonidas made an example of himself and his men; he set a standard of heroic resistance against insuperable odds. This, too, is normal, for artists as well as infantrymen. The living are measured by a standard set by the remembered achievements of the dead. Every maker is shaped and judged by comparison with the memory of famous earlier makers.

Every maker, in other words, is also a survivor. This fact is recognized in many cultures. For instance, the most famous episode in the myth of the poet Orpheus—an episode celebrated in seventeenth-century opera and twentieth-century film alike—is his descent into hell to recover his dead wife Eurydice. A very large proportion of the work we call culture is created from the perspective of a bereaved survivor mourning the loss of someone irreplaceable: from *Gilgamesh*, the earliest fragmentary epic, to the entire genres of epitaph, elegy, and tragedy; from the Taj Mahal to the Requiem Mass to the *Dance of Death* to *Carrington*. The first great biography in English, *Memoirs of the Life of John Hutchinson*, was written by his widow Lucy, mourning in the 1660s the death not only of her husband but of the republican revolution to which he and she had devoted twenty years of their lives.

As these examples suggest, if every maker is a survivor, every survivor is also a re-maker. How do we know whether to believe the images of the dead created for us by Herodotus or Lucy Hutchinson or Nadezhda Mandelstam? What if there is more than one survivor and their versions disagree?

A Struggle

If a memory prevails and multiplies, if an image of the departed is held in more than one head, what inevitably ensues is a struggle between survivors—all of them committed to remembering the dead but bitterly divided over what those memories mean. Different interpretations compete for dominance. In that competition, each party allies itself, consciously or unconsciously, with larger social forces, which are themselves competing for different kinds of dominance. Thus, modern interpretations of Leonidas are obviously dependent upon the Greek victory in the Persian wars, on Alexander the Great's imposition of Greek culture throughout the Middle East, on the Roman adoption and transformation of Greek civilization, on the Roman conquest of western Europe, and so forth. Is it just a coincidence that the "Modern Library" edition of

Herodotus, with its heroic account of the victory of democratic allies over a militaristic autocratic empire, was published in New York in 1942? Interpretations of Mandelstam, just as clearly, cannot be disentangled from larger political struggles, from Khrushchev's repudiation of Stalinism in 1956 to the first publication of Mandelstam's collected works in New York in 1967, to the collapse of the Soviet empire in 1991. Memory does not simply happen; it is always motivated, always mediated, by complex mechanisms.

The devices and desires of memory were spectacularly visible in the wave of cultural fundamentalism that dominated the 1980s. An assortment of cultural critics rose up to protest the end of memory, the end of history, the progressive deterioration of our collective memory of our own great past. Like the political policies of the Reagan and Bush years, these cultural polemics were controversial. But the liberal response to this cultural challenge was ineffectual. At academic conferences, in faculty lounges, a thousand sarcasms bloomed and died, while Allan Bloom's *The Closing of the American Mind* and Joseph Campbell's *The Power of Myth* rode the *New York Times* best-seller list and conservatives in America, Canada, Great Britain, and Germany won election after election. Liberal intellectuals in the West lost the culture wars of the 1980s in part because they surrendered the mechanisms of cultural selection to their opponents. They made no secret of their contempt for the public. While condemning the closed shop of Western culture, the academic establishment has increasingly separated itself from the rest of society. One of the social realities of university life is that scholars who engage the mass media, or attempt to address a large audience outside their own discipline, are almost inevitably despised and distrusted by their colleagues. Any intellectual who appears on television is, by definition, no longer an intellectual.

Culture is the memory of human achievement, but those memories are not the exclusive property of the political right. In writing this book, I hope to offer an interpretation of culture compatible with a more progressive social agenda. That is, I, too, am a survivor, competing with other survivors for the right to speak for the dead.

THEORIES

Someone dies; someone else survives; there is a struggle over what should be remembered. This is a simple story, but it becomes more complicated each time we tell it. After only two cycles of death-survivor-struggle, my narrative has become extraordinarily entangled: from Mandelstam to postmodernism, from postmodernism to the culture wars, from culture wars to the crucifixion, from crucifixions to Thermopylae.

A mathematician would not be at all surprised by the increasing complexity of my story. A single logistic difference equation, repeated enough times, with the right values, produces chaos. Orderly disorder is a function of simple processes. Every human culture, after all, is a dynamic nonlinear system—a collection of interrelated parts, never standing still, and never repeating itself exactly. The vastness and complexity, the order and the disorder, are just what we would expect to happen when a single simple sequence is repeated, with slight variations, by innumerable agents innumerable times. So many deaths, so many survivors, so many struggles, all slightly different—and the result is something colossally, unpredictably rich and moving, an ocean of culture, with occasional islands of stability. Not a telephone book, but *Finnegans Wake*.

The complexities of the results are real, but so is the simplicity of the causes. The constant in all these stories is memory. One person does something that impresses itself on the memory of a second person; the second person's memory persists after the death of the first person. Moreover, every first person is also a second person. That is, every person has been impressed by memories of an earlier person and in turn tries to impress the memory of a later person. There is no original human. Every human has memories of predecessors.

What is worth remembering about our predecessors? That is the question at the root of all human cultures, and it is the basis of all the struggles in all the individual stories of deaths and survivors. What are the most important things to know? What models are worth imitating? Who can tell us what is worth remembering? Why is it worth remembering?

These are simple questions, but they have profound consequences, personal and political. Memory, the mother of the Muses, is also the mother of self: we are what we remember. And societies, like individuals, remember, misremember, and forget. Indeed, the French sociologist Maurice Halbwachs pointed out that even the memories we regard as private are structured within and by a public group (family, school, church, workplace, neighborhood, class, nation). Halbwachs founded the analysis of what he called "collective memory," what recent anthropologists and historians have called "social memory"—the memories that a group shares and by which it defines itself. Every identity, personal or ethnic or national, is founded upon memory; our egos and our societies are sustained by the circulation of recollection.

Societies therefore do everything they can to control the circulation of recollection, generally by supervising the mechanisms of memory exchange, particularly by censoring or promoting certain memories. In the United States, for instance, memory exchange is affected by the Freedom of Information Act, the Federal Communications Commission, the antitrust division of the Justice Department, the Central Intelligence Agency, the Interior Department's Register of Historic Buildings, and other regulatory bodies. Discouragement or promotion of particular memories is performed by the National Endowment for the Humanities, the National Endowment for the Arts, the Education Department. There are comparable institutions within individual states and localities and within self-governing bodies like the Motion Picture Association of America and the National Academy of Science. The regulation of memory affects every aspect of human government, from debates at the United Nations about whether freedom of the press is a parochially "Western" concept being imperialistically imposed upon other cultures, down to decisions made in individual living rooms about whether a child can watch a particular movie. All these decisions, political and personal, have economic determinants and consequences. Budgets for local schools and national museums, subsidies for university research, profits for conglomerates like Time Warner or Panasonic—all are intertwined in a vast educational-cultural complex devoted to the reproduction of desired memories.

This catalog of memory police may persuade you that I am paranoid, or that you should be. But while it is true that any society, including our own, can quickly succumb to conspiracies of lies or silence, there is nothing intrinsically sinister about the regulation of memory. Every individual and every society does it; it is unavoidable. No one can escape from the institutions of memory. The fact that you are reading this book is the result, in part, of decisions made by the publishing house, which is itself one division of a multinational corporation.

This book, consequently, is a specimen of the very phenomena it attempts to describe. How could it be otherwise? From quantum mechanics to anthropology, theorists have come to realize that we transform the systems we observe. Like every other culture worker, like every other bookmaker, I want to shape the institutions of memory. In struggling to think and write, I am struggling to impress my thoughts upon your memory, and through you upon the memories of others.

But I am also, like every other maker, a survivor. I am in part the product of memories impressed upon me by other people. I do not know how to read Russian. My quotation of Osip Mandelstam's poetry at the beginning of this chapter is from an English translation published in New York in 1974, coauthored by a scholar of Russian literature (Clarence Brown) and a poet (W. S. Merwin); that translation was based upon a text of Mandelstam's *Sobranie sochinenii*, in Russian, published in New York in 1967 and edited by Gleb Struve and Boris Filippov, that used many texts preserved by Nadezhda Mandelstam. In quoting Mandelstam, in knowing about Mandelstam at all, I am quoting all these other people. In an even more fundamental way, I am quoting my mother, who taught me to take pleasure in words and rhythms by reading poems aloud to me before I started school. To translate Herodotus, I took from an upstairs shelf a book I had bought in Oxford, England, ten years ago and took from a mental shelf a set of skills I had learned in Lawrence, Kansas, twenty-three years ago in a class in elementary Greek taught at eight in the morning five days a week by Professor Michael Shaw, who had himself been taught by Professor William Arrowsmith. Each teacher had a teacher, and the one who taught me Greek belongs to a human chain that stretches back to the Italian Renaissance and beyond.

That my own memories have been shaped by other people will hardly come as a revelation to anyone, but the theoretical consequences are not always appreciated. If I had had other teachers, this would be a different book. It might, for instance, take fewer of its examples from English and American literature. Such works occupy a disproportionate share of space in this book simply because those are the works best represented in my own memory, because those were the works that dominated my education. Maybe I should have postponed writing the book until I had learned everything my teachers did not teach me, and unlearned some of the things they did teach me. But I could postpone this book for fifty years, and at the end I would still not have learned enough, still not be able to include enough, still not remember enough.

Culture is itself the ad hoc never-adequate solution to this problem. No one person can remember everything; no one book can include everything. The memory of culture is selective. Given the limits of memory, we have to decide what to leave out. In turn, the inevitability of such selection creates the struggle to be selected. At its crudest, you might characterize human cultural history as a struggle to get remembered in this book, or some other book.

By necessity, the memory of culture is partial: selective and subjectively motivated. Comprehensive objectivity will not be found in this book, because it cannot be found in this subject. In this respect, *Cultural Selection* might be usefully contrasted with Northrop Frye's *Anatomy of Criticism*, published in 1957. Twenty-three years ago, when I was learning Greek, I was also reading Frye's book, which had been recommended to me by another teacher,

Professor Margaret Arnold. Arnold had her doubts about the book, but at the time Frye was the most influential literary theorist in North America, and she felt that I needed to know his work. She was right: *Anatomy of Criticism* remains in print in paperback, still visible in college bookstores, a recognizable landmark on every map of twentieth-century criticism.

The influence of Frye's book is closely related to the word *anatomy* in its title. An anatomy textbook provides a precise, complete, disinterested map of a finite and stable physical structure (a body), listing and describing all of its parts (skeleton, circulatory system, nervous system, and so on). Frye's *Anatomy* systematically describes a finite structure (literature) composed of functional categories (modes, symbols, myths, genres). Like the human body, literature changes over time, but according to Frye, those changes are themselves predictable, simply "different forms of rotary or cyclical movement" (like sleeping and waking, birth and death, summer and winter). The proper business of "criticism," then, is to put individual literary works in the right boxes by identifying the formal features that indicate their proper place in this anatomical structure. In this way, criticism can escape from mere subjective "value judgments" ("A is better than B") and construct instead a scientific description of the whole system ("A goes next to B").

A memory obviously differs from an anatomy. Most obviously, memories, unlike anatomies, are motivated and selective. We *select* an experience for recollection, after *evaluating* its importance to *us*. Literature, like every other aspect of human culture, is stimulated and organized by unnatural selection, by perpetual evaluation and reevaluation. For instance, Frye believed that all literature can be understood in terms of myths related to "the solstitial cycle of the solar year," and he interprets tragedy in particular as "the mythos of autumn." This equation seems odd, given that Greek tragedies were written for a one-day dramatic festival held every *spring*. But more important than the date of the festival is the fact that a single date was selected. Holding a dramatic festival on only one day of the year severely restricts the number of plays produced. Only three tragedians a year could see their work performed; only three could be given a chance to impress the memories of spectators and posterity. Cultural time, like cultural space, is always limited, and those limits create competition for access to the available resources. That competition, in turn, has to be arbitrated by some *subjective* person(s), who must *evaluate* the relative claims of the competitors and *select* some over others. And those individual local evaluations, at what we might call the quantum level of culture, are as unpredictable as the movement of individual atoms.

The history of literature, then, is the history of innumerable struggles for cultural space and time, and the results are as unforeseeable as the outcome of any competition. The struggle is not periodic; it does not happen in recurring cycles. Moreover, the randomness created by competition and individual evaluation is multiplied by the fact that literature is not a closed system. The tragedies performed at Athenian festivals are not simply literary texts; like Broadway musicals, they compound verbal with visual, musical, and choreographic art in an unstable mixture that emphasizes first one constituent, then another. And all these arts interact in complex unique combinations with the larger human social environment in which they are evaluated and selected for recollection or oblivion. Even if literature, politics, and economics were all stable and predictable, their combinations would not be. Accordingly, this book, unlike Frye's, cannot confine itself to literature; the following chapters also examine music, painting, movies, architecture, philosophy, sculpture, criticism, political constitutions, and religious scriptures.

Nevertheless, *Cultural Selection* does have at least one thing in common with *Anatomy of Criticism*: like Frye, I believe that individual works of art can be understood only as part of a complex system. But whereas the system Frye perceived in literature was fixed, closed, and predictable in its operations, I believe that culture is dynamic, open, and unperiodic. This difference of approach represents more than a shift in intellectual fashion. It is simply easier to understand unstable systems once you have devised methods for analyzing stable ones. The gradual shift in interest from stable to unstable systems, in both the physical and the human sciences, represents a natural learning curve.

An unpredictable system is, nevertheless, still a system, an arrangement of things related to each other in such a way that, taken together, they form a whole. The elements of culture are related to one another by means of memory. To understand the system called culture, we need to understand the system called memory. This book is accordingly divided into three sections, corresponding to the three actions that, in combination, constitute the phenomenon of memory. First, we must be affected by some stimulus (an electric shock, a movie). Second, we must translate that stimulus into some form of representation (a mental image, a videocassette). Third, we must recollect that stimulus by accessing the representation we made of it (racking our brains to recall the image, putting the video-tape in a VCR). Selection—the central activity of memory—operates in all three.

My understanding of selection, stimulus, representation, and recollection is informed by the current specialist literature on memory in half a dozen disciplines. But this is not a book about neurons, dendritic spines, or chemical cascades; it is not a book about rats, flatworms, sponges, day-old chicks, or chimpanzees; it is not a book about anonymous human subjects performing bizarre routines in laboratory environments. Instead, this is a book about the most common and intimate of human transactions, the intercourse of memories. It is a theory about the stories we tell each other. It is a collection of stories, and in all of them the first person says to the second, "You must remember this!"

PART I

Stimulate.

2.

You Must
Remember This.

The fundamental things apply
As time goes by.

HERMAN HUPFELD

Lee Katz, the assistant director of *Casablanca*, recalls that when the film was in production half a century ago, "nobody thought it was a memorable picture." But the movie continues to be remembered, to be rented, to be watched and rewatched, to feature in lists of the best American films, to inspire books and essays. Can it really be true that a flagrantly commercial piece of romantic wartime propaganda is one of those "fundamental things" that still applies, no matter how much time goes by?

Why do we remember *Casablanca*?

Why do we remember anything?

Memory is, from an evolutionary point of view, simply a survival mechanism. We are biologically better equipped and more predisposed to remember than any other species on this planet, and memory has given us dominion over the earth. Memory augments instinct.

The most fundamental thing about memory, then, is that it occurs as part of the interactive relationship between a biological organism and its environment. It enables an organism to recognize and adapt to its surroundings. Memory is, in the first instance, an internal response to an external stimulus. This is not all there is to say about memory or culture, and a reductionist formula like $x{\rightarrow}y$ will not explain how you feel when you listen to Beethoven's Ninth Symphony or "I Heard It through the Grapevine." But just as a complex culture is built up from innumerable individual variations on a simple sequence like death-survivor-struggle, so the complex and wholly individual pattern of your millions of memories begins with a simple sequence of stimulus-response. At the most basic level, *Casablanca* is a stimulus from the outside world that provokes a sequence of changes in our brains and/or minds that, in turn, we call memory.

STIMULI

To study memory, psychologists and neuroscientists create an artificial environment in which they can regulate the stimuli that initiate memory. In the classic experiment, Ivan Pavlov rang a bell before feeding a dog; soon the dog remembered that the bell always preceded feeding and began to salivate in response to the bell. The intensity and timing of the bell stimulus could be varied in order to chart the relation between the nature of the stimulus and the process of memory formation. In another classic genre of experiments, associated particularly with B. F. Skinner, rats were placed in a box; they were rewarded for certain behaviors and punished for others. These stimuli fostered the formation of memories, which enabled the rats to perform certain tasks more quickly or reliably. By varying every aspect of the stimuli in the rats' constricted world— the voltage of the electric shock, the supply and nature of a rewarding food or drug, the difficulty of the task to be learned, the time between experimental runs, and so on—it was possible to determine which combinations of stimuli were most efficient in generating rat-remembering.

More recent experiments, usually performed by biologists rather than psychologists, have diversified the range of experimental victims, selecting organisms particularly well suited to the investigation of some aspect of the chemistry of stimulus and memory. Newborn kittens are particularly suited to the study of visual memory, and octopuses to the study of tactile memory. In smaller creatures with less complex nervous systems, the chain of reactions is shorter and hence easier to study, but the range of behaviors and memories is correspondingly limited. Nevertheless, the governing procedure in all such experiments, from mollusks to chicks to chimpanzees, is the application and regulation of stimuli. For instance, flatworms can be poked with a glass rod; memory formation will be affected by which part of the body is poked, how many times, how frequently, how lightly.

It has even been possible to investigate directly some aspects of memory in human subjects. Psychologists can control the quantity of information and the speed of its delivery ("You will have ten seconds to look at these seven numbers"); they can vary the number of times the stimulus is repeated, the intervals between repetitions, the complexity of the data, the sense organs to which data is directed. Patients who have suffered serious brain damage, from accident or disease or medical mistake, have been subjected to extraordinarily varied experimental routines to trace the connections between certain kinds of stimulus, certain parts of the brain, and certain memory effects. Wilder Penfield, in a famous sequence of experiments on eleven hundred epileptic patients, directly applied an electric shock to specific areas of their brains; different areas stimulated different kinds of memory. Most recently, people injected with (apparently harmless) radioactive isotopes have been given various verbal or mathematical tasks, while PET-scans monitor changes in brain functioning.

Many of my statements about the functioning of memory in the rest of this book are based upon experiments such as these (admirably described in Steven Rose's *The Making of Memory*). But for now the details of these experiments and their conclusions are less important than the primary fact that, in all of them, we have to understand the stimulus before we can understand the memory. Before we can remember *Casablanca*, *Casablanca* first has to exist, and it has to possess certain qualities that interact with features of our own physical and mental apparatus. If we are to form a memory of *Casablanca*, *Casablanca* has to impress itself upon us. And what is true of our memories of *Casablanca* is true of all the other memories of which culture is composed. Each cultural memory is a response to a particular cultural stimulus.

But not every stimulus leads to a memory. Some stimuli, like *Casablanca*, have proven strong enough to initiate the creation of long-term memories; other stimuli—including other movies made in the same year by the same studio, like *Princess O'Rourke* and *Air Force*—are apparently not strong enough to produce the same response.

Not all stimuli are equal. The stimuli to which we are subjected vary among themselves. Those variations affect whether or not memories are formed and the nature of the ones that are formed.

RELATIVELY SPEAKING

These axioms will seem obvious enough in the context of memory research, whether the kind conducted in laboratories and paid for by governments and corporations or the unpaid kind conducted by people playing Trivial Pursuit. But they are not obvious to a lot of people currently engaged in the study of culture. If, in the preceding paragraph, I had written "poems" or "films" instead of "stimuli," the axioms would not have seemed so self-evident.

One school of contemporary criticism insists that all cultural artifacts are created equal. (To misquote *The Communist Manifesto*: Art is born free, but everywhere it is in chains.) Any poem is as good as any other, and any newspaper article is as good as any poem; if we claim one is better than the other, then we have arbitrarily "privileged" a certain class of texts and so created an oppressive "hierarchy." Particular examples of this kind of reasoning provide wonderful anecdotes for those conservative polemicists who are out to persuade the public that the academic world is populated by a herd of incompetent automatons programmed by one mad Marxist.

These claims, so easy to parody, originate in an awareness of the real and powerful social pressures that influence aesthetic judgments. But the fact that luck and politics play a big part in reputation-making does not justify the conclusion that they play all the parts. Recognizing the imaginative activity of readers should not lead us to ignore the imaginative activity of authors, or to equate the two contributions. Nadezhda Mandelstam and Herodotus are important, and so are their translators, but they all subordinated their own contributions to the work of someone else. To say that culture is remade by survivors is not to deny the existence or the importance of the original makers. The world is not that simple.

Most of the American students I have taught insist that it *is* that simple, that interpretation and evaluation are "just your opinion," and that "what's true for you isn't necessarily true for other people." All of them realize that this logic will not convince the police, and few of them try to apply it in their math classes, but in the humanities they expect it to prevail. All cultural stimuli are equal; all cultural evaluation is arbitrary.

This seemingly egalitarian attitude quickly leads to the most ferocious critical dictatorship. For instance, if you read "Dulce et Decorum Est," you will see that the description of war by the English poet Wilfrid Owen directly and explicitly contradicts the description of war by the Roman poet Horace. Owen's title and conclusion quote Horace in Latin, the language of cultural authority for two thousand years, now as alien to the poet as the lesson it and his teachers taught him. You must remember this: *dulce et decorum est pro patria mori* ("precious and proper it is, for the fatherland dying"). When I ask my students which poet is right, they almost invariably declare, "They are both right!" But that conclusion is logically impossible. Owen declares that Horace is wrong; if Horace is right, then Owen has to be wrong. The eager little relativists reply

Dulce et Decorum Est

Bent double, like old beggars under sacks,
Knock-kneed, coughing like hags, we cursed through sludge,
Till on the haunting flares we turned our backs
And towards our distant rest began to trudge.
Men marched asleep. Many had lost their boots
But limped on, blood-shod. All went lame; all blind;
Drunk with fatigue; deaf even to the hoots
Of tired, outstripped Five-Nines that dropped behind.

Gas! Gas! Quick, boys!—An ecstasy of fumbling,
Fitting the clumsy helmets just in time;
But someone still was yelling out and stumbling
And flound'ring like a man in fire or lime . . .
Dim, through the misty panes and thick green light,
As under a green sea, I saw him drowning.

In all my dreams, before my helpless sight,
He plunges at me, guttering, choking, drowning.

If in some smothering dreams you too could pace
Behind the wagon that we flung him in,
And watch the white eyes writhing in his face,
His hanging face, like a devil's sick of sin;
If you could hear, at every jolt, the blood
Come gargling from the froth-corrupted lungs,
Obscene as cancer, bitter as the cud
Of vile, incurable sores on innocent tongues,—
My friend, you would not tell with such high zest
To children ardent for some desperate glory,
The old Lie: Dulce et decorum est
Pro patria mori.

WILFRID OWEN (1893–1918)

that both poets are describing different aspects of the same phenomenon; the two views are complementary, not contradictory. But that is not what either Horace or Owen actually said, nor what either (apparently) believed. Neither poet recognizes the legitimacy or complementarity of the other poet's point of view. So the theoretical premise that "both authors are right" quickly leads to the practical conclusion that "both authors are wrong." And who is right? The relativist critic, of course.

This paradox afflicts every form of relativist thinking: relativists are absolutists about relativism, and have to deny the validity of all the truth claims made by people who do not share their relativist views. In the very act of rejecting hierarchies of value, relativism constructs a hierarchy, which values its own relativism above any absolutism. More specifically, in rejecting all hierarchies of cultural value, relativism constructs a cultural hierarchy in which the opinions of critics and readers are valued more than those of artists. An artist, after all, is never, in practice, a relativist. When artists are laboring to create a new work, a new stimulus, they cannot honestly believe that their efforts are wasted, that their investment of time and energy won't make any difference, that their work is no better than anyone else's. In practice, relativist critics have to conclude that all artists are deluded absolutists. They have to privilege the survivor over the maker.

If we approach culture from the perspective of memory, if we acknowledge the existence of any reality outside the mind itself, then we have to accept the existence of hierarchies of value. The mind constructs a hierarchy out of the stimuli it receives; only a fraction of those stimuli initiate long-term memory. To misquote *Animal Farm*: some stimuli are more equal than others.

This insistence on cultural inequality may cheer traditionalists. But when it comes to describing or measuring such inequalities, traditionalists behave like a herd of incompetent automatons programmed by one mad white pig. Conservative critics from Edmund Burke in the 1790s to Arthur Schlesinger in the 1990s act as though it were self-evident which works of art are greatest, which are medium great, which are ungreat. Such traditionalists deny—even in the midst of a cultural struggle whose outcome they cannot guarantee— that culture is the result of an unpredictable struggle. They can tell which stimulus they remember, but they cannot tell why one stimulus was greater than another. When you ask, "How do you know this is great?" they are likely to stare at you with incomprehension, pity, or contempt. The fact that you are even asking the question testifies to your incompetence—as though you were in some way physically handicapped and lacked the sense organ that detects greatness. But if you insist on your question, their answers boil down to some variety of, "Because that's what they taught me when I went to school," or, "Because I convened a committee, and this is what they said." They remember certain stimuli, and not others, because someone they trusted once told them, "You must remember this!"

The defense of cultural tradition is based upon the evidence, as dubious in science as in law, of hearsay ("Someone told me"). This fact is as obvious (and as embarrassing to certain political programs) as the inequality of stimuli. One way in which humans are distinguished from other animals is that our remembering a stimulus depends, to some extent, on whether we are told to remember it—and who told us.

PLAYING IT AGAIN

When in the movie the piano player Sam plays the song "As Time Goes By," he is replaying it. The central characters have heard it before, and they remember it. Many people in the original audience may have remembered it, too, because the song did not originate in the movie of 1942 but in a Broadway show of 1931. Rudy Vallee had made a record of it then, and when the movie became popular, Vallee's recording was rereleased and became a hit single. Even now, people seeing *Casablanca* for the first time usually recognize the song.

This remembered song is, of course, a song about memory, a text that explicitly tells us to remember it. Its most important words are not very original but very common: the auxiliary verb *must* and the adverb *still*. "You *must* remember this" because "It's *still* the same old story." What does *still* mean? It declares that something has been true in the past and remains true in the present. Some things have changed ("time goes by"), but some few, specified, privileged aspects of the world remain the same ("the fundamental things apply").

Will they continue to apply? That depends on how we understand the word *still*. When the commercial tells us, "You can still get this car at a fantastic discount price!" we are encouraged to believe that the discount will not last much longer. Tonight a kiss is still a kiss, but I cannot make any guarantees about its status tomorrow morning; in 1942, when *Casablanca* premiered, the world was burning and dying, and the film's first audiences could not be sure that the Allies would win the war. Anyway, amid the global dementia that piled up more corpses than any other event in human history, "the problems of three little people," as Bogart says, "don't amount to a hill o' beans." A kiss is still (only) a kiss, a sigh is just a sigh.

But we can also interpret the still-ness more optimistically. The song slips easily from the fragility of "A kiss is still a kiss" to the confidence of "The world will always welcome lovers." Moonlight and love songs, the love song promises, are "never out of date." ("Still going!" another commercial triumphantly announces.)

This promise of permanence is made by all injunctions to remember; it is the motive of culture. A past experience is worth recording and recalling because it will remain true and therefore potentially relevant to our future survival. But this fundamental promise is, of course, fundamentally unreliable. Indeed, the promise memory makes is contradicted by the very purpose of memory. If our environment were permanent and predictable, we would not need memory software at all. Instinct would be sufficient; we could be hardwired for survival in a hardwired world. But no environment is permanent, and we humans have survived so well (so far) because memory is more changeable than instinct, more easily adjusted to altered precariousnesses. Yesterday's preserving truths are today's or tomorrow's dangerous myths. In 1942 moonlight suggested romance; to the ancient Greeks, it suggested chastity—or madness. In World War II, "Woman needs man, and man must have his mate"; in the overpopulated future of J. R. Haldeman's *The Forever War*, heterosexuality is regarded as an antisocial perversion.

Haldeman and other science fiction writers have to predict what the future will remember of the present. In Haldeman's future, they remember the Rolling Stones. In Jack Womack's *Ambient*, Christianity has been displaced by the worship of Elvis (whose resurrection has been widely reported); in *Star Trek IV*, Jackie Collins is remembered as one of "the greats" of earth literature. Modern audiences laugh at the cultural elevation of Jackie Collins, but Renaissance audiences might have laughed if someone had predicted the cultural elevation of a popular entertainer like William Shakespeare. The obvious but embarrassing truth is that we don't know what the future will consider important. Look at how most of us respond to our children's taste in music.

It may seem strange that I have slipped from analysis of a nostalgic song into speculative science fiction. But memory is aimed, in *Casablanca* and everywhere else, from the present at the future. If a stimulus is to be recalled in the future, it must first be recorded in the present, and so the injunction "Remember!" is actually two injunctions: record now, and recall later. Like all commands, this command is powered by a promise, and the promise, like the command, has two parts. If you remember, you will be rewarded (sweet liquid); if you forget, you will regret it (electric shock). Someone orders us to do something *now* so that something else will or will not happen *later*. In other words, when people order us to remember the past, they are in fact predicting the future. But how can anyone predict the future? Why do we believe these demanding prophets?

We believe them because they are our parents. It is our parents who first teach us to heed these promising commands, and if very young humans did not believe their parents, few of them would survive. Of course, it doesn't matter whether these "parents" are the two people who mixed their genes to make us. For memory's purposes, biological progenitors, adoptive parents, older siblings, wet-nurses, nannies, au pairs, day-care workers, and mentors are interchangeable: they are all older humans who teach younger humans to remember. Like the scientists in the lab, these larger, smarter, and more powerful beings administer pain and pleasure in order to stimulate the formation of certain memories.

If humans remember a stimulus at least in part because someone tells them to, then stimuli that come from our "parents" will be particularly powerful and, as a result, particularly likely to be remembered. "This is great because Mommy told me it's great; I remember this because my teacher said I should remember it." Memories and the evaluations inevitably attached to them are bound up with our emotional attitudes toward the human sources who first enjoined us to remember certain things. The more powerful those human sources, the more likely we are to remember their injunctions. This is a conclusion that most relativists, Marxists, and cultural materialists would readily endorse: memory is a function of social power.

But this explanation of cultural memory, though necessary, is clearly insufficient. If we remembered everything our parents told us, and nothing else, societies would never change. Childhood is not a controlled experiment. (Ask any parent.) Unlike the scientist in the laboratory, the parent in the world cannot control all the stimuli, all the rewards and punishments, that will affect the formation of a child's memories. For one thing, every child always has more than one "parent." This is not just biologically but socially true. Take, for instance, a standard two-parent nuclear family. When the two parents openly disagree, children are taught to remember different things; they are also forced to evaluate which of those memories is most important. Even when one parent clearly dominates the other, or when a couple makes a habit of working out parental policies they can both apply, children will detect differences of style and substance, will sense unexpressed conflicts. As a result, within even the most restricted, well-run home-schooled family there are uncontrollable and unpredictable variations in the stimuli to which children are subjected. And every increase in the number of a child's "parents"—aunts, uncles, grandmothers, grandfathers, older siblings, family friends, adult neighbors, teachers—multiplies the potential for conflict and the unpredictability of variation.

If individual parents are not omnipotent in their own homes, reigning elites are even less omnipotent in the societies they govern. Every elite will, like every family, contain competing subgroups with their own agendas; the differences between those subgroups will be sensed by others and will create conflicting imperatives to memory and choice. But even if the governing institutions of a society could be homogeneous and constant in their commands, they would not be able to control every stimulus their subjects experience as children, partly because they would not be able to control every "parent" who might influence each child's memories. A society can reduce unpredictable variation only by attempting to control more and more of the experience of all its members. But in order to do that, it has to enlist more and more of its members into the apparatus for enforcing memories. But such a burgeoning apparatus simply increases the number of "parents." In societies as in families, every increase in the number of "parents"—teachers, police, critics, censors, informers, regulators—creates a corresponding increase in unpredictable variation. The monolithic stability imagined in George Orwell's dystopian novel *Nineteen Eighty-Four* is a powerful nightmare, but a social impossibility.

Radical relativists who treat cultural memory as nothing but a function of political power exaggerate the stability and predictability of human societies. They also do not solve the problem of memory. You may remember the story of the person who believed that the earth was not a globe but a flat surface supported by the shell of a vast turtle; when asked what was under the turtle, he replied triumphantly, "It's turtles all the way down!" If we remember a stimulus because our "parents" told us to remember it, then why did *they* remember it? Because their "parents" told them? It's not enough to proclaim, "It's parents all the way down!" At some point, someone had to be directly impressed by the stimulus itself, impressed so powerfully that he or she told other people, "You must remember this!"

Moreover, within the mind itself there seems to be a difference between the way we remember what we are told and the way we remember what we experience directly. The psychologist Endel Tulving calls the first kind of memory "semantic," and the second, stronger kind "episodic." My children have only a semantic memory of the Vietnam War; it is something they have heard about, but it ended before they were born, and they acquired information about it in circumstances and on occasions that were not in themselves remarkable. They know, without remembering when they learned what they know. By contrast, they have an episodic memory of the Vietnam Veterans Memorial because visits to it have been episodes in their own lives. If you have been to the memorial yourself, the episodic memory you already have of it will be triggered by these words; if you have not been there, my words can create only a semantic memory or remind you of something you have heard or read.

Our "parents" give us semantic memories about things that were done in the past, including cultural things, like memorials and other works of art. Our "parents" can even encourage or require us to experience those cultural things ourselves: to visit the Vietnam Veterans Memorial, to read *Animal Farm*, to see *Casablanca*. And once we experience the memorial or the book or the movie for ourselves, it becomes part of our own episodic memory. But our memories will still differ from theirs. As every teacher and parent soon realizes, a child's personal episodic memory may not confirm, or even resemble, the public semantic memory her "parents" have given her.

What stimulates us does not necessarily stimulate our children or our parents, our students or our teachers. This fact distresses traditionalists, who want to blame the difference on inadequate teachers or parents. ("If only we had the right textbooks, if only we could get rid of all these radical teachers, if only we had a national curriculum, if only parents would read to their children more often, then this generation would appreciate what the previous generation appreciated.") But the value of memory for biological survival actually depends upon this difference between semantic and episodic memory. Semantic memory represents the long-term experience of the species; episodic memory represents the short-term experience of a single living organism interacting with its immediate environment. The long-term memory may often be useful, but sensitivity to the immediate environment will always be necessary. Episodic memory needs to be stronger than semantic memory precisely in order to create differences between one human generation and the next.

If it is obviously true that *the stimuli to which we are subjected vary among themselves*, it is just as obviously true that *different human beings respond differently to the same stimulus*. Any analysis of human memory, and particularly any analysis of the memories we call culture, must begin with these variations. But which variation should we measure first? Should we begin with the differences in the human beings or with the differences in the stimuli to which those human beings are subjected?

STANDING STILL

Let's begin with the differences in human beings. We've all seen *Casablanca* enough times; for a change, let's go to a performance of *Romeo and Juliet*, another story of star-crossed lovers and a violent social struggle. In the play's best- remembered scene, Juliet is on her balcony, and Romeo stands below.

JULIET: I have forgot why I did call thee back.

ROMEO: Let me stand here till thou remember it.

JULIET: I shall forget, to have thee still stand there,

    Rememb'ring how I love thy company.

ROMEO: And I'll still stay, to have thee still forget,

    Forgetting any other home but this.

If *Romeo and Juliet* amuses and moves us, we say, "You see, it's obvious, Shakespeare was a genius." But what if the play does not amuse or move us? Then we say it was a bad performance. When the play stimulates us, we identify Shakespeare as the cause of our response; when the play does not stimulate us, we identify the performers as the cause of our response. We may even go as far as the Romantic essayist Charles Lamb and declare that no performance is ever adequate to the greatness of Shakespeare's text. And so we may subtract the performers: rather than go to see *Romeo and Juliet*, we may stay at home and read it. And if the printed text moves and amuses us, we say, "You see, it's obvious, Shakespeare was a genius." But what if the text does not amuse or move us? What if, like the Victorian scientist Charles Darwin, we find ourselves admitting, "I have tried lately to read Shakespeare, and found it so intolerably dull that it nauseated me"? Then we blame the reader, not the text, as Darwin blamed himself for his failure to appreciate Shakespeare. We say, "I must be getting old, *Romeo and Juliet* doesn't appeal to me much anymore," or we say, "This job is drying up my soul, I can't even read poetry anymore," or we say, "Would you kids shut up and let me concentrate! I've had to read this passage six times already, and I still don't know what it means," or we say, "Our old critical theories are inadequate, continuing to think that way makes everything seem boring, even *Romeo and Juliet*."

If we are willing to blame ourselves when Shakespeare does not give us pleasure, then we will certainly be willing to blame others when Shakespeare does not give them pleasure. If Coleridge describes *Measure for Measure* as a "hateful" and "disgusting" play, then it must be because Coleridge himself belonged to a sexually repressed generation, a generation that could not tolerate the play's seedy sexuality, the same generation that first bowdlerized Shakespeare's plays. If Tolstoy does not like *King Lear*, then it must be because *King Lear* is so psychologically astute, so relevant to Tolstoy's own obsessions, that Tolstoy simply vented his rage on the therapist who was telling him something he did not want to hear. If Ezra Pound records that "hunks of Shakespeare bore me," then it must be because Pound was a madman and a fascist. And if millions of Americans turn their backs on Shakespeare, close their minds to Shakespeare, it is, as the best-selling Shakespeare scholar Allan Bloom will tell you, because "Higher Education Has Failed Democracy and Impoverished the Souls of Today's Students." Just as Shakespeare condemns Shylock as a man who cannot appreciate music, so we condemn Coleridge and Tolstoy and Pound and even ourselves if necessary for not properly appreciating the music of Shakespeare.

If Shakespeare fails us, we blame the player, we blame the reader. We may even, if we are very clever, blame the text itself, arguing that it was corrupted in transmission or has been interfered with by a theatrical adapter or a modern editor in ways that obscure the greatness of Shakespeare's intentions. Shakespeare's greatness is never proven; it is simply postulated. Any evidence that appears to deny that postulate is dismissed as a failure of instrumentation: the performances, the readers, the texts, are inadequate, and whatever data they record are untrustworthy. We no longer use our critical instruments to measure the stimulus provided by Shakespeare; instead, we measure our instruments by the fidelity of their responses to the Shakespeare stimulus. Shakespeare is treated as the standard of value, the standard of measurement.

A standard—as the etymology of the word tells us—is something that stands still ("It's *still* the same old story"). A standard of measurement has to be a constant, something that stays the same, something we can rely on, and yet history demonstrates that the standards of literary value have, over the centuries, changed and changed again. Anyone at all familiar with literary history knows that Shakespeare was not always the standard; he became so long after his death. If you had walked into your local betting shop in 1616 or 1659, you would have been given very long odds against Shakespeare becoming the most famous of English writers, let alone the writer most familiar to educated readers everywhere on the planet in the late twentieth century.

If we are going to measure individuals or generations by how well they respond to certain cultural stimuli, then we have to decide that particular works of art are reliable standards, that they "stand still." But how can we know which stimuli are reliable standards? You cannot measure what you measure with. There can be no measure for measure.

To misquote *Hamlet*: we must find grounds less relative than this. We cannot begin the study of culture by assuming that certain works are standards and then use those standards to judge other people. We have to begin instead with the works themselves, and then find some standard by which to measure them.

MEASURE FOR MEASURE

If stimuli vary, and if those variations in the stimuli are crucial to the operation of memory, then in order to analyze memory we need to be able to describe those variations. In particular, we want to identify which variations are crucial to the formation of memories. Investigators in the hard and soft sciences consequently regulate and measure each stimulus to memory as precisely as possible: the voltage of an electric shock, the pressure of a poke, the timing of a message.

Culture is a memory of human achievement. Achievement is the stimulus that initiates the response we call memory. In some fields, like sports, we know how to measure human achievement. Every day whole sections of most newspapers are filled with freshly updated charts and tables, summarizing the performance of individual athletes and teams. These statistics break those performances down into a series of component actions: runs batted in, earned run average, errors, hits, home runs; goals, free throws, assists, rebounds;

passing yards, completions, sacks, time of possession, points allowed. A few blocks from my house, at a shop specializing in sports cards, my youngest son buys a popular commodity that translates a recognizable human being in action (the photograph on the front) into a numerical profile (the statistics on the back). On cards, in newspapers, during broadcasts, the sport is supported and defined by a subsidiary industry of analysts who provide the public with instant, ongoing measurements of its progress. These measurements enable us to situate any individual performance within a clearly defined conceptual field. That field includes all contemporary and past performances in the sport. On the basis of such evidence, we can determine, for instance, that Michael Jordan is the greatest basketball player ever—that is, the greatest stimulus to basketball memory. Or at least we can reduce the field of candidates ("Who was the greatest, Willie, Mickey, or the Duke?") and then debate their merits by hurling statistics back and forth.

We can measure economic achievement, too. The same newspapers that update sports statistics every day also update business statistics. In fact, business statistics—stock markets, currency valuations—are updated continuously, at a speed limited only by the time it takes to transmit information around the globe. As with sports, the activity itself has developed a symbiotic relationship to the accountants, analysts, and investment brokers who evaluate the performance of individual players and teams in terms of a series of component features. Individuals can be characterized by income, debt, assets, liquidity; companies by sales, growth, market share, profit margins; and national economies by inflation, unemployment, government debt, interest rates, trade balances. Again, as with sports, these measurements enable us to situate any individual performance within a clearly defined conceptual field. It is easy to demonstrate that in the last half-century Japan has been a more memorable player, has generated a greater stimulus to economic memory, than Burundi.

Many people will object to any suggestion that we can or should measure art as though it were a sport or a business. But the connection between art and sport is itself ancient. Pindar, widely regarded as the greatest of Greek lyric poets, wrote most of his odes to celebrate victors in the Olympic games. The Greeks, who founded the Olympics, also founded the tragic festivals in which three playwrights competed against each other for a prize. Records were kept of who won first, second, and third place (gold, silver, and bronze, as it were); scholars trying to measure the achievement of Sophocles note that he always took the first or second prize, never the third. Artists continue to compete against each other for prizes of every kind, from the one hundred dollars given by the town arts committee for the best watercolor in the annual amateur show to the Nobel Prize for Literature.

Art is also a business. Homer was blind; he earned his living as a minstrel, reciting before audiences who were willing to pay to listen. The business of art varies in different times and places, for like other businesses it depends on the nature of the market in which it operates. In a feudal economy, artists are rewarded by the patronage of an elite, with whom they develop personal relationships. In a capitalist economy, artists are rewarded by consumers, often with no direct relation to the artist, who purchase artistic works as they do other leisure commodities. People can often buy theater tickets, concert tickets, and sports tickets from the same vendors.

The connections between sports, business, and art suggest that we should be able to measure artists in some of the same ways we measure athletes and corporations. We can quantify the sales of records and books, the prices for which paintings and sculptures are sold, the sizes of audiences, the number of reviews, and of column inches in those reviews. We can count—as scientists already do systematically among themselves—how often a work is cited in other publications. We can make these purely quantitative measurements more sophisticated by recognizing social hierarchies of value. Prizes, for instance, are signs not simply of popularity but of esteem. Reviews may be positive or negative or mixed. Some reviews, some venues, and some prizes are more important than others.

All this evidence measures the response to an artistic stimulus within the generation that initially receives it. *Casablanca*, for instance, made more money for Warner Brothers than all but two other films the company released during the war years; it also won Oscars for Best Picture, Best Director, and Best Screenplay, and "As Time Goes By" was on the "Hit Parade" for twenty-one weeks in 1943.

Of course, such evidence does not tell us everything we need to know to understand culture. (If it did, there would be no need for the rest of this book.) But it does give us one way of measuring the initial stimulus. It recognizes the fact that some stimuli are stronger than others, and it enables us to distinguish the initial impact of *Casablanca* from the initial impact of other movies. It tells us how people *did* respond before their "parents" told them how they *should* respond. And it gives us a way to begin relating a stimulus to a memory, relating a work of art to the human environment with which it interacts—relating, for instance, "You Must Remember This" to a place called Casablanca (or Hollywood). Every song is sung in a place.

3

The Origin of Cultural Species.

There seems something more speakingly incompre-
hensible in the powers, the failures, the inequalities
of memory, than in any other of our intelligences.

JANE AUSTEN

In 1859 Charles Darwin proposed that new forms of life arise gradually, by "very short and slow steps." But a century of further
research weakened this theory, and in 1977 Niles Eldredge and
Stephen Jay Gould proposed an alternative model, which is now
widely accepted among paleobiologists. According to Eldredge and
Gould, evolution proceeds, not by the drip-drip-drip of random
genetic break and spill over many generations, but by "punctuated
equilibrium."

When I was growing up in Kansas, there were endless airless
summer days when it was all the universe could do to push the
heavy second hand around an ancient clock; then, abruptly, dark
clouds would pile up across an accelerating sky, the world began to
whip and crack, hail was bouncing on the roof and rain torrenting
down the gutters, the sky itself started splitting, and I could glimpse,
fitfully, through the torn black curtain, another world, a world of
radiance and rage; and then, just as abruptly, the power was gone,
everything was still again, still but dripping new. The evolution of
life is like those days in Kansas: long epochs of equilibrium punctuated and punctured by brief thunderstorms of desperate change.

The evolution of civilizations is also characterized by punctuated equilibrium. Sometimes, as Kenneth Clarke has noted, whole
cultures are simultaneously transformed:

> One such time was about the year 3000 B.C., when quite suddenly
> civilisation appeared, not only in Egypt and Mesopotamia but in
> the Indus valley; another was in the late sixth century B.C., when
> there was not only the miracle of Ionia and Greece—philosophy,
> science, art, poetry, all reaching a point that wasn't reached again for
> 2000 years—but also in India a spiritual enlightenment that has
> perhaps never been equalled. Another was round about the year
> 1100.

Such changes are usually more local, though no less abrupt. The history of every art form in every area of the world conforms to the
same pattern. Ovid, Horace, Virgil, and Propertius were literary
contemporaries; Bosch, Botticelli, da Vinci, Dürer, Giorgione, Man-
tegna, Michelangelo, Raphael, and Titian were all painting between
1490 and 1505; Handel and Bach were born in the same year.

Cultural achievement is not randomly or gradually distributed; it comes in clumps. Why?

This question assumes the validity of the conclusions I reached
in the preceding chapter—that there are in fact real differences in
human achievement between different periods that account for our
"inequalities of memory." Having argued that *not all stimuli are created equal*, I am now proposing that *strong stimuli cluster*.

If we were talking about anything except art, this claim would
not seem controversial at all. It would, for instance, not surprise or
distress historians of science. Throughout history, the giants of science, within any particular discipline, have tended to travel in gangs.
Modern physics, for instance, is founded upon theories about relativity, probability, the structure of matter, and quantum mechanics
that were produced by Niels Bohr, Albert Einstein, Werner Heisen-
berg, Ernest Rutherford, and others in the first decades of the twentieth century. In his book *The Structure of Scientific Revolutions*,
Thomas Kuhn argues that science does not "progress" in the orderly,
incremental way we usually assume; instead, scientific revolutions

turn the established worldview on its head, replacing one paradigm with another. The new paradigm is not necessarily better; it is just different, so different that it cannot really be compared with the old paradigm, because there is no common standard of measurement that both paradigms would accept. Kuhn divides the history of science into brief periods of revolution, when paradigms shift, and much longer periods of normal science, when researchers investigate technical problems defined by the prevailing stable paradigm. We especially remember the revolutionary periods and the scientists associated with them because they generated an exceptionally large intellectual stimulus. Some periods of science and some scientists are more important than others.

Again, I am assuming that there is a relationship between stimulus and memory. Strong stimuli cluster; so do strong memories. As individuals, our personal memories are not evenly distributed over every minute of our lives; our strongest, most vivid, most plentiful memories cluster around certain events, certain people, certain periods. As a society, we remember certain epochs of art and science better than others.

For instance, we remember Elizabethan drama better than any other period of playwriting in the English language. Our most admired dramatists—William Shakespeare, Christopher Marlowe, Ben Jonson, Thomas Middleton, John Webster, John Ford, John Fletcher—were all contemporaries, born within a twenty-year period; each lived most or all of his adult life in London, which, with only one to two hundred thousand inhabitants, was by modern standards a small city. The achievement of this generation of playwrights was recognized in their own lifetimes as new and extraordinary; the generation of their grandchildren would look back upon them as, in John Dryden's words, "the giant race before the flood." Our classrooms, anthologies, and theaters still recollect a dense concatenation of dramatic masterpieces, by several authors in several genres, that all premiered in London between 1585 (Marlowe's *Tamburlaine*) and 1633 (Ford's *Perkin Warbeck*). By contrast, most people—including professional writers and teachers—could not name a single stage play written in the English language between 1779 and 1894. Sheridan is the only eighteenth-century playwright still regularly revived; the literary canon and the theatrical repertoire then skip ahead to Shaw and Wilde at the very end of the nineteenth century. These later periods produced few remembered plays and not a single memorable tragedy. How can we account for such a pattern, for what Darwin called "distribution, rarity, abundance, extinction, and variation"?

The most fully developed explanations of such clustering are biological, and in analyzing the clusterings of cultural memory, I will draw heavily on biological theories. Though works of art are not themselves living organisms, their creators are, and culture—like life—is created by endlessly reiterated combinations of struggle, death, and survival. *On the Origin of Species* described a "principle of preservation" by which desirable innovations are "preserved, accumulated, and inherited," a process that sounds like the memory of nature. And much as our biological ability to remember has been preserved, accumulated, and inherited over forty thousand human generations, our memories of culture have been shaped by similar laws.

OPENINGS

If organisms, or artists, are to thrive, then they must find for themselves a viable niche. But, as Darwin observed, "the number of places in the polity of nature is not indefinitely great," and the same is true of the polity of culture. Artists must choose one of two strategies for survival: either they develop a niche that has never been occupied before, or they invade and conquer a niche developed by the occupant they will displace.

The first strategy, filling a new niche—finding what Darwin called "some place in the polity not so perfectly occupied as might be"—is the strategy of originality. This description may seem to fit Romantic notions of the isolated genius who creates works never before imagined. But, unromantically, the availability of unoccupied niches fluctuates historically. Society creates those new openings in the environment that permit originality to thrive.

Great dramatists, for instance, almost always come in localized groups: in addition to the group in Elizabethan England, similar groups of playwrights flourished in Athens in the fifth century B.C., in Spain in the early seventeenth century, and in France and Japan in the later seventeenth century.

Such groupings could not occur if cultural prowess was merely a matter of individual genius or genetic splendor. True enough, artistic gifts are often passed from parent to child. Both Mozart and Bach came from notable musical families; Sophocles' son Ariston was a dramatist; Noh drama was shaped by two actors, Kan'ami and his son Zeami. But in most cases, genetic inheritance, or even familial training, is less important than social context. After all, the overwhelming majority of the contributors to a cultural boom are strangers, who converge on the same spot at the same time; Shakespeare, Marlowe, and Ford were not even native Londoners, and none of the great Elizabethan playwrights came from a theatrical family. Something in the environment must *attract* geniuses to a particular art form in some periods and places but not in others. That something can only be the opening of a new cultural niche.

How is it that such "new places in the natural economy of the country are left open"? Something in the cultural environment has to have changed; for dramatists, the most crucial environment is the theater itself, the architectural and social site where plays are performed. The most prodigious flourishing of English drama came within a single human lifetime of the building, in London in 1576, of the Theater, the beachhead of a commercial secular vernacular drama in England's most populous urban market. (The most prodigious flourishing of Spanish drama came, within the same human lifetime, in Madrid, the capital city of what was then Europe's richest nation, where the first theater was built in 1575.)

Enclosed, purpose-built theaters transformed the economics of playgoing by enabling actors to charge in advance for admission and to hierarchize prices in relation to a fixed hierarchy of architectural space. But a profitable return on such investments in the purchase or lease of land and buildings could be sustained only in those areas where thousands of people were able and willing to pay for admission many times each year. The new European theaters thus depended on the historical evolution of concentrated urban populations, which provided a market dense enough and affluent enough to support a capital-intensive leisure industry.

This new cultural environment was protected and enriched by its insularity. As Darwin learned from his study of the Galápagos Islands, "isolation, by checking immigration and consequently competition, will give time for any new variety" to be "improved." England, too, is an island, much more effectively separated from its European neighbors then than it is now. In 1596, London theaters did not have to compete with those in Paris, still less with those in Madrid (from which England was separated not only by ocean and language but by religion and geopolitical rivalry). London did not even have to compete with other English towns: no other boasted a population large enough to support commercial theaters, and sixteenth-century changes in religion and town government had enfeebled and finally extirpated noncommercial religious drama, like the great cycles of York and Wakefield. The London theater companies virtually monopolized the market for drama in England, and the number of such companies was—for political reasons—always strictly limited by the city and the monarchy. The Elizabethan theater community was thus protected from any serious competition in a market that had no other forms of commercial entertainment: no cinema, television, video, radio, opera, ballet, circus—not even music concerts, except for those performed in the theaters.

Thus isolated, this profitable new industry generated a demand for fresh wit, which in turn transformed the economics of playwriting. Because the potential playgoing population of London was relatively small, a new play could quickly be seen by most of its potential customers; consequently, the new theaters needed large numbers of new plays, so that audiences could be continually offered new theatrical experiences to purchase. Because there was no indigenous tradition of professional playwriting, this sudden high demand for plays coincided with a dearth of writers who could supply that demand. This gap rapidly inflated the economic value of an ability to write plays that audiences would pay to see. In 1601 experienced dramatists sometimes received eight pounds per play; by 1613, a time when a schoolteacher's average annual salary was only ten pounds, a single script could be worth as much as twenty pounds. A successful playwright could easily make two or three times as much money as most university graduates—and far more than he could make by any other kind of writing. Moreover, the theater's appeal was not just financial. The poet and playwright Michael Drayton confessed that his "pride of wit" and "heat of blood" could not help being moved by the "shouts and claps at every little pause."

The makers attracted to this exciting and rewarding new arena could exploit a nutrient-rich environment. The humanist Renaissance had given educated Englishmen access to a treasury of ancient models and materials, which could be adapted to the new niche; the Tudor regime had encouraged vernacular translations of classical works and new vernacular histories of England. The impact of such work—like Arthur Golding's Ovid, Thomas North's Plutarch, and Raphael Holinshed's *Chronicles*, on which Shakespeare so often relied—was intensified by the transformation of the book trade, initiated by Gutenberg's invention of the printing press. The first books printed in England had appeared a century before the rise of the London theaters, and by the 1580s London had a flourishing print economy of its own. By multiplying copies and reducing costs, print increased the accessibility of texts; what technology made possible, ideology made desirable, as the Reformation urged Christians to learn to read so they could encounter the Word of God firsthand. Supply and demand began to spiral around each other in an ascending double helix: a demand for original vernacular literature began to emerge, and the new playwrights could appropriate and adapt new works by a cluster of nondramatic English authors like Philip Sidney, Edmund Spenser, Thomas Nashe, and John Donne. They also read and translated into their own theatrical forms plays and novels from France, Italy, and Spain. No copyright laws limited their ability to steal from any source, foreign or native.

The new niche created a demand, and the wider environment created rich materials. Of course, only the individual organism—the playwright—could refashion those materials to create something that would satisfy the new demand. But the artist's ability to refashion his materials was also, to a large extent, provided by society. Stephen Jay Gould and Elizabeth Vrba argue that much biological evolution results not from adaptation (the environment changes and then the organism changes in ways that fit the new environment), but from "exaptation" (the organism has already changed in ways that, coincidentally, fit it for changes that subsequently happen to take place in the environment). The relationship between Elizabethan education and drama provides a perfect example of this process.

English schools in the second half of the sixteenth century followed a pedagogical model articulated by the Dutch humanist Desiderius Erasmus. This educational regime slighted women, mathematics, science, technology, any vocational skill; it was designed to produce male eloquence. Erasmus demanded that students range as widely as possible over the writers and genres of antiquity: oratory, philosophy, epic, satire, comedy, tragedy, fable. By memorizing, explicating, and imitating, students internalized this cornucopia of texts as a storehouse of human possibilities and verbal strategies that could be immediately accessed and applied as occasion demanded. As intended, these schools produced princes, civil servants, churchmen, and humanist scholars; the system was not deliberately designed to produce dramatists, a profession that did not, at the time, exist. But Erasmus's curriculum provided a set of skills that, coincidentally, perfectly fitted its students to succeed in the new theatrical environment. Their abilities, in turn, strengthened the commercial appeal of the new institution.

As Darwin observed, the origin of species "depends on many complex contingencies," and Elizabethan drama originated in a niche created by a combination of circumstances peculiar to one time and place. Other niches have been differently constructed, but in every case a similar pattern can be discerned. A new cultural niche satisfies a demand that has been created or focused by significant developments in the social, economic, political, or technological environment (change); the new niche is somehow protected in its formative stages from excessive external pressure (insulation); it offers strong incentives for success (reward); early successes in the new niche are further enabled by preexisting features of the larger environment (exaptation); those successes enrich the niche, thereby initiating a cycle that progressively strengthens the niche and its inhabitants (feedback loop). The combination of all these elements—change, insulation, reward, exaptation, feedback loop—creates an enormously attractive and powerful new niche.

Most of the makers whose achievements will be remembered are simply those lucky enough to be born at a time and in a place where such a cultural vacancy is emerging. What could be easier? The world builds a vacant mansion next door to your hovel; you take possession and are thereafter acclaimed as a master of real estate investment.

Actually, it's more complicated than that. For one thing, you will not be the only person to notice the lucrative vacancy: there will be a sudden rush of applicants for the new position.

COHABITATION

"The Struggle for Existence" that Darwin posited in biology is intensified within the turbulent and rewarding environment of a new cultural niche. The sudden clustering of ambition produces open, fierce, and direct competition. Whatever the particular mechanisms of competition in a given culture, any cluster of geniuses is, in its own time, a society of rivals, competing for whatever rewards attracted them to the new niche in the first place.

A new niche attracts talented people, and those people then become more accomplished by competing among themselves, seeking to outdo one another, adapting themselves "so as better to fill up the unoccupied place." Kabuki and joruri puppet theater developed side by side during the seventeenth and early eighteenth centuries, vying for audiences and dramatists, continuously stealing and learning from each other; Jean Baptiste Racine's *Bérénice* opened only a week before Pierre Corneille's tragedy based on the same story, and Racine's *Phèdre* within two days of Pradon's; Aristophanes, in *The Frogs*, imagined Euripides and Aeschylus continuing to contend even in Hades.

The Elizabethan theater was ferociously competitive. The stability of its niche was achieved at the expense of extreme instability for individuals within it. Theaters and acting companies were constantly going bust; only one troupe, the Chamberlain's-King's Men, survived until the 1640s, when it, too, was finally destroyed by parliamentary decrees. Most individual playwrights were imprisoned at one time or another for debt or political indiscretion. Companies poached each other's actors, playwrights, and subject matter. Shakespeare's *Richard II* (written for one company) answers Marlowe's *Edward II* (written for another), just as *The Merchant of Venice* answers *The Jew of Malta*; *Henry V* was the third or fourth dramatization of that monarch's reign within little more than a decade; *Henry IV* immediately provoked an indignant revisionist play on the same reign by a rival company; *Hamlet* laments the rise of the "little eyases" who are driving the adult actors out of business.

Once an innovation had demonstrated its competitive value, it was likely to be adopted by other playwrights and companies. The building of the first enclosed amphitheater was followed almost immediately by the building of a second; when one company of adult actors moved to an indoor theater with artificial lighting, others followed; the custom of dividing a play into five acts, with music played during each interval, originated in the companies of child actor-singers, but within a few years such intermissions had become universal. Examples of adaptive similarity, however, are less striking and less pervasive than examples of adaptive dissimilarity. In Darwin's formula, "more living beings can be supported on the same area the more they diverge in structure, habits, and constitution."

The new London theaters produced, as critics have long recognized, an extraordinary supermarket of styles (monumental, colloquial, clotted, elliptical, transparent, smooth, jagged) and structures (romantic, satiric, heroic, historic, tragic, sentimental, sadistic).

Diversifying competition intensely and directly among a group of talented contemporaries provides the best possible breeding ground for works that will be able, in turn, to survive competition with centuries of yet unborn rivals. As Darwin says, circumstances of "very severe competition" tend to produce "many new forms of life, likely to endure long and to spread widely." Certainly, this process applies to Elizabethan drama as well: "The new forms . . . which already have been victorious over many competitors, will be those that will spread most widely, will give rise to most new varieties and species, and will thus play an important part in the changing history of the organic world." Successful competition leads to diversification, which makes the organism suitable to a greater variety of environments.

An artist's contemporary rivals are surrogates for future rivals. If your contemporary rivals are few, weak, or homogeneous, your work will not be well prepared "to endure long," to overcome the diversified challenges from future aspirants to your niche. The stronger your contemporary competition, the stronger your work will have to become simply to survive in its own time; the stronger your work, the better its chances of surviving the cultural struggles of the future.

But competition is not the only means by which strong contemporaries help to create great art; various forms of interspecies symbiosis and interdependency are equally important. Darwin himself recognized that a so-called social plant "could exist only where the conditions of its life were so favourable that many could exist together, and thus save each other from utter destruction," and modern biologists place much greater emphasis on the importance of cooperation within and between species. In culture, too, collaboration is common, and often difficult to distinguish from competition. Were the Elizabethans rivals or partners? Certainly, each was better because of the others, and their rivalry was often carried on by imitation. Shakespeare cowrote plays with Thomas Nashe, Thomas Middleton, John Fletcher, George Wilkins, and probably others; he also encouraged his company to perform Ben Jonson's first important play. Jonson in turn introduced and praised, famously, the posthumous collection of Shakespeare's *Comedies, Histories, and Tragedies*. It has been estimated that at least half of the plays of the English Renaissance were cowritten by two or more playwrights. Such collaboration is still common among modern screenwriters: the final script of *Casablanca* was created by seven Warner Brothers writers who adapted an eighth person's play (and incorporated a song written by a ninth). Collaboration is a kind of artistic interbreeding; sometimes the results are sterile, but cross-fertilization can also produce new varieties, different from the normal offspring of either collaborator. Some of the most famous and unique plays of the period were cross-fertilized: Beaumont and Fletcher's *The Knight of the Burning Pestle*, Middleton and Dekker's *The Roaring Girl*, Middleton and Rowley's *The Changeling*, Middleton's adaptation of Shakespeare's *Macbeth*.

These incidental collaborations—individual artists briefly combining their talents to produce individual works—are supported by the more fundamental shared labor through which they all help to sustain and expand their shared habitat. Each playwright's individual success contributes to the collective health of the theatrical economy on which they all depend. Spectators who enjoy one play will probably attend another; tourists are drawn to the theaters of London, New York, and Tokyo not by a particular play but by the variety on each city's theatrical menu. *Casablanca* came out of the Hollywood studio system, under which the success of any single Warner Brothers picture contributed to the familiarity and box-office appeal of the stars contracted to appear in other Warner Brothers pictures; *Casablanca* itself was pivotal to the future careers of Humphrey Bogart and Ingrid Bergman.

The success of any individual playwright, or team of playwrights, depends upon and makes possible the success of the other professionals who inhabit different parts of the same niche: actors, musicians, costume-makers, designers, technicians, directors, choreographers, makeup artists, theater managers. *Casablanca*, like every other film, has a long list of credits; so does the theater program for any good production of *The Oresteia* or *Our Town*. Even a "one-man" show like Spalding Gray's *Monster in a Box* is trailed by a roll call of collaborators. Mutual interdependence strengthens the profession as a whole, but at the same time, dependence on others makes every individual professional more vulnerable. Innumerable writers have blamed the failure of a play on the incompetence of actors, and actors can be equally caustic about writers.

I have taken these examples from drama, but they can be duplicated in other forms of cultural work. Collaboration is common enough outside the theater. Citing numerous examples from poets and prose writers of the last two centuries, the editor and critic Jack Stillinger has attacked "the myth of solitary genius." The most influential of all Western texts, the Bible, contains many separate books, most of which contain the work of more than one writer; they were not collected into a single volume until the sixth century, twenty-six hundred years after the first texts were written down. The most magnificent of all Christian churches, St. Peter's Basilica in Rome, owes its completed shape to a succession of great architects: Donato Bramante, Michelangelo, Giacomo della Porta, and Gianlorenzo Bernini. The most magnificent of pagan churches, the Parthenon, represents a combination of the talents of the politician Pericles, the architect Ictinus, and the sculptor Phidias. The theory of punctuated equilibrium was itself articulated in a paper cowritten by two scientists. Many successful artists have run studios in which the master's work was often difficult to disentangle from the work of subordinates; "Henry Moore" may have begun as the signature of a single sculptor, but it became something closer to the trademark of a factory. And even when cultural work originates with a single intelligence, it cannot be completed without help from others. Not only playwrights and actors but novelists and publishers, painters and dealers, composers and musicians, choreographers and dancers, architects and builders, scientists and technicians, depend upon and denigrate each other, collaborating and competing to build a shared environment.

RISK

Organisms are often forced to adapt to new circumstances or die. But nobody is forced to become an artist, and certainly no one was ever forced to enter a new artistic niche.

There are, in fact, always good reasons not to do so. An unoccupied niche may be uninhabitable, or precarious and marginal, supporting only a severely limited range of activities. Because the position has never been occupied before, it will almost certainly be regarded skeptically by the reigning cultural authorities. Sir Philip Sidney was not alone when he complained about the idiotic tackiness of Elizabethan popular drama. When young men sold their talents to the rowdy commercial theaters, they would have seemed to many of their most respected contemporaries to be committing cultural suicide. When you try to do something no one has done before, you have no guarantee that it is worth doing, or doable.

Occupying a new niche is like boarding a small leaky boat, overcrowded with opinionated passengers, bound for an unknown destination. To embark on such a career and succeed in creating new cultural species, you have to be willing to take risks.

The sense of risk is one of the things that attracted Elizabethan spectators to live performances—and still attracts audiences. Few of us go to see actors groping helplessly for forgotten lines, or to hear musicians screech the wrong note, or to watch stand-up comics flop like gasping fish on the shore of a stubbornly silent crowd. Few of us want the performance to fail, but most of us want to know that it *could* fail at any moment, and that it succeeds only by a fragile, perpetually patched union of hard work and good luck, of ability and serendipity, of nature and fortune. We relish the overcoming of obstacles.

We are therefore enormously interested in characters who must overcome obstacles. It doesn't really matter what the obstacle is, though most great plays are about the two greatest obstacles to human happiness—death (of which there is always too much) and sex (of which there is never enough). In some sense, it doesn't really matter whether the characters succeed in overcoming the obstacle (as they do in comedy) or fail (as they do in tragedy). We are fascinated by the situations themselves, which pit a strong individual desire against a strong obstacle.

This is, of course, a human survival mechanism: we are born with a sense of what W. B. Yeats called "the fascination of what's difficult." We are programmed to be deeply curious about how Odysseus will overcome the many obstacles between him and home, or how a couple of mere humans will stop an unstoppable inhuman Terminator, or how Romeo and Juliet's love will or will not defuse and elude the civil war between their families. What most people remember most vividly about *Romeo and Juliet* is, in fact, a simple physical obstacle, the balcony that separates the two lovers at that once-in-a-romance moment when love declares itself, reciprocally. We are fascinated by Shakespeare's Henry V and Marlowe's Tamburlaine because they are such superb, triumphing obstacle-crushers; we love revenge plays like Middleton's *The Revenger's Tragedy* or the movie *Death Wish* because we want to see how the revenger will overcome the seemingly insuperable obstacles that stand between him and the execution of a perfect justice.

Great characters must face great obstacles; so must great artists. History is an obstacle course for artistic reputations, and the best preparation is to have met and overcome as many obstacles as possible in one's own lifetime. (In the Zen formula: "Having many difficulties perfects the soul.") Sometimes those obstacles are purely personal. Homer and Milton composed their epics when they were blind; Dante composed his epic in exile; Joseph Conrad wrote novels in a foreign language; Emily Dickinson was a woman in nineteenth-century rural Massachusetts; Walt Whitman in Victorian America and C. P. Cavafy in turn-of-the-century Alexandria were homosexuals;

Osip Mandelstam and Anna Akhmatova and Aleksandr Solzhenit-syn were politically persecuted; Alexander Pope and Christy Brown and Christopher Nolan were physically handicapped. In such circumstances, to write at all, to write the *kind* of work these artists wanted to write, requires a titanic commitment, a desperate, ferocious will to create.

But you don't have to be disabled, disadvantaged, or persecuted to create great art. Even when there are no personal obstacles, there will always be technical ones—that is, obstacles created by a cultural niche. A villanelle or a haiku or a sonnet, for instance, is a severely artificial, constricting, difficult structure—a self-imposed formal obstacle by which poets make it *harder* to say what they want. Meter serves the same purpose. In the late sixteenth century, iambic pentameter was a new niche. The first important long poem in iambic pentameter in modern English was Spenser's *The Faerie Queene*, begun in the 1580s; the first important play in iambic pentameter in English was Marlowe's *Tamburlaine*, written in the same decade. Iambic pentameter—especially dramatic iambic pentameter—was new; no one knew how to do it, or what you could do with it. Blank verse was as difficult for Marlowe to write as free verse was for Whitman; in both cases, what made the writing so difficult was the absence of models, of teachers, of formal memories.

The dramatists of the English Renaissance were writing works in a new formal medium (iambic pentameter) for a new economic and architectural institution (the commercial theater). They had no one to show them how to turn prose narratives into verse plays, how to dramatize the complex history of *Hengist, King of Kent* in two and a half hours, how to convey an impression of the whole of Roman or London society with a small cast, how to empower visual spectacle with very limited technical resources, how to stimulate and sustain theatrical suspense, how to create opportunities for actors, how to interweave plots and subplots, how to enact convincing heterosexual love stories without any female performers, or how to write about politics without being censored or thrown in jail.

When you occupy a new niche, you have to overcome a whole

new set of obstacles; you have to solve new problems. "Make it new," Ezra Pound demanded. You can make something new only by solving a new problem, and a new niche presents the most new problems, making it the greatest training ground for artistic problem-solving. The most successful competitors in any new niche will be those who are the most imaginative problem-solvers. In this respect, great artists are not so different from great scientists. This is perhaps most obvious in the case of architects, whose work combines visual art and mathematical science. Hagia Sofia, the great church in Istanbul built by Emperor Justinian, encloses in stone more space than anyone had ever before attempted to subdue to architectural or religious ambition. The problem was solved by two men—Isidore of Miletus and Anthemius of Tralles, working in collaboration—whom some critics call "architects" and others "engineers." In other cases we have less difficulty distinguishing scientists from artists, but the mental facility is more similar than we tend to suppose. In the work of Aristophanes and Aristotle, of Darwin and Whitman, of Shakespeare and Bacon, the struggle to solve new problems leads to the creation of a new paradigm, a flexible, complex, comprehensive new model for thought and practice. There follows a period of imitation in which the principles of the new paradigm are widely applied and its limits explored. After Petrarch, we have Petrarchan love poems; after Andrea Palladio, Palladian architecture; after Newton, Newtonian physics. A proper name becomes a common adjective; a man becomes a manner; a scientific revolution becomes routine science. In the long wake of every revolution in the arts or the sciences, many people solve minor variations on the old problems by using minor variations of the old solutions. They plug up the gaps, nail down the supports, finish off the rough sketch, fill out the architectural outline of a new world. But that world was found by someone else, and the founder will be celebrated longer than the followers.

The works of art most likely to be long remembered are those produced by superb problem-solvers, working in the challenging, rewarding, training environment of a competitive, collaborative, problem-laden new niche.

INCUMBENCY

Niches fill up. The richer they are, the faster they fill.

The Elizabethan niche filled extraordinarily quickly. As the decades passed, acting companies accumulated, in their chests and memories, stocks of old reliables that could be revived without paying living playwrights for new scripts. By the 1620s, the most successful company, the King's Men, was licensing only four new plays a year; almost three-fourths of known court performances in the reign of Charles I (1625–42) were revivals of old plays. Dramatists found themselves working in an increasingly constricted marketplace. Moderate success for one meant utter failure for another; worse, a playwright with a long career was eventually competing with his own past successes. The problem deepened as the century wore on. In 1660, when the theaters were reopened after an eighteen-year hiatus, a new generation of inexperienced dramatists was pitted against a full, nostalgic, venerated repertoire of plays that had already been defined as classics. Moreover, these dramatists were competing for places in a diminished niche: the authorities had licensed only two theaters. This cramped niche had also been stripped of some of its cultural insulation. English plays now had to compete in the urban entertainment market with musical concerts, operas, coffeehouses, and newspapers. English playwrights had to compete for cultural prestige with older London drama and with new Parisian drama, which was not only experiencing a genius burst of its own but had become much more familiar in England through the long Continental exile of the English court. The Restoration playwrights managed, despite these obstacles, to produce some memorable work, but by doing so they overcrowded the repertoire even more. In the eighteenth century, the theater's hospitability for new plays was further weakened by social, architectural, and political changes. Not surprisingly, literary talent migrated to other, newer, more rewarding niches—first satirical verse, then novels.

But new niches are not the only cultural environments capable of supporting memorable art. The Elizabethan niche filled, and so does every other eventually. If no new niches are available, organisms must invade a niche already occupied by another species and displace those occupants. This is the agonistic, antagonistic, "war with the mighty dead" strategy much discussed by the critic Harold Bloom.

In such an artistic struggle—as in warfare and congressional elections—the incumbent has enormous advantages, and the invasion of a well-defended niche is at least as risky as pioneering in an empty one. The more important the niche, the more powerful its incumbent is likely to be, and the harder to dislodge. To take over a strong niche, the invaders must be exceptionally strong and must dedicate all their resources to the task—as Virgil committed himself to the emulation of Homer, as Dante committed himself to the emulation of Virgil. The incumbent is in effect one big brain-busting obstacle, and anyone who can leap such a hurdle, anyone who can survive competition with an opponent so potent and entrenched, is well equipped to avoid oblivion.

The power and function of incumbency is critical to the dynamics of both biological and cultural evolution; its importance can be demonstrated in the history of every long-lived artistic reputation. Whoever occupies a niche first will be easy to imitate but terrifically difficult to displace. Shakespeare has stimulated and influenced many artists, but the most successful beneficiaries of his influence have worked in a different medium (the painters Hogarth and Fuseli, the composers Mendelssohn and Verdi) or in a different language (Goethe, Stendhal, Hugo, Pasternak). Shakespeare provided these artists with imaginative ammunition that they used in conquering their own niches without challenging his incumbency in his own. On the contrary, their imitations enormously strengthened Shakespeare's position; his imitators became in effect allies of his reputation. Since their work was in part dependent on his, any attack on their niches entailed an attack on his, and vice versa.

Nevertheless, no cultural incumbent can hold a niche forever; no matter how dominant a species is, "sooner or later, it gradually decreases." First Homer, and then Virgil, and then Dante, and then Milton, were successively weakened by the passage of time, which changes the niche itself. Age weakens memory, and age eventually undoes every incumbent. The emergent vitality of Elizabethan drama was not seriously threatened by the rival cultural achievements of Greek or Latin drama; those earlier ages could provide useful materials and models, but despite their educational prestige, they were so foreign to the experience of English men and women in the early modern period that they could easily be displaced by new vernacular varieties.

Culturally, age is relative; what matters is not the recording of minutes on an atomic clock but the quantity of change in an environment. Chaucer was weakened unusually quickly because he lived just before a radical phonetic shift in the dialect of his tribe; Virgil, by contrast, commanded the pinnacle of European culture for more than fifteen centuries—that is, as long as the Latin language dominated educational institutions. Shakespeare has had a longer run than Chaucer, but he will probably not last nearly as long as Virgil, simply because cultural change is continuing to accelerate. It is no accident that the last fifty years have seen such a varied flourishing of dramatists writing in English: Eugene O'Neill, Arthur Miller, Tennessee Williams, Samuel Beckett, Harold Pinter, Tom Stoppard, David Hare, Alan Ayckbourn, Neil Simon, David Mamet, Sam Shepard, Tony Kushner, Wole Soyinka. These playwrights, though talented, are not strong enough to displace Shakespeare, but Shakespeare is no longer intimidating enough to keep such challengers from knocking on the door to his niche.

Sooner or later, the old always succumb to the young. The aging dominant male has to defend his status more and more frequently, and eventually he will lose. That struggle between the old and the young is the stuff of tragedy—and comedy (depending on your point of view).

ARTIFICIAL NICHES

Soyinka is competing with Shakespeare on a different continent, four centuries later. Soyinka is competing, that is, against the memory of Shakespeare. Human memory creates the possibility of permanent competition and collaboration in cultural niches that contain both the living and the dead.

The nature of that collaboration and competition will depend upon the parameters of the niche. In fact, niches are a large part of the answer to the problem of measurement that I raised in the last chapter. To measure a stimulus, we need an agreed standard of reference. We use performance statistics when measuring athletes and financial statistics when measuring companies or economies; we do not evaluate the Japanese economy by counting the number of runs scored by Japanese baseball teams. A niche like sports or economics is defined by a set of boundary conditions, and those conditions in turn help to define what counts within that niche.

Of course, I am here using *niche* in a sense more familiar in biology than in cultural studies. But this sense of *niche*—that part, within a total environment, that is particularly suitable for a certain organism—is clearly related to several key terms and concepts in analysis of the arts. In writing, just now, of tragedy and comedy, I was referring to two recognizable cultural categories. Literary critics often call these categories "genres." But those genres are themselves part of a larger category that we could call drama. In turn, drama is part of a still larger category that we might call performance—a category that has been studied by many people besides literary critics. For instance, Richard Bauman and other anthropologists, describing the nature of verbal performance, have defined "performance" as "an action marked in such a way that it invites evaluation." All verbal performance is marked and framed in a way that invites attention to, and judgment of, the way a player plays. Different cultures frame such performances differently, and different cultures frame different kinds of material as performance, but every human culture includes verbal performance, and every verbal performance is framed for evaluation. Evaluation is made possible by the frame itself, which determines what actions and persons are being compared. And evaluation is always part of the game. Some players play better than others; the quality of their play determines the character of their reward. Evaluation, the measurement of the significance of a stimulus, is only possible within frames that determine the nature of performance in a game. A game, by its rules or conventions, defines what will constitute success or failure, a brilliant move or an error.

What all these concepts—niche, genre, frame, game—have in common is the idea of an environment in which competition occurs, a competition governed by the conditions of the environment itself. Genres and games and frames are all artificial niches created by human beings to enable an interpretive community to evaluate the performances of its members, living and dead. Different artificial environments enable us to measure different human qualities: strength, speed, leadership, intelligence, military power, economic ingenuity, political coalition-building, artistic creativity.

The reliability of such measurements depends upon the stability of the niche itself. As long as the niche—the frame, the game, the genre—remains the same, we can compare all the performances within it, because each is keyed to the same standard of measurement, the same reference grid. But if the rules of the game change, it becomes harder to compare one performance (under old rules) to another performance (under new rules). Roger Maris hit more home runs in a single season than Babe Ruth did, but his season was longer than Ruth's. Any change in the niche represents a change of standards. That change does not prevent comparisons between contemporary performers playing together in the altered niche: Maris was clearly the best home-run hitter of 1961. But changes of standard do complicate any comparison between the living and the dead. Babe Ruth cannot be brought back to life to demonstrate how he would compete under the new rules. Shakespeare cannot be brought back to life to answer the question I was asked on a British television program: "Would Shakespeare be a successful dramatist if he were alive today?"

Rules change with the passage of years and frontiers. If this is true of sports and other games with very explicit rules, it is even more obviously true of genres of art. The best players, competing for dominance within their niche, will change the niche itself in order to give themselves an advantage, or others will change the niche when an exceptional player takes advantage of one of its features. The rules of basketball were changed to prevent Wilt Chamberlain from completely dominating the game: for example, because Chamberlain could dunk his free throws, players were forbidden to pass the plane of the free-throw line until after the ball hit the rim or the backboard. Within every game, the desire to preserve the rules (to maintain continuity with past performances and preserve the constancy of certain standards) competes with the desire to change the rules (and thereby either improve the way performances are measured or measure different features of performance). The existing rules always seem "natural" because we are accustomed to them, but because these niches are artificial and arbitrary, they are always subject to pressure to deconstruct and reconstruct them.

Such changes are not confined to cultural niches. Even in the physical world, organisms change the niches they inhabit. Human beings in particular have transformed every niche we have occupied. That is why we need memory.

NICHES OF MEMORY

A niche is the setting where the innumerable individual struggles of culture are fought. The conditions of the niche (genre, frame, game) enable us to determine the winner. Or to put it another way: by constructing an artificial niche, we make it possible to measure which human stimuli are strongest.

Earlier I treated the problem of measurement as though it were just a technical difficulty in setting up memory experiments: we need to measure the stimuli in order to analyze the relationship between stimulus and response. But this technical problem is just one example of a much more fundamental problem. In trying to measure which stimuli are greatest, we are trying to determine what are the most important features of our environment and experience. If we can identify which features and events are most important, then we will know *what* to remember.

The conditions of the niche help us to compare performances and to identify which are most important, and hence most memorable. *Casablanca* was judged the "Best Picture" produced in the United States in a particular year, 1942; its theme song was a "hit" according to the mixed criteria of sales and on-air time that prevailed in the music industry; marketed as a "war" movie, its box-office performance was later evaluated by comparison with that of other war movies; in the 1970s it was judged in a poll against all other Warner Brothers pictures (it came in first), and later against all other American pictures (it came in third). In all these different niches, *Casablanca* can be identified as a significant event, one worth remembering.

Such categories—niches, genres, frames, games, whatever we call them, however we categorize them—are necessary, but they are also necessarily arbitrary. Being arbitrary, they may be arbitrarily created, destroyed, or transformed. As happened in Elizabethan England and in many other times and places, change opens up new niches into which cultural talent may move; change also alters old niches, weakening the power of cultural incumbents. Or the inhabitants of a cultural niche may themselves change it in order to alter or preserve the balance of power within it. Niches and memories are attempts to create a constant field against which we can measure individual events separated in time, but those very niches and memories are themselves subject to change. Our constants are inconstant.

Memory is particularly sensitive to environmental change. There is a good biological reason for that sensitivity: when the equilibrium of its niche is punctured, the very existence of an organism may be threatened. Such changes must be carefully noted so that the organism will remember the new constants, which may be literally a matter of life and death. Our memories are particularly active and plastic in infancy and early childhood, when we are building the basic category-niches that will largely determine the way we sort and remember experience for the rest of our lives; they intensify again in adolescence, when our bodies and our social status undergo a major metamorphosis. We also tend to remember other less predictable and more individual experiences that resulted, or seemed about to result, in major changes in our personal niche: an intense love affair, a marriage, an alteration of career or status, the death of someone especially close to us, an experience that brought us close to death ourselves.

In short, *we are particularly prone to remember stimuli associated with changes in a niche.* In cultural terms, this tendency reinforces our attention to the strong stimuli that cluster around the opening of a new niche or the radical transformation of an old one. It takes great power to create or cultivate a new cultural niche, or to invade an old one; that power itself is a stimulus to memory. But the power of that stimulus is intensified to the degree that it succeeds in changing the niche. We remember the strength of the stimulus, but we also remember the change it effected. Those changes to the niche, moreover, will determine the way we categorize future events there.

American citizens remember, within the niche of their histories, the first colonists; the Founding Fathers of the American Revolution, the Declaration of Independence, and the Constitutional Convention; the heroes and battles of the Civil War and the civil rights movement. (We also remember John F. Kennedy—I am writing this paragraph on November 22, 1993—because he was shot, and that shot changed a very big niche.) Scientists remember within the niche of their disciplines the giants of relativity and quantum physics because they changed the categories by which we organize our memories of the physical world. Literary historians remember, within the niche of their genres, the playwrights of early modern England because they created new forms of vernacular drama that were radically different from classical models and fundamental to the way subsequent generations conceived of theater, poetry, and personality. *Strong stimuli cluster at radical changes in a niche.*

The preceding arguments may sound like a form of cultural Darwinism: the "constantly-recurrent Struggle for Existence" works its impartial and irresistible magic, "favouring the good and rejecting the bad." The Victorian ideologue Herbert Spencer and the contemporary pop-intellectual Camille Paglia might both be expected to approve. Whatever is still remembered deserves its supremacy; whatever has been forgotten deserves its oblivion; there should be no changes to our textbooks, our niches, or our social practices. It might appear that, in culture as in nature, in the niches of memory and of biology, everything is determined by that single simple law that Spencer called "the survival of the fittest."

But we have forgotten to ask, "Fittest *for what*?"

4.

Chosen People.

Once I went, there would be no reunion:
Perpetually separated, dead
Alive. How could I bear to turn away?
The children, clinging to my neck, cried, "Mother,
Where are you going? When will you be back?"

Ts'AI YEN

"*D*ad is writing a book about *memory*?"
My children express incredulity because I have, apparently, the lousiest memory in the family. Rebecca remembers the names and natures of innumerable flora; Isaac, almost anything mechanical or electrical; Josh, the songs, habits, and plumage of birds; Jess, the style and color of everyone's clothes; Michael, three-dimensional visual configurations. I, by contrast, cannot even recall, reliably, something so basic as each child's hot-dog condiment preferences. If writing this book depended on remembering any of those things, I would be unfit to finish it; if survival depended on them, I would be unfit to live.

Fit, as dictionaries remind us, means "well adapted or suited to the conditions or circumstances of the case, answering the purpose, proper or appropriate." Fitness is not an absolute quality, present in one thing; fitness describes instead the relationship between two things. These clothes fit me; they wouldn't fit you—or rather, they wouldn't fit you as well as they fit me. Fitness is a continuum, from least to most fit; statisticians can determine "degrees of goodness of fit" between a set of figures and a set of probabilities.

Fitness is—as these examples indicate—a way of measuring relationships. In other words, the concept of fitness does not solve the problem of measurement; it is just another way of looking at that problem. When we try to measure a cultural stimulus that might initiate a cultural memory, we do so in terms of fitness. ("This is a fitting way to remember the dead." "This is unfit for the memories of children.") So it should not surprise us that the most fundamental of all critical categories, in all the arts, is the concept of "decorum"—an English word derived from the Latin *decorus*, meaning "seemly, fitting, proper" (*Dulce et decorum est . . .*). The critical analysis of decorum attempts to describe which features are most appropriate, or fittest, to comedies, elegies, symphonies, folk songs, portraits, historical paintings, war memorials, churches, or any other genre.

Decorum, then, is a way of measuring fitness to a genre, game, or frame, fitness to any of those categories I am calling niches. But as we have already seen, niches change over time as new cultural stimuli enter them. Since fitness describes a relationship to a niche, if the niche changes, then so does what is fittest for that niche. What is appropriate to the niche at one time will not be appropriate at another time. As Ecclesiastes puts it:

> *For every thing there is a season, and a time for every matter*
> *   under heaven:*
> *a time to be born, and a time to die;*
> *a time to plant, and a time to pluck up what is planted;*
> *a time to kill, and a time to heal;*
> *a time to break down, and a time to build up;*
> *a time to weep, and a time to laugh;*
> *a time to mourn, and a time to dance;*
> *a time to cast away stones, and a time to gather stones together;*
> *a time to embrace, and a time to refrain from embracing;*
> *a time to get, and a time to lose;*
> *a time to keep, and a time to cast away. . . .*

A time to remember, and a time to forget.

A TIME TO DIE

As I learned in my most memorable science class (taught by Mr. Runyan in an air force school in Dover, Delaware), the phrase and the concept "survival of the fittest" originated as an interpretation of the process Darwin called "natural selection." For more than a century, we have visualized biological evolution in terms of a tree, an ordered cone of continually expanding possibility, or a ladder, an ordered ascent to inevitably increasing complexity. Both models are essentially deterministic and optimistic. In this vision of organic evolution, life gets better all the time—richer, more varied, more sophisticated—by a process that weeds out incompetence and culminates in the inevitable, glorious arrival of *homo sapiens sapiens.*

Throughout the nineteenth and twentieth centuries, while scientists were busy reading this mega-history in the rocks, humanists were busy reading and writing local histories of individual artistic reputations, and those minihistories were based upon a model of cultural evolution as optimistic and deterministic as its biological counterpart. According to the humanists, it was inevitable that Michelangelo would eventually be recognized as the greatest of visual artists, Shakespeare as the greatest of writers, Rembrandt as the greatest of portrait painters, Darwin as the greatest of biologists, and so on. They were "fittest," and therefore they inevitably survived and flourished. Moreover, the history of interpretations of a great artist's work can be visualized as an ordered cone of continually expanding critical activity, or as a ladder, an ordered ascent to inevitably increasing complexity and sophistication. Just as "Man" would eventually claim his rightful, foreordained place at the pinnacle of evolution, so the great artist would eventually claim his rightful, foreordained niche in the pantheon of culture.

These two optimistic histories, biological and cultural, reinforce each other by assuring us that the best will survive: we are the best, we have the best, we know the best ("Vanity of vanities, says the Lecturer; all is vanity").

But both theories are untenable. The biological theory has collapsed because it cannot account for the most spectacular features of the fossil record. In the late 1970s, Louis Alvarez, the winner of a Nobel Prize in physics, proposed that the extinction of the dinosaurs resulted from the global environmental effects of collision with a large interplanetary body. This theory has since been confirmed almost to the point of certainty, and similar explanations seem increasingly plausible for most of the other mass extinctions that punctuate the geological record, including the late Permian catastrophe 225 million years ago that exterminated up to 96 percent of marine species.

The history of life on earth no longer looks tidily optimistic or inevitable ("the race is not to the swift, nor the battle to the strong"). In the new theories articulated by Stephen Jay Gould, evolution is governed by contingency. Life could have happened differently; alternative candidates lost out, not because they were less deserving, but because, in the cosmic lottery, they were less lucky. An organism cannot thrive in a hostile environment, and environments change unpredictably, sometimes rapidly, sometimes radically. What is fittest in one environment may be fatal in another. A species can become dominant in an ecosystem only through a series of environmental contingencies.

If biological survival has always been, in part, contingent on luck, then *homo sapiens sapiens* must be cast down from his allegedly inevitable roost at the top of the evolutionary tree. And if *homo sapiens sapiens* tumbles from the top of the biological tree, Artist X plummets off the pinnacle of the cultural pyramid. Contingency has a finger in both pies.

I do not know if any artists or works of art have succumbed, like the dinosaurs, to meteorites, but Aeschylus, the first great Greek tragedian, is said to have died when he was struck on the head by a turtle dropped by an eagle. This story is so bizarre that most scholars have trouble believing it, but there can be no doubt that the young Hungarian dramatist Ödön von Horváth was killed in 1938 when a tree he was standing under was struck by lightning. Other artistic careers have gone extinct as a result of contingencies less singular but no less fatal ("For the fate of the sons of men and the fate of beasts is the same; as one dies, so dies the other"). In 1625 the playwright John Fletcher stayed in London an extra day to pick up a new suit from his tailor, and as a result was struck down by bubonic plague; a year later Francis Bacon fell to pneumonia, apparently contracted while conducting an experiment in the snow. The story of culture begins, after all, with the death of a creator, and those deaths—like the deaths of other human beings—are often accidental, premature, or violent ("How dies the wise man? like the fool").

Such unpredictable deaths not only deprive us of particular memorable works that those creators might have produced; they may also affect the development of an entire niche. If Christopher Marlowe had not been murdered in a tavern when he was twenty-nine, if he had lived (like Shakespeare) another twenty years, we might all now regard him as the superior artist; certainly, Marlowe's career had a more impressive beginning than Shakespeare's. The future of Elizabethan drama would have been at least different— perhaps even greater—if Marlowe had lived, because Marlowe was an exceptionally active, potent, and destabilizing part of that niche.

To biological evolution, it matters only that an organism survive long enough to reproduce; in cultural evolution, what matters is not physical offspring but memory. Makers must, accordingly, survive long enough to produce something that seems to others memorable. Longevity may or may not be an advantage. If makers live a long time, they may produce more memorable works. On the other hand, if they die young, the works they do produce may be especially cherished by survivors. The death itself, by its unexpectedness or unfairness, may intensify the stimulus created by the work; the sense of bereavement may be sharpened or prolonged by an awareness of promise unfulfilled, of what might have been achieved if the gifted victim had lived longer. In the biological world, early death can hardly ever be an advantage, but in the cultural world, early death can actually enhance a reputation—as with Mandelstam, Chopin, Keats, Byron, Shelley, Pushkin, Lermontov, Kennedy, King.

To some critics, the preceding observations will seem irrelevant—or worse, undisciplined. Some would say that our responses to art ought not to be contaminated by the fluff and clutter of biography, or trivialized by daydreams that begin "What if . . . ?" But such objections are based upon a misunderstanding of the nature of culture. We remember works of culture because we remember persons. We are all survivors remembering memorable work done by the memorable dead. Our responses to such canonical cultural artifacts as the pyramid of Cheops (built by persons now dead to entomb other persons now dead) or Robert Browning's poem "My Last Duchess" (in which a person long dead when the poem was written, by another person now dead, describes a painting modeled upon a third person already dead when the speaker spoke) cannot be disentangled from the emotions we attach to persons. That is why biographies are more popular than disciplined disciplinary criticism. Moreover, how can we remember the dead without asking ourselves, "What if . . . ?" Memory allows us to carry with us into the present (what is now) images of the past (what is not now). Consequently, memory of the past (what is not now) cannot easily be divorced from speculation about an alternative present or future (also what is not now). How can anyone who is convinced of the importance of human fictions be dismissive of the question "What if . . . ?"

A TIME TO LOSE

Not only the artist but the artist's work is subject to the accidents of mortality. If the minimum condition for avoiding biological extinction is that one specimen of the species must be preserved at all times, then the minimum condition for avoiding cultural extinction is that a work survive in at least one memory, living or artificial.

Once created, memories can be amazingly durable. But they can easily be lost, permanently, if something disrupts the initial response to a stimulus. On a foggy spring morning in Kansas in 1975, I was driving my Volkswagen Beetle from Topeka to Lawrence on old Highway 24; just ahead, I saw a car cross the highway, and I braked to avoid hitting it. The next thing I remember was regaining consciousness in my smashed car, which was in a ditch on the far side of the intersection. I had been hit, not by the car I saw, but by a second car following the taillights of the first, but I remember nothing between braking and awaking. Many accident victims suffer such memory gaps, and the lost moments cannot be recalled, even under hypnosis. Such episodes of amnesia result from a severe but temporary disruption of the physical processes by which memories are created in the brain. My moments between braking and awaking can never be retrieved because they were never successfully recorded.

Cultural memory suffers from the same weakness. Works of art, like human beings, are particularly vulnerable just after birth. They may perish before they have a chance to stimulate any permanent memories. "In the summer of the year 1797," Samuel Taylor Coleridge fell into "a profound sleep" (actually induced by opium) for about three hours, during which time, as he described the experience (writing of himself in the third person),

> he has the most vivid confidence, that he could not have composed less than from two to three hundred lines; if that indeed can be called composition in which all the images rose up before him as *things*, with a parallel production of the correspondent expressions, without any sensation or consciousness of effort. On awaking he appeared to himself to have a distinct recollection of the whole, and taking his pen, ink, and paper, instantly and eagerly wrote down the lines that are here preserved. At this moment he was unfortunately called out by a person on business from Porlock, and detained by him above an hour, and on his return to his room, found, to his no small surprise and mortification, that though he still retained some vague and dim recollection of the general purport of the vision, yet, with the exception of some eight or ten scattered lines and images, all the rest had passed away like the images on the surface of a stream into which a stone has been cast.

So perished—if we believe Coleridge—all but the first fifty-four lines of "Kubla Khan."

The process Coleridge described is, like the brief amnesia brought on by physical shock, familiar enough to psychologists. When a set of twelve numbers (in three rows of four) is flashed momentarily on a screen, subjects can recall on average only four numbers; but if, having seen the whole set, they are asked to recall the numbers in one specific row, they can recall three of those four. Therefore, since they can recall three of any four numbers, they must actually have perceived at least nine of the twelve. Nine numbers are available for recall, but *in the time it takes to write down four numbers, the other five are forgotten.* This simple experiment, like many others, measures the transience of short-term memory. Literary scholars have expressed skepticism about the alleged arrival of "a person on business from Porlock," but even without such an intruder, Coleridge could easily have forgotten most of the lines in the time it took to write down fifty-four. His poem, like a dream vividly remembered when we wake but forgotten by the time we finish breakfast, perished before he could transfer it to the long-term memory provided by pen, ink, and paper.

The other two-hundred-odd lines of "Kubla Khan" are not the only works to have failed to make the transfer from short-term holding to long-term storage. Anyone who uses a word processor has lost passages, or whole files, before they could be backed up or hard-copied. In the 1950s, a taxi drove off with the only copy of I. A. Shapiro's completed typescript of the letters of John Donne; we are, as a result, still without a complete edition of Donne's letters. In the 1730s, fifty-five rare or unique manuscripts of Renaissance plays perished when Betsy Baker—the household servant of John Warburton, an English antiquary—used the pages as scrap paper under pie bottoms. Half of Shakespeare's plays—the ones that had not yet been printed—could have been lost in one day in July 1613 when the Globe Theater burned down. Shakespeare would not have cast so large a shadow across the subsequent history of Western culture if *The Two Gentlemen of Verona, The Taming of the Shrew, King John, Julius Caesar, As You Like It, Twelfth Night, Measure for Measure, Othello, All's Well That Ends Well, Timon of Athens, Macbeth, Antony and Cleopatra, Coriolanus, The Winter's Tale, Cymbeline, The Tempest, All Is True* (also called *Henry VIII*), and *The Two Noble Kinsmen* had never been published.

All written works, until recently, have begun life by crossing the vulnerable bridge of a single text, but some have had to cross that bridge twice. We owe to a single late manuscript—now housed in the breathtakingly beautiful Biblioteca Medicea-Laurenziana in Florence, designed by Michelangelo—our only text of nine plays by Euripides. All the surviving manuscripts of Lucretius's epic *De rerum natura* derive from a single damaged copy made centuries after the poet's death, in the twilight of the Roman empire in the West. The poems of Catullus and Propertius, the prose of Petronius and Tacitus, barely squeezed through the Dark Ages and were damaged in the long transit. The perseverance of *Beowulf* was secured by a single manuscript, its final page charred by the fire from which the text was rescued ("I only am escaped to tell thee"). Such incidents— the cliffhangers of bibliography—remind us of how fragile and solitary the transmission of culture can be. And these, after all, are the stories with happy endings: the battered survivor somehow clings to the raft and is saved. But for every romance of rescue there is at least one documentary of extinction. Umberto Eco's *The Name of the Rose* supposed that a single copy of Aristotle's lost treatise on comedy had survived until the twelfth century in a remote Italian monastery—only to be destroyed, with the library that housed it, at the end of the novel. Reading of the burning of Aristotle's treatise induces the same wrenching sense of poignancy (and guilt) as watching film of the last passenger pigeon dying in a Cincinnati zoo.

Such extinctions are as common in culture as in biology. In 1623 a fire in Ben Jonson's study consumed the manuscripts of his translation of Horace's *Ars poetica*, his English grammar, his history of the reign of Henry V, and a long poem narrating his journey into Scotland. The destruction of these works inspired the creation of another, "An Execration upon Vulcan," in which Jonson upbraids the mythological "lord of fire" who devoured "So many my years-labors in an hour" and "ravished all hence in a minute's rage." But even while mourning his losses, Jonson recognizes that fire has always been the enemy of "arts" and "wit." It destroyed the Temple of Diana at Ephesus, the library of Alexandria, and (closer in time and space) both the Globe Theater and the Banqueting House at Whitehall.

Buildings are, paradoxically, more perishable than poems. Of magnificent buildings (or paintings, or carvings) there is only one specimen; survival depends upon the perpetual preservation of that solitary original. The most celebrated works of the most celebrated sculptors of antiquity—the young Aphrodite by Praxiteles, the Zeus in Olympia and the Athene in Athens, both by Phidias—have all perished.

It has always been apparent to historians of the physical arts that survival is often fortuitous, that excellence does not guarantee endurance. Material things are subject to material misfortunes ("the silver cord is snapped, and the golden bowl is broken, and the pitcher is broken at the fountain, and the wheel broken at the cistern"). But sometimes more than random fracture is involved. Perversely, the very fame of a work often endangers it. The Temple of Diana at Ephesus did not burn down accidentally; it was arsoned, in 356 B.C., by Herostratus. In 47 B.C. Julius Caesar deliberately started a fire near the port at Alexandria because he calculated that the Egyptians would rush to put it out; the destruction of forty thousand high-quality book scrolls was part of a tactical diversion. In 1687 the Parthenon was badly damaged when Venetian bombardment ignited gunpowder that had been stored there by the Turks—precisely because they figured that no one would attack so revered a site. In 1972 a deranged atheist attacked and damaged Michelangelo's *Pietà*. What many value, some will loathe, simply because others value it.

Such motives for vandalism are purely human, but the vulnerability of singular works of art has corollaries in the natural world. If all the members of a species are confined to one place, they may all be extirpated by a single local catastrophe: a meteor, an earthquake, an oil spill. A building, painting, or manuscript is so susceptible to fortuitous or deliberate destruction because at any one time it can be in only one place. A statue occupies a very small niche; it can be annihilated by even a teensy calamity.

A TIME TO PLANT

An act of planting, as Ecclesiastes recognizes, is always balanced by an act of plucking up. In North America, my European ancestors cut down and uprooted trees in order to plant grains. Deforestation is not a uniquely human activity. Some of the fires that burn each summer in our national parks are started by hapless campers, but massive burn-off is a recurring feature in the history of forests on an oxygenated planet flickering with lightning. Humans create artificial catastrophes, but there would be catastrophes enough without us. We were not around to witness the Atlantic Ocean spilling into the Mediterranean basin, or a North American glacial lake emptying with such explosive force that it left scars in rocks hundreds of miles south.

Agriculture simply domesticates biological disaster by deploying it for human convenience. Fires, earthquakes, floods, and new diseases wipe out the inhabitants of a particular niche, and thereby create a vacancy for another set of inhabitants; agriculture does the same. From the perspective of the trees and their dependents, the European invasion of North America brought sudden devastation; from the perspective of the grains and their dependents, it brought sudden opportunity. Cataclysms tend to empty an ecosystem; whatever survives or moves in will find itself in an environment with many unoccupied niches and few competitors. Mammals—including ourselves—have done quite nicely thanks to the extinction of the dinosaurs. Every grave is an opening.

In cultural history, as in evolution, it is hard to overestimate the importance of cataclysm. Minoan civilization was devastated by a massive volcanic eruption on the island of Thera; Tokyo was destroyed by an earthquake in 1923; Venice and Florence have been flooded; London and Moscow have burned. Natural devastation is regularly supplemented by man-made demolition. In innumerable incidents—the razing of Carthage in 146 B.C., the sack of Constantinople in 1453, the firebombing of Dresden in 1945—the destruction of memories has simply been incidental to the routine work of military conquest. Libraries and museums and architectural wonders tend to be located at the center of power, sometimes literally within the palace walls. The Library of Congress and the Folger Library are both within a block of the Capitol, and as any visitor to the Mall realizes, a single small atomic bomb targeted at the U.S. government would obliterate a large proportion of America's cultural treasures.

Other changes to cultural niches have been less violent but no less devastating. From the perspective of makers of silent films, the development of talkies was a calamity; the development of motion pictures weakened the demand for live theater; the development of television weakened the demand for movies.

Wars and technological breakthroughs resemble earthquakes, fires, and floods: they devastate cultural niches well enough, but inadvertently. In other cases, cultural niches are deliberately singled out for destruction or neglect. In 641 the Caliph Omar ordered the destruction of all the books in the great library at Alexandria: "If their content is in accordance with the book of Allah, we may do without them, for in that case the book of Allah more than suffices. If, on the other hand, they contain matter not in accordance with the book of Allah, there can be no need to preserve them. Proceed, then, and destroy them."

For six months, the artificial memories represented in those books fed the fires that warmed the water in the city's four thousand public baths. Acts of bibliogenocide are, of course, not unique to Islam. Christians have burned pagan books, pulled down pagan temples, and melted gold and silver statues and vases. The first Chinese emperor, Shi Huangdi, ordered all Confucian books to be burned; he supplemented this edict by banning the teaching of Confucianism and killing many Confucian scholars. On April 4, 1865, Union troops burned down most of the University of Alabama, deliberately destroying some of the most elegant architecture, and one of the finest libraries, in the South—in a town, in fact, whose representatives had campaigned against secession.

Sometimes a particular work is singled out for repression. Pope Clement VII ordered the burning of all copies of the 1524 edition of Marcantonio Raimondi's engravings of Giulio Romano's *I Modi*, sixteen depictions of sexual intercourse in different positions; a second edition, containing caption-poems by Pietro Aretino, was also suppressed. We may (or may not) regret the loss of this collaborative work by three important figures of the Italian Renaissance, but in such cases we are clearly dealing with a response directly stimulated by the features of a particular work. By contrast, if the fascist powers had won World War II, *Casablanca* would not now be so famous or familiar a film; indeed, the movie might already have joined the ranks of extinct species. But unlike *I Modi*, *Casablanca* would not have been singled out for censorship; it would simply have belonged to a whole class of cultural works disliked by a new regime. The qualities of an individual specimen are irrelevant when a whole niche is bulldozed. The best and the worst, the fittest and the unfittest, get flushed down the same vast toilet.

A TIME TO GATHER

Accidents to persons, accidents to works, inadvertent destruction of niches, deliberate destruction of niches—these cultural calamities, large and small, are indifferent to individual fitness. The wise, the skillful, the intelligent—"time and chance happen to them all." *Any individual artist or work, any niche, is subject to indifferent desolation.*

But the desolation is not evenly distributed, because the niches themselves are not egalitarian. Anyone can die young, but premature mortality clusters among slaves and the poor (and until recently, among women, worn out by pregnancies). Dominant males are likely to live longer and better. They are also likelier to be admitted to a niche in the first place. Cultural niches are, after all, artificially constructed, and their construction will be affected by the same social, sexual, racial, and political preferences and prejudices that shape other genres of human organization. As a result, cultural niches are seldom if ever zones of uncontaminated free competition. (Women were not even permitted to act in the Elizabethan theater.) A cultural niche is almost always dominated by persons from the class that dominates the host society.

Significant achievement in any art requires long periods of training or practice; most people are never taught and do not have the leisure or the instruments necessary for practice; training, leisure, and materials will be concentrated in the dominant class. As Virginia Woolf complained, Shakespeare had no female rivals because no woman could have competed with him without a room of her own. ("Again I saw all the oppressions that are practiced under the sun. And behold, the tears of the oppressed, and they had no one to comfort them! On the side of their oppressors there was power, and there was no one to comfort them.")

Just as certain groups may dominate a society, so certain societies may dominate others. Human beings are no more consistently distributed than stimuli. "Men did not spread evenly over the world like a layer of oil, but originally clustered together like coral polyps," the French geographer Paul Vidal de la Blanche observed in 1922. Some clusters are larger and stronger than others. The strongest clusters, for at least three thousand years, belonged to a geographical band from the Mediterranean through India to China, and each strong cluster has exerted its influence over a penumbra of satellite peoples. Influence easily shades into incorporation: the unification of China, the growth of the Roman empire, the Islamic conquests from Spain to India, the continental expansion of the United States. The western European colonization of North and South America, five centuries ago, decisively altered the global balance of power, but only by moving onto a larger scale a pattern of inequality that has characterized all of human history.

This inequality, this gathering of powers, is directly related to the distribution of cultural achievement. As we saw in chapter 3, strong stimuli cluster; these cultural clusters, in turn, tend to be found in politically, militarily, and economically dominant societies. Such societies are, obviously enough, attractive niches, rich with the nutrients that feed human achievement. Cultural historians speak naturally of the "silver age" of Roman literature, the "golden age" of Spanish or Dutch culture, because cultural pinnacles coincide with periods of material abundance.

These periods and places have another advantage. Dominance results from technological or organizational or ideological change in the expanding society, a change that enables it to sustain a larger population or to accumulate more wealth or to motivate more sacrifice or to deploy its military power more effectively. Some such radical change initiates a process of expansion, and that expansion in turn brings a society into intimate contact with other societies, some of whose peoples and memories it will inevitably incorporate into itself. Although the expanding society massively introjects itself into those societies it comes to dominate, there is also always a backwash of counterinfluence. In some cases, this retrofluence of the repressed is glaringly obvious (the impact of conquered Greek culture upon an expanding Roman empire). But to a lesser or greater degree, the colonized always transform the niche of the colonizer. Moreover, because of the delay between simple military or economic conquest and this backwash of retrofluence, these changes will percolate through the dominant society for some time, reinvigorating cultural activity.

In this feedback loop, change within a demographic niche leads to dominance, which leads to further change. These changes, in turn, precipitate the clustering of strong cultural stimuli in particular places associated with particular peoples. There is nothing remotely egalitarian about the geographical distribution of cultural achievement.

Moreover, these hierarchies within a society and between societies are complemented by a hierarchy of genres, which can be seen not only in the clustering of genius in a particular cultural arena at a particular time, but also in shifts in the favored arena over time. Consider, for instance, three incidents in the history of English literature.

On August 5, 1624, a new play was performed at the Globe Theater in London. Thomas Middleton's *A Game at Chess* was, as several witnesses report, "followed with extraordinary concourse, and frequented by all sorts of people, old and young, rich and poor, masters and servants, papists and puritans, wise men etc, churchmen and statesmen . . . and a world besides." So great was the demand for tickets that the actors raised the price of admission, and still the house was packed to capacity at every performance and would-be spectators waited in line for hours to get in. Before it was closed by the government, Middleton's play had the longest and most profitable consecutive run any English play had ever enjoyed. *A Game at Chess* stimulated more contemporary comment than any play of the English Renaissance and survives in more manuscripts than any other play of the period. It also provoked an international diplomatic incident, followed by the closing of the theater and the arrest of the author. In the next century in the same city, on May 18, 1728, Alexander Pope's poem *The Dunciad* was published, and provoked a comparable explosion of interest. As one contemporary observed, "On the day the book was first vended, a crowd of authors besieged the shop . . . to hinder the coming out of the *Dunciad*; on the other side, the booksellers and hawkers made as great efforts to procure it." An unprecedented commercial success, Pope's satirical pamphlet about pamphlet writers was followed by innumerable pamphlet replies and by Pope's own *Dunciad Variorum* in 1729 and *The New Dunciad* in 1744. The poem provoked such outrage that for some time after its publication Pope never ventured out without pistols in his pocket and his Great Dane at his side for fear of being attacked. In the next century in the same city, on November 24, 1859, every copy of the first edition of Charles Darwin's *On the Origin of Species* was bought on the day of its publication; a second and third edition quickly followed, and within a couple of years, twenty-five thousand copies had been sold. Even before it was published, a friend had warned Darwin of "the considerable abuse . . . which, unless I greatly mistake, is in store for you," and indeed, Darwin immediately became the target of intense vituperation from opponents in the scientific and religious establishment.

These three events happened in the same geographical place to a single people who were not much changed in the interim by invasion or immigration. In each case, a native, white, well-educated, upper-class male produced a cultural stimulus of extraordinary force, the impact of which we can measure by entirely objective criteria. In each case, the response was not the result of marketing departments or engineered hype, but initiated or expressed a kind of collective spontaneous combustion. In each case, the new stimulus provoked a storm of conservative hostility. Across only 235 years, however, the focus of this society's cultural attention shifted from a play to a satirical pamphlet to a scientific treatise. It is impossible to imagine an English scientific treatise in 1624 having the same impact as *A Game at Chess*, and equally impossible to imagine an English play in 1859 having the same impact as *On the Origin of Species*—or a satirical pamphlet, in either year, doing what *The Dunciad* did in 1728.

This shift can be charted not only in the impact of particular remarkable works but in the demographics of genius. Middleton's play was performed by the same acting company that was producing revivals of Shakespeare's plays and new plays by Jonson, Fletcher, and Philip Massinger; Pope's pamphlet was inspired in part by his friend and collaborator Jonathan Swift; Darwin rushed his book into print, after decades of gestation, so that his theory would not be preempted by the very similar conclusions being reached by Alfred Russel Wallace.

Comparable shifts have occurred in other times and places. Fifth-century Athens, for instance, produced a cluster of great dramatists, and fourth-century Athens a cluster of great philosophers. Within any society at a particular point in time, some cultural activities will be valued more than others. But strong societies can remain strong only if they keep changing; when they do, such changes produce changes in the hierarchy of cultural genres.

Genres are niches, and niches exist partly to enable us to measure human performances so that we can judge which ones are worth remembering. I have just measured *A Game at Chess* against other Renaissance plays, *The Dunciad* against other Augustan pamphlets, *On the Origin of Species* against other Victorian treatises. Such measurements make it possible to say, with some confidence, that within this niche, within this game or frame or genre, X is a stronger performance than Y. Cultural activity within a genre is always hierarchized. Moreover, the hierarchy within genres exists inside another hierarchy, the hierarchy between genres, which tells us which cultural games are most important; and the hierarchy between genres exists inside another hierarchy, the hierarchy between social groups (genders, classes, races, populations), which tells us whose cultural games are most important. Pyramids within pyramids within pyramids. The strongest human achievements tend to cluster in what the most important group in the most important society considers the most important genre. *Strong stimuli cluster in dominant niches.*

But as we have just seen, dominant niches do not stay dominant forever. Accordingly, the reputations that have lasted longest are those that were earned in more than one niche. Homer, according to tradition, wrote both the tragic *Iliad* and the comic *Odyssey*; Virgil wrote both the pastoral *Georgics* and the epic *Aeneid*; Chaucer wrote both the tragic *Troilus and Criseyde* and the comic *Canterbury Tales*; Chikamatsu wrote, for both the Kabuki and the puppet theaters, domestic plays as well as historical ones (*sewa-mono* and *jidai-mono*); Tolstoy wrote both the domestic *Anna Karenina* and the epic *War and Peace*; Michelangelo wrote poems, painted frescoes, carved statues, designed buildings; Aristotle made major contributions to the study of ethics, rhetoric, politics, biology, physics, and tragedy; Newton was a master of mathematics, physics, and optics. A maker's adaptability in mastering different genres increases the likelihood that his work will continue to be remembered, even at times, in places, and by persons hostile or apathetic toward certain kinds of cultural work.

Of course, there is more to a maker's adaptability than a quick count of genres. Genre is itself important in part because different genres usually deal, in different styles, with different topics and materials, and so the mastery of more genres implies a greater variety of human stuff. The greater the variety, the more likely that at least *some* of that stuff will continue to seem interesting, accurate, relevant, or vital in the unpredictable cultural environments of the future.

You can also get a rough measure of the amount of human stuff in a cultural artifact by measuring the size of the container. Aristotle said that in order to be magnificent a literary work must have magnitude; after all, in one sense *great* and *large* are synonyms. It is more difficult to create large works than small ones; larger works create more obstacles and therefore give a maker greater challenges—and more opportunities to dazzle us by seeming to overcome those obstacles effortlessly. Moreover, a large work is capable of far more complexity than a small one. The more parts to an entity, the more connections can be made between parts. Naturally, if all the parts are identical, the connections between them will be utterly predictable and boring. But if the parts of an entity are not only numerous but various, then the kind and number of possible interactions becomes enormous. Hence, the possible interpretations of the Katsura Palace in Kyoto, Rembrandt's *Nightwatch,* Goethe's *Faust,* Wagner's *Ring,* or Dostoevsky's *The Brothers Karamazov* are, for all practical purposes, incalculable. And the more interpretations, the more likely that some will seem particularly relevant and important to the unpredictable changing cultures of the future. The more variously interpretable a work is, the more adaptable it is—and the more likely to survive.

A TIME TO CAST AWAY

With the conclusion I have just reached, I may seem to have abandoned my tale of random destruction, returning at last to law, predictability, and the survival of the fittest. But dominant groups or societies or genres do not become dominant because they are fittest for survival in some purely aesthetic sense; their survival and supremacy are based upon physical, military, or economic power. The English did not colonize so much of the globe *because* they had Shakespeare. Shakespeare was like a local parasite—attached to a species that eventually dominated its own niche and migrated out into others, taking the parasite along and introducing it into new ecosystems that had, often, no defenses against it.

Moreover, what is true of reputations is true also of societies: the influence of a *social* container is also partly dependent upon its size, upon the amount of human stuff contained within it. Societies that have influenced others, that have conquered or colonized many niches, are, like makers who have conquered or colonized many genres, likeliest to be remembered. If the societies are remembered, their makers will be, too.

The intensity and duration of a cultural stimulus thus depends upon the density and duration of the niche in which it occurs. Genres become dominant because they are valued by social groups that have the power to set social agendas. Any individual's cultural achievement is fitted to niches created by other people. Cultural fitness is contingent in a fundamental way upon the fitness and the interests of its host class or society.

There are biological parallels for this pattern. Humans have not achieved dominion over the earth because we have an appendix; the appendix has been carried along because it belongs to humans, organisms with other features that have given them dominance in the struggle for survival. Similarly, culture is the appendix of social dominance: not a cause, but a corollary.

But this analogy is not perfect: the human appendix does not grow or shrink or change its position in the body depending upon the ecological success of its host organism. Culture does. Culture is shifty and supplementary. On the one hand, cultural achievement is *only* a supplement to social dominance; on the other hand, cultural achievement is *inevitably* a supplement to social dominance.

The complex relationship between "only" and "inevitably" will keep me busy in other chapters of this book. For now, I want to emphasize only the inevitable contingency of cultural achievement. The efforts of makers to create strong cultural stimuli are fundamentally dependent upon the efforts of other members of their society to create strong governments, economies, and armies—that is, in practice, the efforts of the latter group to create inequalities that favor some people over others. There can be no "survival of the fittest" when most members of the population are prevented or discouraged from demonstrating their superior fitness. We may acknowledge, for instance, that virtually all of the strongest literary achievements before the eighteenth century were produced by men, without believing for a moment that men are intrinsically better fitted than women to produce significant literature. The male dominance of literature for those many centuries is only/inevitably a corollary of the male dominance of almost everything else.

Such arbitrary inequalities imposed among potential makers are compounded by the same inequalities among survivors. For most of human history, socially dominant males were much likelier to have access to a cultural niche and to the resources that fitted them for success in that niche; socially dominant males were also much likelier to succeed in any struggle over what from the past was fittest to be remembered ("I hated all my toil in which I had toiled under the sun, seeing that I must leave it to the man who will come after me; and who knows whether he will be a wise man or a fool?").

Culture is not what was done but what is passed on. Culture therefore depends not only upon the maker who stimulates but upon the survivor who remembers, preserves, and transmits the stimulus. Even if a person from a dominated gender, class, race, or society succeeds, through extraordinary wisdom and toil, in overcoming circumstances and creating a strong cultural stimulus, her legacy will be subordinated and neglected to the extent that it depends upon the memories of a subordinated and neglected group of survivors. Often memory simply denies that the exceptional individual belonged to the despised group: Saint Augustine ceases to be African, Jesus is seldom Semitic, Shakespeare's homoerotic sonnets to a beloved male become heterosexual sonnets to a beloved female.

But which groups will be subordinated or neglected? The struggle for primacy within and between societies is endless and unpredictable. If a new group or a new genre becomes dominant, the achievements of an old group in an old genre (however extraordinary) may be deliberately destroyed or simply neglected to death. The cultural stimuli that have been gathered together may be thrown away or dispersed.

The fate of a reputation depends upon the fate of the niche in which it was earned. Niches, too, are mortal.

A TIME TO MOURN, AND A TIME TO DANCE

A century before Darwin, Samuel Johnson declared that "length of duration and continuance of esteem"—that is, survival—is the only true measure of the merit of a work of art. Johnson was half right. He was right to affirm that those works that survive for long deserve to survive ("The fundamental things apply, as time goes by"). And how do we know that a thing is fundamental? Because it continues to apply as considerable time goes by. Whatever has lasted must be, for us, fundamental. Human consciousness is not just the subject of art; it is the very environment in which a given species of art survives (or does not). Whatever flourishes for centuries must in some way suit the human environment.

Take, as an example, Ecclesiastes. It was probably written between 250 and 200 B.C.; it has been called "the most heretical book of the third century B.C." It remained controversial for more than a century, and it was not admitted into the canon of Judaic scripture until the Synod of Jamnia around A.D. 100. That decision—over the issue of whether this text was worth remembering—represented a social victory for one faction over another within the Jewish intellectual class. That victory probably owed something to deliberate alterations of the text; virtually all modern scholars agree that the received text contains several interpolations by later scribes that introduce conventional pieties flatly at odds with the general argument, which is deeply skeptical. But these interpolations themselves are a tribute to the extraordinary power and impact of the original. So is its eventual canonization.

Once this group of survivors had won the struggle to have this text, written by a dead author, incorporated into Jewish scripture, it became part of a very large, many-genred cultural container central to the memory of its people; as long as those people survived, the text would. But those scriptures were later appropriated by the break-away ideology of Christianity and translated into Greek, the language of the New Testament; once Christianity had successfully colonized the Roman empire, both testaments were translated into Latin, in which form they were widely distributed in manuscript throughout the Christian Roman West and the Orthodox Byzantine East. The first book produced by the new technology of the printing press, developed in the fifteenth century, was a Bible, and it was followed in the sixteenth century by printed translations of the Bible into most vernacular European languages. By the middle of the seventeenth century, two thousand years after its composition, the text of Ecclesiastes was a familiar, often-quoted part of the most widely distributed, translated, and revered text in Europe—and in South America, North America, and other European outposts. The Jewish nation had been destroyed and its population dispersed by the Romans, and Jews continued to be persecuted, deported, and murdered by Christians; nevertheless, the memory of the words composed in Hebrew by a teacher in one of the Jewish wisdom schools survived and multiplied.

Does this story of "length of duration and continuance of esteem" vindicate or undermine Johnson's maxim? Is survival equivalent to greatness? The author of Ecclesiastes did not think so: "For of the wise man as of the fool there is no enduring remembrance, seeing that in the days to come all will have been forgotten." The works that survive must have some qualities that make them memorable; they must contain some quality that continues to stimulate new minds in new niches. But possessing those qualities is no guarantee of survival. My ability to quote Ecclesiastes and your ability to recognize at least some of those quotations are clearly dependent upon the outcome of a complex sequence of historical struggles that the human author of Ecclesiastes could not have predicted and did not influence.

Good work can have bad luck. Luck is, after all, part of the human environment. Successful people often realize that their success owes at least something to the occasional lucky break, and we can all see that the success of *other* people owes a little or a lot to luck and muck. Why should this law of life suddenly cease to apply when we talk about literature or music? The story of culture is about deaths, survivors, and struggles, and the outcome of some struggles will owe more to chance than talent.

Even if you recognized all my quotations from Ecclesiastes, even if you have read *The Dunciad* and *On the Origin of Species*, you probably are less familiar with *A Game at Chess*. And yet the author of *A Game at Chess*, Thomas Middleton, satisfies every one of the criteria for a great maker. He is the author of a large and varied body of texts; he was extraordinarily successful in the extraordinarily rich, competitive, changing niche of the dominant genre in the expanding society of early modern England, a society on the road to dominating much of the global history of the next three centuries. *A Game at Chess* itself is a unique and powerful representation of contingency and survival. The characters are all identified as chess pieces, but several are clearly based on contemporary political figures; the two sides, White and Black, Protestants and Catholics, English and Spanish, struggle for dominance throughout the play, and at the end the White House wins. In this struggle between competing ideologies and societies, God does not intervene. He makes no appearance onstage, and he does not visibly favor his chosen people; he might as well not exist at all. But because the struggle is represented as a chess game, we cannot help but wonder who is playing. What moves these pieces? The individual characters believe that they are acting independently and unpredictably, but are they? Is everything a matter of chance, or is everything fated? Does chaos result from the absence of law or from the operation of a law we cannot apprehend? Is God nowhere or everywhere?

I cannot answer the final question. I will try instead to answer one that is a little simpler. Why do we remember the author of Ecclesiastes but not the author of *A Game at Chess*? In both cases, the stimulus was, in its own time, in its own niche, very strong; in both cases, the stimulus and the niche have both survived into our time. But one is now familiar, and the other is not. Why?

We cannot answer that question by analyzing, as I have been doing in these last three chapters, the stimulus itself, the work of the maker. The stimuli were similar, but the responses have been very different. The difference must therefore have something to do, not with the way the makers produced a stimulus, but with how the survivors represented and recollected the stimulus in their memories.

PART II

Represent.

5.

Family Likenesses.

*Nothing can please many, and please long, but
just representations of general nature.*

SAMUEL JOHNSON

Forget about everything that has been permanently lost or
destroyed. Forget about all the masterpieces never created
because the men and women who could have created them were
crushed by poverty or bigotry or just bad luck. From now on, let us
limit our attention to what has been created and has, in at least the
most minimal way, survived—that is, to what has been preserved in
at least one memory.

What does it mean to be preserved in memory? A stimulus in
your cultural environment—Darwin's *On the Origin of Species* or
Middleton's *A Game at Chess*—has affected you strongly enough
that you want to remember it. How do you do it? What exactly is
happening when you remember?

REPRESENTATION

The complicated process we call memory has traditionally been
divided into two parts: first we store the memory, and later we
retrieve it. There are problems with these words *store* and *retrieve*,
which is why I have avoided them, but it is clear that two separate
processes occur. The distinction between them was recognized at
least as long ago as Aristotle's treatise *On Memory and Reminiscence.*
Aristotle's assumptions have governed thinking about memory for

more than two thousand years, and as a result, they probably seem to most people as uncomplicated and obvious as any other bit of common sense. Of course, as Galileo and then Newton and then Einstein demonstrated, Aristotle and common sense were wrong about gravity; they are also wrong about memory.

According to Aristotle, this thing memory that we store or retrieve is an image, a likeness, "like a portrait." In my own case, as it happens, a memory is *never* like a portrait, for I have no visual recall. I have seen my wife Rebecca's face almost every day for more than twenty-five years, but if I stand in front of her and close my eyes, I cannot summon up a mental image of what she looks like. I could describe her appearance in words; I have a capacious verbal memory and a strong narrative memory. And I do recognize her: I can identify what I have seen before, I can distinguish one face I have seen from another I have seen. But I cannot picture her. Or anyone else. Or anything else. If I close my eyes now, I cannot visualize the computer screen in front of me (although I am typing this sentence with my eyes closed, because my hands know where the keys are). I lack what psychologists call "eidetic memory"; I do not remember with an image (*eidos*, in Greek).

Apparently, most people can—like Aristotle—see their memories. Rebecca, for instance, can close her eyes and visualize me. She can visualize, with an almost hallucinatory vividness, events that happened five minutes ago or when she was five years old; I cannot. It would be hard to claim that her life is intrinsically and continuously more memorable, visually, than mine; indeed, for most of our lives, we have been surrounded every day by the same optical reality. These differences in our responses thus have nothing to do with differences of stimulus; they must be caused by differences in the respondent. Just as some stimuli are stronger than others, so *some memories are more capable than others.*

But the inequities of memory, the unavoidable hierarchy created by the superiority of some memories, should not obscure an underlying fundamental sameness. Rebecca and I both remember, and both of us are human beings, with very similar biological equipment; our memories take different forms, but those forms arise from similar mechanisms, mechanisms that are not *necessarily* visual and not *necessarily* verbal. When I see something, in order to remember it I must translate the image into words. I must make for myself a verbal representation of a visual experience. Rebecca, by contrast, can remember images. But like me, she also must make for herself a mental representation of her sensory experience. Both of us translate the world into a representation of the world. *Every act of memory is an act of representation.*

After all, what are we doing when we remember? We are taking something in the present and storing it so that we can access it again later, when it is no longer present. This sequence of actions creates a philosophical paradox, which Aristotle recognized at the start of his analysis of memory: how can something from the past, something "not present," be "present" in our minds? When we access a memory, we are making something "present again"; we "re-present" it to ourselves. But what we re-present is not the thing itself but only a "re-presentation" of it. The thing itself is not present. When Rebecca closes her eyes and remembers my face, my actual face is not literally there inside her cranium; what she sees is only a representation. Her mental representation of my face is visual, and my mental representation of her face is verbal; but they are both representations.

To understand the world, human beings make representations. And since words and numbers and sounds are all representations, I could use a poem by Behn, an equation by Bohr, or a symphony by Beethoven to illustrate the nature of representation. But for most people, the easiest way to understand representation is by looking at a picture.

MEMORABLE IMAGES

The representation in figure 1, produced in 1656 by Diego Velázquez, is the most famous painting by the most famous artist of the golden age of Spanish culture. As Aristotle would have recommended, it is not only a visual image but, more specifically, a portrait. It is also the subject of the first chapter of the most influential postmodern analysis of representation, Michel Foucault's *Les Mots et les choses* (literally, "Words and Things," although the English translation is entitled *The Order of Things*). In this painting, Foucault argues, "are arranged all the signs and successive forms of representation":

> . . . on the left, the painter with his palette in his hand (a self-portrait of Velázquez); to the right, the visitor, one foot on the step, ready to enter the room; he is taking in the scene from the back, but he can see the royal couple, who are the spectacle itself, from the front; and lastly, in the center, the reflection of the king and the queen, richly dressed, motionless, in the attitude of patient models.

The painter (who makes the representation), the palette, brush, and canvas (the materials from which the representation is made), the model (what is being represented), and the spectator (who observes the representation) are all here. In its own time, this work was described as "the theology of painting," and indeed, as Foucault concludes, "representation seeks to represent itself here in all its elements."

What does any of this have to do with memory? Like any other portrait—like the commissioned painting of the master or mistress of an Oxford college, like the death mask of John Keats, like the photograph and then the sculpture of six infantrymen raising the American flag on Iwo Jima—it is designed to preserve the memory of a person or persons at a certain moment. The painter is Velázquez himself; his models, the figures in the mirror, are King Philip IV and his wife, Queen Mariana; the girl to the right is their daughter, the Infanta Maria, accompanied by an entourage that includes Dona Maria Agustina Sarmiente, Nieto, and Nicolaso Pertusato. Today, centuries after the deaths of every person in it, the painting can still make "present again" for us what is "not present." Velázquez, as court painter, was paid to immortalize his patrons by preserving their likenesses in a memory made of paint.

This portrait, then, is a memory, and Aristotle compares memory specifically to a portrait. But Aristotle's description of memory differs quite strikingly and fundamentally from this painting.

FIGURE 1
Diego Velázquez, *Las Meninas*. Reprinted by permission of Museo del Prado, Madrid.

According to Aristotle, when we perceive something with our senses, that perception produces a change in us—in our soul and in the part of the body that contains the soul. This sequence roughly corresponds to the process of stimulus and response that I described in earlier chapters. But Aristotle uses a particular metaphor to describe the change that occurs within us: "The change that occurs marks [the soul, and body] in a sort of imprint, as it were, of the sense-image, as people do who seal things with signet rings."

Most of us do not use signet rings anymore, but the image is easy enough to understand: a specially designed ring was pushed into hot wax, impressing an image of itself in the wax, which then cooled and hardened, preserving the image in the more permanent form of a seal. This metaphor has proven extraordinarily resilient. Cicero compared "the structure of memory" to "a wax tablet"; Freud compared it to "a magic writing pad"; Kafka imagined a penal colony in which the memory of crimes was written on the body of the condemned by a machine that gradually pressed more and more deeply into his flesh. In all these metaphors and many others like them, a memory is created by pressure exerted from outside on a soft surface. We still speak of someone being "impressionable" or of something "making an impression" on us.

And yet this model of memory and representation is much less satisfactory than the one provided by Velázquez. Aristotle's model makes seven mistakes.

1.   THE WAX IS ACQUIESCENT AND INERT. For Aristotle, the initial act of representation is essentially passive; it is something that happens to us. The outside world, like the seal ring, forcibly imposes itself upon our helplessness. But it is quite clear in Velázquez's painting that representation is an active process; we see the artist doing it. In fact, rather scandalously, Velázquez himself, not the royal couple, dominates the image. Representations are made not by the outside world but by a human agent, a representer.

As F. C. Bartlett demonstrated in his classic study *Remembering* (1932), memory is an active response; it is something we may or may not *do* when confronted with a certain kind of stimulus. After all, there is no direct relationship, no contact, between the thing in the outside world (the signet ring) and the thing in our memories (the wax image). These words before you do not leap from the page, forcibly penetrate your cranium, and make dents in your neurons. That is why I have consistently written not of "impressing" but of "stimulating." These words, if they are working, are stimulating activity in your brain. You are not being impressed; instead, you are making impressions. If you have ever made a "rubbing" from a brass or stone funeral monument, you will know that many hours and calories may be consumed in taking an impression of an object. Having made that rubbing, you then possess your own private representation of something you wish to remember, a representation you can take home with you and reexperience whenever you want. But you cannot have the representation until you do the work. *Memory actively constructs representations.*

2. THE IMPRESSION IS FORMED BY A SINGLE OBJECT IN A SINGLE ACTION, WHICH TRANSFORMS ANOTHER SINGLE OBJECT. For Aristotle, memory is singular. This (ancient) assumption led inevitably to the (modern) conviction that each human memory must be stored in the brain in a single "engram." Neuroscience has now discredited that theory, but a glance at Velázquez's painting would have shown that the search for an engram was always misguided. At the most basic material level, the representation itself was constructed not in a single action but by the weaving of cloth for the canvas, by the manipulation of wood for its frame, by the mixing of natural and chemical ingredients that created the pigments on the artist's palette, by the mixing and juxtaposition of pigments in the palette and on the canvas, by the thousands of separate brush strokes that compounded canvas and pigment. This representation is constructed not by impressing but by combining. Abraham Lincoln spoke of "the mystic chords of memory"—memories, like chords, result from compound simultaneity. Likewise, neuroscientists now describe memory not in terms of wax seals or engrams but in terms of looms, like those that wove the canvas on which this painting was made. *Every representation is a combination.*

3. THE RELATION BETWEEN THE IMAGE IN THE WAX AND THE IMAGE ON THE SIGNET IS RECIPROCAL. We could use the image in the wax to

make a mold and thereby produce a signet identical to the original. In other words, a representation, by definition, must be able to reproduce the same situation in the external world that it originally represented. This works well for signet rings, but it does not work well for human beings. Because human representations and memories are always only partial, they cannot be used to reproduce the original stimuli. We cannot, by decoding Velázquez's painting, bring back to life the Infanta or any of the other persons depicted there. More generally, healthy people can easily distinguish mental images of the past from their perceptions of the present; memories are weaker than physical sensations. *Representations are not equal to the realities they represent.*

4.   THE IMAGE ON THE RING CORRESPONDS PERFECTLY WITH THE IMAGE MADE IN THE WAX. External detail fits internal detail. Of course, Aristotle recognizes that some memories are better than others, but he attributes such deficiencies to accidents in the raw material: if the wax is too hard or too soft, it will be too hard to create a memory, or too easy to forget one. But Velázquez demonstrates that failure of fit is not accidental or occasional but fundamental and unavoidable.

The painting leaves things out. Part of the body of the girl on the far right is amputated by the frame; only the top half of the bodies of the two adults in the right middle distance are visible, the rest being blocked by intervening figures; we see only part of the canvas on the left. More obviously, of course, we see only the back of that canvas; the painting represents one side of a collection of three-dimensional objects. These deficits are compounded by effects of distance and light. It is hard to discern any detail of the ceiling or of the paintings that hang on the far wall. The adult in the doorway is much smaller than any of the children in the foreground, not because his body was actually smaller but because it is meant to be farther away from us. The smallest figures of all are the adult king and queen, partially visible in miniature in the central mirror, which, like other mirrors, presumably reverses their images, left to right.

We could find other paintings that do not commit some of these errors of representation, paintings in which figures are not blocked, amputated, diminished by distance, or obscured by darkness. Even within this painting, there are figures who, like the Infanta in the center foreground, are in no way eclipsed. But even there, if we look very closely at the Infanta's left hand (figure 2), we can see that it consists only of a few brush strokes; as a detailed anatomical representation of a real hand, it is as inaccurate or deficient as the representations of the man in the doorway or the paintings on the wall. Nevertheless, these "defects" are precisely what we admire about the work of Velázquez and his contemporary Rembrandt: their representations seem more real to us precisely because they more closely resemble our own internal representations of the world. Consequently, the fact that this particular representation so obviously fails to correspond with certain realities of our three-dimensional environment does not make it an uncharacteristic or inept representation; rather, those deficiencies actually make it a truer, more representative example of human representation.

Human representation is deficient in part because human perception is. Velázquez's painting was produced in a century that revolutionized our understanding of the visual world. A few decades before its creation, Galileo Galilei had published the first representations of the telescopic world (*Siderius Nuncius*, 1610); while the painting was hanging in Philip IV's private office, Robert Hooke published the first collection of representations of the microscopic world (*Micrographia*, 1665); in 1675, Newton published his *Opticks*. Under a microscope, the skin of a human hand looks as unfamiliar as the hand of Velázquez's Infanta. Infrared photography or magnetic resonance scanning makes it look even more bizarre. Human vision scans only a narrow band of the spectrum of light and,

even within that spectrum, has limited powers of resolution. Human perception is selective. And since representation depends upon perception, representation is always selective.

Because representations are selective, they must therefore be the result of an act of selection performed by a composing/selecting agent. A view requires a point of view. Velázquez's painting, for instance, is compositionally organized by its point of view. Using the laws of perspective, we can quite scientifically project out of the painting the "point of view" from which it was painted and should be viewed (figure 3). An environment is thus represented as it appeared to a particular observer from a particular point in space and time.

This rule can easily be applied to all other forms of representation. Literary critics, as well as art historians and physicists, analyze point of view. But the rules of perspective have more than a physical or formal significance. They remind us that every representation is made by a representer, who is inevitably situated in a particular space, time, and ideology. *Representations are always partial.*

5.   WAX IS INANIMATE. For Aristotle—as for much of twentieth-century psychology and neuroscience—the imprinting of memories is a dispassionate mechanical process. But as Velázquez demonstrates, it is impossible to disentangle memories from feelings. This painting served the same purpose in the seventeenth century as a family snapshot does in the twentieth. Although it is now usually called *Las Meninas* (The Maids of Honor), it was not given that title until 1843; the first known reference to the painting, in an inventory of 1666, describes it as "the family picture." It even includes the family dog. It hung in the king's private office, just as workers in many modern offices keep framed family photographs on their desks or walls. The king and queen are visible only in the mirror, not because Velázquez subversively wanted to diminish or minimize royal authority, but because the painting represents and satisfies parental feeling. The painter looks at them, but they

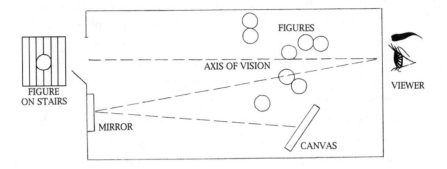

FIGURE 3
Point-of-view sketch of *Las Meninas*. Drawing courtesy of Celia R. Daileader.

look at their daughter, who dominates the center of the painting's light and attention. This is not primarily a painting *of* a
royal couple for others to look at, but a painting *for* a parental
couple to look at, a representation of the intimate community
they most enjoy observing. It is hardly necessary to keep a picture of myself at the office; I keep instead pictures of the people I love. Such pictures remind us during the grind of the day
of pleasures that are not present. We make such representations in the first place because we feel strongly about something or someone, and the representations in turn stimulate
repetitions of those feelings.

This connection between memory and feeling is not limited to representations of domestic life. For Lincoln, the
"chords of memory" were directly linked to "bonds of affec-
tion," and those emotional and memorial cords justified and
demanded political union. Velázquez also produced images of
explicitly public occasions, like *The Surrender of Breda* (figure 4). That painting reflects and stimulates very different feelings than *Las Meninas*: pride in victory (and artistry), awe at
the scale of the scene (and the painting), respect for the sense

of disciplined power the painting conveys, a subordinate but nevertheless real sympathy for the defeated. Human emotions vary in kind and intensity, and human representations reflect that variety.

What does not vary is the centrality of some sort of emotion. For Plato, what made art dangerous was precisely its ability to stir emotions, and Aristotle defined tragedy in terms of its functional relation to pity and fear. What philosophers have recognized about the representations of art they have also recognized about representative memory. Friedrich Nietzsche, in *The Genealogy of Morals*, observes, "If something is to stay in the memory it must be burned in; only that which never ceases to *hurt* stays in the memory." John Locke, in *An Essay Concerning Human Understanding*, realizes that those ideas "which naturally

FIGURE 4
Diego Velázquez, *The Surrender of Breda*. Reprinted by permission of Museo del Prado, Madrid.

at first make the deepest, and most lasting Impression, are those, which are accompanied with *Pleasure* or *Pain*." Locke, remembering the two-thousand-year-old words of Aristotle, still describes memory in terms of an "Impression" that is "imprinted on" and "stamped deep into" the blank wax tablets of the mind, but unlike Aristotle, Locke recognizes how inextricably memories are entangled with what he calls "*Passions*."

Experiments on the biology of memory depend upon, and measure, pleasure and pain. But in the laboratory, pleasure and pain are treated as physical sensations—in part because experimental animals cannot tell us how they feel about the memories inflicted upon them by scientists. The most satisfying documents of twentieth-century neuroscience are much more sensitive to feeling. A. R. Luria's account of *The Mind of a Mnemonist* and the descriptions by Oliver Sacks of persons suffering various memorial disorders recognize that memory decisively shapes the emotional life of every individual, and that a scientific description of mnemonic abnormality must therefore include a description of its affective effect. By attending to the feelings of their subjects, such documents—which Luria called "romantic science"—remember those subjects for us and stimulate our own feelings for them. By contrast, because most twentieth-century academic criticism self-righteously ignores the emotions generated by the art it analyzes, it often seems to the general public irrelevant or misguided. In its anxiety to appear scientific, such criticism disregards a fundamental scientific fact: *memories are emotive*.

6.   THE SIGNET IS ITSELF A REPRESENTATION. The wax image is therefore just a representation of another representation. Aristotle does not, in fact, describe how physical reality is turned into representation; he describes instead how one image (on a ring) is reproduced (in another medium, wax). By contrast, the people and the room represented in *Las Meninas* were physically real; they were things, which Velázquez turned into images, just as Rebecca can turn my real face into an image of that face. But

Velázquez and Rebecca both remain aware of the difference between the real and the remembered face.

This conscious gap between reality and representation (which Aristotle's image does not recognize) is a doorway through which feeling and art enter our representations. We have all been, at one time or another, frustrated, humbled, or enraged by the inadequacies of our memories or our talent. Kafka and Virgil, dissatisfied to the end, asked that their work be destroyed after their deaths; Ezra Pound abandoned his epic poem in despair. In each case, the maker's despair is itself a part of the work; we admire *The Aeneid*, *The Trial*, and the *Cantos* partly for their representations of human beings confronting a world that demands more than any individual can give. Lord Byron did not finish *Don Juan*, as Lady Murasaki Shikibu did not finish *The Tale of Genji*, not because the authors happened to die before they reached the end of the story, but because to end would have been to imply that the representation was complete—and it could never be complete. In both cases, that sense of a world so full and fluid that it can never be contained is itself part of what we admire in the work. A sense of insuperable inadequacy can suffuse with sadness even the best memory or the most finished work of art. I find *Las Meninas* an especially moving painting. It advertises its own incompleteness. Its painter looks out at us, knowing that we will look back not at him but only at his representation.

Nevertheless, the gap between reality and representation is also, and at the same time, a source of artful pride. After all, in *Las Meninas* the figure in the doorway is not really farther away than the dog in the foreground; we know perfectly well that they are both represented on a two-dimensional plane, both at an equal distance from our own eyes. But the representation compensates for its two-dimensionality by deliberate distortions that mimic the effects of perspective in the three-dimensional world. We admire the impression of distance in *Las Meninas* precisely because we know that it is an illusion, an effect constructed by the art of the representer. Likewise, plays and novels do not obey the same laws of space and time as the narrative reality they represent. No novel (not even Richardson's *Clarissa*) is as long as a lifetime. Actors wear masks; women are played by men; people are impersonated by puppets. But we admire these imperfect representations to the extent that they create, from obviously inadequate materials, the successful illusion of real people in real places performing real actions in real time.

Of course, it is possible for a representation to impose upon itself various rules that bring it closer to the laws of nature. Aristotle thought that a play should represent events that took place in a limited time and place; even more rigorously, the baroque neoclassicism that based itself upon Aristotle demanded that the duration of a performance equal the duration represented by the performance. Some of the plays of Jonson, Racine, or Molière impress us in part because we are aware that, by satisfying the neoclassical demand for unity of time, place, and action, they are following the rules of a particularly difficult game; we admire the virtuosity of the player. But those same plays are obviously, in other respects, distorted representations of social reality—not least in the compression and intensity of the language their characters speak. Even more fundamentally, we know that nobody really dies, that nobody really gets married, that stage money is as counterfeit as stage blood.

We know that every representation is a deception. In some languages, the same word means both "poet" and "liar." In our own, "artifice" is deception; we call someone who makes a fraudulent living a "con artist"; "to make" is not too distant from "to make up." In Renaissance England, a painting like *Las Meninas* could be called a "counterfeit." This linguistic overlapping between representation and deception reflects an overlapping of emotions. We detest liars (when they deceive us) but admire them (when we are undeceived) for the executive plausibility of their "memories" of a past that never in fact existed. Knowing that the onstage deaths are counterfeited allows us to applaud them (as accomplished performances), while we also cry real tears (for the real deaths they represent). Although the emotion, and the relation between emotion and art, may vary, emotion and art are always involved.

What is true of professional representations like paintings and plays is true also of personal memory. Because we know memory is inadequate, we try to overcome its natural deficiencies by training it. We can learn to remember just as we can learn to paint or write; the mnemonist Shereskevskii, described by Luria, made a living by displaying his mnemonic talent, just as Velázquez made a living displaying his artistic talent. In both cases, the skill at representation is a source of pride (in the possessor), amazement (in the observer), and, at the same time, curiosity, disbelief, suspicion, sadness, sometimes even rage (in both). The exercise of memorial representation inevitably creates a vacuum into which these skills and emotions pour. *The gap between representation and reality is filled with artifice, imagination, and feeling.*

7.   THE WAX IMPRESSION HAS NO SENDER OR RECEIVER. It engages in no transaction. Aristotle does not explain who is making it, for whom, or why. By contrast, the painter in *Las Meninas*, like every painter outside it, is making a representation for someone.

All representations are for someone; they are all transmissions. As a statement about art or language, this may seem obvious enough; its relevance to memory may be less obvious. After all, we tend to think of memory as personal and internal, as something that takes place inside one person. But what happens when I remember something purely for my own benefit, with no intention of communicating it to anyone else? What happens is this: I-in-the-present transmit a message to I-in-the-future. Depending on our philosophical inclinations, we could describe I-in-the-present and I-in-the-future as one person or two. But either description assumes that memory is a form of communication. If they are two persons, then memory is how one communicates with the other; if he is one person, then his unity, stability, and coherence depend upon the communications link maintained by memory. *All representations are communications, and memory in particular is a representation that communicates across time.*

Perhaps your memory is better than mine, but before I can go any further, I need to remind myself of the seven observations that have been generated by the preceding pages of analysis.

1. Memory actively constructs representations.
2. Every representation is a combination.
3. Representations are not equal to the realities they represent.
4. Representations are always partial.
5. Memories are emotive.
6. The gap between representation and reality is filled with artifice, imagination, and feeling.
7. All representations are communications, and memory in particular is a representation that communicates across time.

THE CONSEQUENCES OF AN IMAGE

These truths about representation account for four common pathologies in the memory of culture.

The first pathology is hostility to all representations. Since representations are imperfect, they should be forbidden. Many religious traditions prohibit any representation of God. The Jews who refused to write out the name of YHWH, the Muslims who forbade images of Allah, the Puritans who smashed stained-glass windows, the Quakers who retreated into spiritual silence—all acted from a belief that any merely human representation of the divine was blasphemous, because inadequate. Plato banished poets from his ideal republic because human representations could provide only a misleading "shadow of a shadow" of the real world of ideal forms. This rejection of representation is the foundation of many different kinds of mysticism, and it is pathological, because human beings cannot escape from representation. We cannot remember, or think, without it. We cannot formulate a critique of representation without representations.

By contrast, postmodern literary theory does not forbid the construction of representations; indeed, it is devoted to them. (The most influential journal in the humanities is called *Representations*.) But the diverse theories that have dominated the last quarter-century of critical practice agree in insisting that all representation is essentially flawed. Politically, representations from the past can be shown to have distorted the portrayal of women, or homosexuals, or the lower classes, or other nations, or other religions, or other races, or some other Other. Philosophically, representations can be shown to be self-contradictory, combining elements that are logically incompatible. Within the academy, the first kind of criticism is associated with Michel Foucault, the second kind with Jacques Derrida. Outside the academy, both tend to be lumped together in a single mysterious and dangerous movement called "deconstruction." Indeed, both tendencies easily slide into a mysticism that legitimates itself by denigrating everything else. Given the inevitable gap between representation and reality, *every* individual work of art can be pilloried from some political or philosophical perspective; such criticisms can quickly become repetitive, pointless, and complacent. Worse, this institutionalized sniping seems indiscriminately ungrateful. Yes, there is something wrong with every representation, but some are better than others, and we care so much about the best of them because they remind us, powerfully, of some reality that moves us.

What the Quakers, the Muslims, and the deconstructionists all have in common is a resistance to idolatry. Idolatry is the belief in perfect representations—the belief that representations can be as singular and whole as Aristotle's impression in wax. The belief in perfect representations leads to the second pathology, the pathology of fundamentalism. Fundamentalists believe that certain representations are simple, certain, transparent, and complete. We do not need priests, critics, or special interpreters of any kind; we need only the representation itself. Fundamentalism is pathological because it depends upon interpreters who deny the need for interpretation, and upon representations that are treated as though they were realities. Representations become dangerous when people forget their inadequacy. The crucifix is not in itself sacred but only a reminder of something sacred. *The Last Supper*, Handel's *Messiah*, and the American flag are not sacred either; they are just representations.

The fundamentalist belief in perfect representations easily shades into a hatred of change. Every change of representational technology, for instance, provokes resistance and a corresponding nostalgia for the old technology. The invention of writing stimulated a nostalgia for the greater authenticity of oral culture; manuscript seems more authentic than print, handwriting more authentic than typewriters, typewriters more authentic than word processors, live theater more authentic than film, painting more authentic than photography, black and white more authentic than color, and so on. This nostalgia is the third pathology: it forgets that the old representations were also technological; they just used a different technology. The old representations were not less artificial; we had simply become accustomed to their artifice, so accustomed that we no longer noticed it and could pretend that the representation put us into spontaneous touch with reality.

This desire for direct contact with reality often leads to the belief that art is, or should be, "realistic." Realism is the fourth pathology: it asks for what no representation can give and rejects much of what any representation does give. The meaning and power of a representation always depend upon its connections with something else. Some of those connections link the representation to the world: *Las Meninas* represents real persons. But some of those connections will link one part of a representation to other parts of the same representation ("form," "structure"), and some will link one representation to other representations ("convention," "allusion," "intertextuality"). Representations, accordingly, need not guiltily strive to close the gap between themselves and reality; they may dance in the gap.

What they can never do is dance alone. If it is pathological to believe that representations can be real, it is equally pathological to believe that they can be isolated.

SYSTEMS OF REPRESENTATION

Combining is, of course, what memory does. It will, for instance, be easier to remember the first three propositions we generated from Aristotle's mistakes if we combine them into a single formula. Representation (R) is an Activity (A). What kind of activity? Combining (C). This gives us the formula

$$R = AC$$

Representation equals activity-combining. But Representation does not equal Reality (R').

$$R \neq R'$$

We can combine these two formulas to produce

$$R = AC \neq R'$$

Now instead of remembering three separate propositions, we need to remember only one.

What I did in the preceding paragraph is what psychologists and cognitive scientists call "chunking." This process was first described by the psychologist George Miller in 1956. Suppose that you are given a random sequence of nine letters to memorize:

$$F C C C N N N B C$$

You will find it much easier to remember this sequence if you break it down into three recognizable groups:

$$F C C \qquad C N N \qquad N B C$$

You have, in this way, turned nine "bits" (nine separate atoms of information) into three "chunks" (three separate molecules of information), which we can further reduce to a single chunk ("The FCC regulates CNN and NBC"). In the same way, I can reel off with great speed and complete accuracy a sequence of sixty digits, consisting of my own phone number in the last three places I have lived, plus the phone numbers of my university office, my mother, and my mother-in-law. For you, that sequence would be sixty random numbers, each equally unpredictable; for me, it is only six chunks of information.

We remember by linking one representation to another. Aristotle himself makes this simple empirical observation when he describes what happens when we try to recollect something: we "hunt up the series" until we arrive at a memory "contiguous with" the one we are seeking, a process that somehow stimulates the release of the desired missing memory. "Accordingly, things arranged in a fixed order," he concluded, "are easy to remember, while badly arranged subjects are remembered with difficulty." True enough—but why should that be true if memory is like the impression made by a signet ring in wax? Aristotle had, by the time he made this observation about retrieving memories, forgotten his own metaphor for the making of memories. How we find memories must have something to do with how they are made in the first place.

"Only connect!" the novelist E. M. Forster prescribed; although he was not referring to memory, that is indeed how memory works. When studying memory in laboratory animals, we are actually inferring memory from the fact that a connection has been made: the dog has connected the stimulus of the bell to the stimulus of the food, the rat has linked different pathways in the maze into a system that connects the starting point to the finish line. Like the representations of a novel, the representations of memory are always connected. Systems for improving personal memory—which are demonstrably efficient—all depend upon this fact. *The Memory Palace of Matteo Ricci*, described by Joseph Spence, or *The Mind of a Mnemonist*, described by A. R. Luria, are much the same; the sixteenth-century Jesuit missionary to China and the twentieth-century Russian showman both made use of a technique first described by the Roman orator Cicero in the first century B.C., who attributed its discovery four centuries earlier to the Greek poet Simonides—the poet who wrote the epitaph for the Spartans who died at Thermopylae.

Simonides had just left a banquet when the roof collapsed on the other guests, killing them all and mangling their bodies so badly that they were unrecognizable; Simonides was able to identify the corpses by recalling where each of the guests had sat around the table. We can recognize this as another story of a survivor remembering the dead. The families wanted him to identify those many bodies, because each family wanted to know which body to mourn; his memory was driven by their grief and by his own relief and guilt at having survived. This anecdote thus confirms the theories about memory, emotion, and culture I have been tracing. But the anecdote also adds something new. Simonides could remember so much because he began with the fixed image of a place and then located the positions of individuals within it by mentally walking around the table. Likewise, Ricci and Shereskevskii began with a fixed imaginary place and placed details they wanted to remember within it; they found the details by mentally walking through the place. All three mnemonists created a machine that would enable them to "chunk" any number of random disparate bits of information.

Simonides, Ricci, and Shereskevskii commanded extraordinary memories, but they did so simply by intensifying and exploiting a natural property of all memories. Memory constructs a system of linked representations. Thus, *Las Meninas*, that exemplary "representation of representation," is a "family picture," a group portrait. As such, it implies that individuals can be properly represented, or remembered, only in terms of their relationships with other persons. Of course, not all portraits are group portraits, and Velázquez himself painted several separate portraits of the Infanta alone. But every representation depends upon relationships: between the representer, the represented, the materials of representation, the observer. It also depends upon and creates a relationship with other paintings—just as every book or film depends upon the memory of others. I am at this moment communicating verbally through an extraordinarily complicated system of representations, the English language, created and maintained by its other users. I am, like Velázquez, playing a game; my ability to play, your judgment of how I play, depends upon our memories of the rules of the game and of the field created by other players.

I am making representations by making new combinations within a complex composite system. Biological memory depends upon complex networks of neurons. Artificial representations—the preservation of memories in speech, in handwritten language, in print, in computers, on audiotapes and compact disks—are all systemic; each individual sign or signal makes sense only within the context of its recording system. No memory is an island; memory cannot occur except as the property of a system of signs. Representation—and the specific subset of representation called memory—always belongs to a system.

Memories, like human beings, always come in families. I am not just speaking metaphorically. Literally, we learn to remember in a family, which need not be biological or nuclear. The family picture by Velázquez that hung in King Philip IV's office portrayed not simply two parents and their child but a small private household. Remember: biological parents, adoptive parents, older children, teachers, mentors—from the perspective of memory, they are all "parents." Our personal memories evolve within the system of relationships, emotions, and representations created by such families. We cannot remember an "I" except within a "we." Individual memory is a part of collective memory. *Every memory is a collective memory.*

Las Meninas is thus a better representation of representation—and memory—than Aristotle's image of wax impressed by a signet ring. But if the foregoing analysis of representation is correct, then no representation is complete in itself—*Las Meninas* must also be inadequate. Which leads us to the next question: what does this "representation of representation" leave out?

6

Invisible Man.

Pay no attention to that man behind the curtain.
THE WIZARD OF OZ

How do we know that Velázquez painted the painting we have been looking at? How do we know that the painter on the canvas is a self-portrait of Velázquez? How do we know the historical identities of the other persons represented in the painting? None of the persons are named on the canvas. How do we know what it is that is being represented (or remembered)?

An even more basic question: how do we know what the painting looks like? My discussion of it, like Foucault's, is illustrated by a photographic reproduction. That reproduction reduces to a few square inches a painting nine feet wide and ten feet tall, translating all its colors into shades of black and white, flattening its variously textured surface into the uniform thin smoothness of a plate. Of course, Foucault or I might have used a different kind of reproduction; we might have used color plates, for instance. But even a color plate cannot reproduce the exact tints of the original, and it certainly cannot reproduce its size or texture. A color plate would simply be a different form of reproduction; it would not be the thing itself.

How can we look at the thing itself? We could fly to Madrid and peer touristically at the canvas in the Museo del Prado. But the painting hanging there does not look the way it did in 1656. A collaborative study by an art historian, a conservator, and a conservation scientist concluded in the early 1980s that "*Las Meninas* has grown noticeably darker," that the "impasto has also been flattened by lining," that the whole scene "is less optically persuasive than it was in 1656." The original is no longer the original. In 1984 *Las Meninas* was cleaned by John Brealey of the Metropolitan Museum of Art. Any such pictorial restoration is complicated and controversial, as was demonstrated by the arguments over the recent restoration of the Sistine Chapel. But whether we observe *Las Meninas* before or after its most recent cleaning, we are looking at an image that is different from the original.

Moreover, one of the ways in which the-painting-now differs from the-painting-then is the very fact that we can look at it at all. The Museo del Prado places the painting in a context—a particular position in an edited collection of works of art, a visual anthology— and every such contextualization alters the meaning of the work in question. By contrast to its current public position in the Prado, we know that the painting was originally hung in the king's small personal office. The painting has been displaced; if it were returned to the king's personal office, it would become inaccessible to our gaze.

Las Meninas, the original representation composed by Velázquez in 1656, no longer exists; all that survives is the memory of *Las Meninas*. All that is left to us is a representation of that representation.

Obviously, not all representations suffer exactly this fate. But if a representation becomes a collective memory, if it is dispersed among many members of a society, it will have to be passed from one set of memories to another. In the process of that passage, it will become subject to four transformations.

1. We can fully understand a representation only by surrounding it with information that it does not actually contain. The farther we move from the origin of the representation, the greater the amount of information that will have to be supplied as a supplement to the representation itself.
2. Reproducing a representation alters it.
3. The representation itself decays or is altered by changes in its human and physical environment; thus, to preserve its

original force, it must be repeatedly "restored" (physically or imaginatively).

4. Whether or not the representation is restored, it will eventually occupy an environment in some ways different from its original environment, and its new environment will alter its significance.

The effect of each of these transformations increases with distance. The more effectively and extensively a representation circulates, the more fundamentally and extensively it will be altered.

But the image does not transform itself. Who supplies the elaborate informational apparatus that the image itself does not? Who reproduces the image? Who restores it? Who places it in new environments?

The person who made the representation cannot do any of these things: the maker is dead—or at least, not present. The transformations must therefore be performed by a survivor. But not all survivors do so. From the perspective of Velázquez, you are a survivor; you are alive after his death, and *Las Meninas* is now, if it was not before, in your memory; but you have not (I assume) recontextualized, reproduced, restored, or resituated it. Of the multitude of survivors, only a small subset transform representations in any of these ways. In the case of *Las Meninas*, these four transformations have been performed by, respectively, an art historian, a photographer, a restorer, and a curator. For other art forms, different words would be used.

We do not have a single term that covers all these activities, but I will call these people "editors." For a literary text, an editor supplies the informational apparatus of introduction and notes, reproduces the text, restores it by correcting errors, and resituates it in an anthology or in the "Collected Works" of a particular author or in an expensive and forbidding "Critical Edition" or in an accessible paperback or in an electronic file. An editor may also be a translator; most of the "Great Books" are translated. If the text is a play, the directors, designers, and actors who produce it will also "edit" it. Similar activities are performed on paintings and drawings, musical compositions, buildings, silent films, and every other species of representation. For a text, as for other representations, these activities may be performed by one editor or several, and the differences between these functions may be important. But the difference between one kind of editor and another is less important than the fact that every cultural representation that becomes a collective memory is edited, one way or another. There is no culture, or memory, without an editor. *There are no unedited collective memories.*

Michel Foucault's influential book on representation begins with an examination of *Las Meninas*. Although he singles it out as a classic "representation of representation," nowhere does his analysis acknowledge the function or the inevitability of editors. Foucault dismisses as trivial the elaborate informational apparatus that names, attributes, and contextualizes the painting. He ignores the differences between his photographic reproduction and the original, and he never recognizes the reproducers, restorers, and curators who have made possible and also conditioned his attention to the painting. Foucault's interpretation of representation is systematically dependent upon editors whom it systematically does not acknowledge.

This silence is not unique to Foucault. In general, people looking at works of art do not see or acknowledge the editors who make it possible to look at them. In 1959 America's then most influential editor, Professor Fredson Bowers, lamented that America's most influential literary theory at that time, New Criticism, paid no attention to the editorial problems of the texts it routinely interpreted. In 1990 America's then most prestigious editor, G. Thomas Tanselle, made the same complaint about the then most prestigious literary theorists of the day: Jacques Derrida, Paul de Man, Harold Bloom, and J. Hillis Miller, he demonstrated, were systematically ignorant of the editorial theory and practice that had reconstructed the very texts they were busy deconstructing.

This may seem like a local dispute about scholarly footnotes, or the kind of meaningless miniature civil war for which academics are notorious. But, in fact, the editorial process fundamentally affects everything we remember about the achievements of the past. And nevertheless, the invisibility of the editor is neither an accident nor a failure of professional ethics by a few theorists. Why is the editor, who is so crucial to the collective memory of representation, so consistently invisible?

> I am an invisible man ... I am a man of substance, of flesh and bone, fiber and liquids—and I might even be said to possess a mind. I am invisible, understand, simply because people refuse to see me. Like the bodiless heads you see sometimes in circus sideshows, it is as though I have been surrounded by mirrors of hard, distorting glass. When they approach me they see only my surroundings, themselves, or figments of their imagination—indeed, everything and anything except me.

ART IN THE MIRROR

Historically, persons who have performed functions conventionally described as authorial have also performed functions conventionally described as editorial. The great Italian poet Petrarch, the great Italian prose writer Boccaccio, the great Dutch humanist Erasmus, and the great English poet Pope are all as important to the history of editing as to the history of literature. Joseph Addison, A. E. Housman, Samuel Johnson, Richard Steele, Walt Whitman, and W. B. Yeats were all editors; Toni Morrison edited at Random House, T. S. Eliot at Faber and Faber. In the apparatus of modern editions of the Greek tragic playwright Aeschylus, you will discover that certain corrections to the Greek text were first made by the English epic poet John Milton. The tenth-century Japanese poet and prose writer Ki No Tsurayuki was also the principal editor of the canonical *Kokinshū* anthology.

The most influential editor in the history of China—perhaps the most influential editor in human history—was Confucius. Confucius edited the *Spring and Autumn Annals* and the *Book of Songs*; "I love the past," he said, describing himself as "someone who seeks for it earnestly." Confucius insisted that he was only an editor, only a survivor recording the glories of others. "I transmit," he said, "I do not make." But this saying was itself transmitted in the *Analects*, an anthology of the sayings of the Master edited by the disciples who survived him, a text venerated for as many centuries as the New Testament has been. As much as Confucius may have wanted to separate the two activities, his transmitting became indistinguishable from making.

What is true of editing is equally true of translation. Many writers have also been translators, and translations can powerfully stimulate memories that would never be touched by the originals. St. Jerome's translation of the Hebrew Old Testament and the Greek New Testament into the Latin Vulgate was the most important European text for a thousand years. Martin Luther's translation of the New Testament laid the foundations not only of a massive theological and political revolution but also of German literary prose. William Tyndale's English translation of the Bible, and the various revisions of it that culminated in the Authorized Version of 1611, for centuries influenced speakers of the English language more than any other text. When John Keats compared the experience of reading Homer to the experience of a Spanish conquistador first sighting the Pacific Ocean, he was inspired not by the Greek text but by George Chapman's translation. Of the greatest English poets, Chaucer, Wyatt, Dryden, and Pope all devoted much of their talent to translation, and the "original" work of most of the others—including Shakespeare, Middleton, and Milton—often incorporates images, passages, and episodes edited/translated from other languages.

Why should makers so often also be editors? *Las Meninas* is a better guide than Aristotle or Foucault. At least one detail of the painting was altered three years or more after its original composition in 1656: the painter wears the red cross of a knight of Saint James, an honor not bestowed upon Velázquez until 1659. Was the addition of that cross to the painting an act of vanity or homage? That is, was the addition authorial or editorial? Did Velázquez change the painting to reflect his new status, or did someone else change the painting as a tribute to the painter's new status? There is, so far as I know, no way of knowing. If the painter of the cross was an editor, he stood, literally, in the same position as the author: in front of the canvas, holding a palette in one hand and a brush in the other. This is the very position in which John Brealey stood in 1983 when he cleaned *Las Meninas*. It is the very position in which all copyists of *Las Meninas* must stand—including the photographer responsible for the image of *Las Meninas* reproduced in this book. The reviser, the interpolator, the restorer, the copyist, the translator, the director, the actor, the dancer, the musician—that is, in all these incarnations, the editor—always stands in the place of the maker.

Editors as a class perform all of the local functions performed by makers as a class. They add images to paintings, and words to texts. They delete, alter, substitute, and transpose words; they choose among variants that have already been written down or introduce new variants of their own. They collect and arrange works; they reclaim or disown works; they divide works into sections. (The biblical chapters and verses are an editorial addition, supplied for convenience of reference.) Editors punctuate; they situate; they annotate; they titulate. *The Prelude* was a title given to Wordsworth's poem by its first posthumous editor, his wife; *The Art of the Novel* was the title given to a collection of essays by Henry James first gathered together and arranged by R. P. Blackmur in what he mistakenly believed was their order of composition, eighteen years after the author's death; *Las Meninas* was the title that a Spanish art historian in the nineteenth century gave to an untitled seventeenth-century painting by Velázquez.

These correspondences between editorial and authorial activity are generated by the circumstances of all reproduction. No representation can be finished in a way that forestalls subsequent refinishing. No representation can be *fixed* (established definitively, secured permanently, rendered nonvolatile) in a way that prevents subsequent *fixing* (manipulation, repair, amendment). The religious conflicts that have dominated the history of the Middle East for the last two thousand years are based upon this simple fact. Was the Bible finished with the completion of the Old Testament? Or was it only completed with the addition of the New Testament? Or are both the Old and the New Testaments only prefaces to the last and most important holy book, the Koran? Is the Book of Mormon a holy text or a hoax? Representations are always partial, and therefore they can always be supplemented, in an effort to make them less partial. Representations are made by combinations, and further combinations are therefore always possible. Representations connect, and there is consequently no way to prevent them from being reconnected.

From the perspective of the original work, there is no distinction between authorial revision, corrupted transmission, and editorial emendation. All makers at one time or another revise their own work. And just as every authorial revision of a composition is an editorial act, so every composition is an act of editorial revision. All representations are made by adopting, altering, and recombining features of preceding representations. (The book you are reading recombines words that already exist in the English language.) And within this circulating economy of representations, the shape of new authorial artifacts may be generated by preceding editorial artifacts. The division of Elizabethan plays into five acts was based upon (mistaken) editorial conventions in Renaissance textbooks of classical drama; the division of *Paradise Lost* into twelve books derives from a late editorial division of Homer's *Iliad* and *Odyssey* into twenty-four books.

This fusion and confusion of editing and authoring makes it easy for authors to represent themselves as editors. The eighteenth-century French text *Les Liaisons dangereuses* was transformed in the 1980s into an English play written by Christopher Hampton (*Liaisons dangereuses*) and an American movie directed by Stephen Frears (*Dangerous Liaisons*); these creative transformations were part authorial, part editorial. But the original book advertised itself in 1782 not as a novel but simply as a collection of private letters, published and edited by "Monsieur C—— de L——." The editor, by his own admission, omitted many letters and could not find others; he printed and labeled first drafts of some letters; he arranged "the letters . . . in an order which is nearly always chronological"; he identified quotations, corrected errors, interrogated the text's claims. Of course, "Monsieur C—— de L——" (Choderlos de Laclos) was the author of the entire collection, and his portrayal of himself as a mere editor demonstrates yet again the similarity of editorial and authorial functions.

From one perspective, then, editors are indistinguishable from the makers who transmit a message. From another perspective, though, editors are indistinguishable from the survivors who receive the message. They are survivors, admiring the past, attempting to preserve and transmit its memories.

This confusion about what it is that editors do, or who they are, is evident even in attempts to visualize editorial subjects—as demonstrated by any of the many images of Saint Jerome, editor and translator of the Latin Vulgate edition of the Bible. In Antonello da Messina's painting of *Saint Jerome in His Study*, for instance, Jerome is sitting in a chair before a desk with both of his hands upon an open book; other books populate the shelves around him. Who is this person?

I realized that I no longer knew my own name.

He looks like a man reading, nothing else. At most, he might be an author. What kind of iconography would specifically identify him as an *editor*?

It's all mixed up. First I think it's one thing, then I think it's another.

Turning from sacred to secular editing, we can see the same ambiguity. The British neoclassical artist John Flaxman designed a memorial plaque to commemorate the eighteenth-century Shakespeare editor George Steevens. Like the images of Saint Jerome, this image was produced by a survivor to celebrate a past achievement, an achievement that was specifically editorial. In Flaxman's representation, Steevens sits on the left; he is looking at a book propped on his knee; just beyond the book, on the right, a bust of Shakespeare looks down upon the editor and his book. If we did not know that Steevens was an editor, what in this image would tell us that he was anything but a reader? What would tell us that the "text" Steevens is apparently reading was constructed, in part, by the reader himself? Indeed, what would tell us that Steevens is editing

Shakespeare's text rather than authoring a new text of his own, as Keats would do, with a bust of Shakespeare as his presiding muse?

> I tried, thinking vainly of many names, but none seemed to fit, and yet it was as though I was somehow a part of all of them, had become submerged within them and lost.

Many of Steevens's emendations and commentary notes can still be found in editions of Shakespeare. Jerome was famous enough to be sainted and painted. Most of the greatest poets in English were either editors or translators or both. Confucius was worshiped. How can I describe such people as invisible? Clearly, editors as persons are often visible enough. What is invisible is the editorial function. Velázquez could represent a painter as a person with brush in hand, and an observer as a person pausing in the doorway to look at a canvas. Likewise, we can represent composition by showing a person with pen in hand or fingers on keyboard; we can represent reading by showing a person looking at, often holding, a text. But how can we display the cultural function performed by editors? Editing is visually unrepresentable.

It is equally unrepresentable in law. An editor may claim copyright to introductions or commentaries; after all, the editor is the author of those texts. But how can an editor copyright a rediscovered variant reading, or even an emendation, of a text by a dead author? Others will want to copy that variant or emendation only if the editor persuades them that it represents not the editor's act of invention but the author's. In the nineteenth century, the influential British editor John Payne Collier precipitated a major scandal by insisting that the manuscript readings in a particular early printed edition of Shakespeare's plays were his property, protected by his copyright, and hence not usable by other editors without his permission. Collier was eventually accused of having forged the readings he claimed to have discovered, to which he replied, "If I were the real author of them, what could have induced me *to foist them into an old folio and to give anybody else the credit of them*?" If he were the author, why should he pretend to be only the editor? But if he were only the editor, why should he, like an author, claim copyright?

Legally, an emendation is simply a labeled forgery; a forgery is simply an unlabeled emendation. (As the historian Anthony Grafton has observed, there is a long and intimate relationship between the technologies and personnel of forgery and textual criticism.)

Editors devote their lives to proving that their best work belongs to someone else; as Collier's case demonstrates, editors will be vilified to the extent that they do legally *own* what they wish to *disown*. Only an editor's mistakes are truly his property. If an editor's work is perfect, the editor is invisible; editors become visible only when they make mistakes. Editing can be represented only as a failure of representation.

This failure can be represented as deficiency or excess, as dullness or madness. In fact, the editor is, impossibly, represented as both excessive and deficient, the epitome of, at the same time, too much and too little . . .

> as though I stood simultaneously at opposite ends of a tunnel . . .

These characteristics make the editor a natural target of satire, and the best of those satires have been written by authors who were also editors. Vladimir Nabokov, who translated and edited Pushkin's great Russian verse-novel *Eugene Onegin*, also wrote a novel about a fictional author and editor, *Pale Fire. Pale Fire* is the title of a poem, putatively by John Francis Shade; it occupies pages 33–69 of the book. The rest of the book (pages 13–29 and 73–315) consists of the foreword, commentary, and index prepared by a putative editor, Charles Kinbote. Shade was killed shortly after completing the poem; Shade is the dead maker, and Kinbote the surviving editor. In Nabokov's portrait of the editor, dullness and madness, too small and too big, too hot and too cold, too hard and too soft, acrobatically miscegenetically intertwine, like text and apparatus. Like all editors, Kinbote is, as the poet's widow describes him, "an elephantine tick . . . the monstrous parasite of a genius."

Kinbote's deficiencies are evident from first to last. His marginal instructions to the printer—on where to place a sentence evidently added in the galley proofs of the book ("Insert before a professional")—are literally inserted, nonsensically, before the words "a

professional" in the middle of a paragraph of Kinbote's own foreword. Confronted with "hal . . . . . s" in his author's poem, Kinbote
stupidly emends it to (poetic) *hallucinations* instead of the (unpo-
etic) word obviously required by the context, *halitosis*. Kinbote does
not understand a pun on *Homer* (a Greek epic poet; an American
baseball term), and he cannot locate the source of the phrase "pale
fire," which the poet took from Shakespeare and Middleton's play
Timon of Athens. But if Kinbote's editing is obviously deficient, it is
just as obviously excessive. The very bulk of his obsessive editorial
apparatus enfolds and dwarfs its object (as Nabokov's own commentary enfolds and dwarfs his translation of *Eugene Onegin*). Kinbote encourages readers of Shade's poem to read his editorial prose
before, during, and after the poet's verse, asserting that "without my
notes Shade's text simply has no human reality." And from this
allegedly "unambiguous *apparatus criticus*," Kinbote/Nabokov constructs "the monstrous semblance of a novel."

Kinbote is fictional, and through him Nabokov can caricature
editors shamelessly. But something similar happens even when the
editor is real and beloved. The twelfth-century widow Li Ch'ing-
chao could write of her husband,

> *The wind subsides—a fragrance*
> *of petals freshly fallen;*
> *it's late in the day—I'm too tired*
> *to comb my hair.*
> *Things remain but he is gone*
> *and with him everything.*
> *On the verge of words: tears flow.*

Li Ch'ing-chao, like other makers, was also an editor, who published
in 1132 the unfinished text of her husband's monumental work on
ancient Chinese epigraphy, *Chin-shih lu* (Records on metal and
stone). Her postscript to this catalog, commemorating her husband's life, fondly remembers their years of idyllic collaboration;
when he brought scrolls home, "we would sit facing one another,
rolling them out before us, examining and munching." "Whenever
he got a book, we would collate it with other editions and make cor-

rections together, repair it, and label it with the correct title." But reality eventually punctures this conjugal editorial dream. As the Sung empire is invaded by Chin Tartars, the enormous collection of books and artifacts in which they had invested their shared life is gradually destroyed. "In the twelfth month Chin forces sacked Ch'ing-chou, and those ten or so rooms I spoke of were all reduced to ashes." Later, "those books which . . . took a string of boats to ferry across the Yangtse were scattered into clouds of smoke." Others are stolen. She saves "six or so baskets of books, paintings, ink and ink-stones"; five are stolen. "Maybe it is Heaven's will that beings as insignificant as ourselves are not fit to enjoy these superb things." In the very act of gathering these memorials of the past, in the act of trying to preserve them, Li Ch'ing-chao and her husband made them more vulnerable to destruction and theft. "When there is possession, there must be lack of possession; when there is gathering together, there must be dissolution—that is the constant principle of things. Someone loses a bow; someone else happens to find a bow—what's worth noticing in that?" The entire editorial enterprise that had dominated her life from age eighteen to fifty-two and filled the pages of the book she is publishing becomes, retrospectively, trivial, futile, and mad. Her husband was "deluded," his achievement evidence of a "disease," no more dignified than an obsession with hoarding pepper.

It will do editors no good to complain that these authors misrepresent an honorable profession. The only possible representation of that profession is a misrepresentation.

GHOSTS

> The trouble is that there is little the dead can do; otherwise they wouldn't be the dead. No! But on the other hand, it would be a great mistake to assume that the dead are absolutely powerless.

In the 1990 movie *Ghost*, the ghost of a dead man (Patrick Swayze) enters the body of a medium (Whoopi Goldberg) so that he can speak to and touch his beloved (Demi Moore) one last time. But what the film shows us at this climactic romantic moment is not the black female body of Whoopi Goldberg lovingly connecting with the white female body of Demi Moore. That would have seemed, to the heterosexual audiences for which the movie was designed, wrong; it would have provoked embarrassed tittering in the theater; the scene would have been represented that way only by someone intent on satirizing it, someone who wanted to parody its sentimental falsehood. No, at that moment, what we saw was the white male body of Patrick Swayze touching the white female body of Demi Moore. The medium simply disappeared from the screen.

> It was as though they hadn't seen me, as though I were here, and yet not here.

The dead maker is a ghost. We are in love with that ghost, but we can keep in touch with it only through a medium, the editor. At the moment of contact, the ghost and the medium (the maker and the editor) occupy the same position. The medium therefore is unrepresentable: we cannot see the medium at the very moment when it performs the function that makes it a medium.

An editor, like a medium, must represent what she is not. In the movie, a black woman is the medium for a white man. This discrepancy is not fortuitous. Imagine how different the movie would have been if the medium had been played by another attractive white male like Swayze. We would immediately, inevitably, have sensed a conflict of loyalties. The medium might wish to touch Demi Moore for his own reasons. Indeed, the medium might have become the movie's villain, the man trying to seduce the bereaved young woman, the man who wants to take the place of the dead in the bed of the living.

A medium must be different from what she mediates. The very qualities that qualify one as an editor distance one from the author. No conductor of Beethoven could be deaf. Milton's amanuensis could not be blind.

> Whoever else I was, I was no Samson.

Authors can be—and often are—sloppy; editors must be relatively tidy. Authors usually write one work at a time; editors edit any given work in the context of an entire oeuvre, parts of which did not yet exist at the time of the given work's composition. Authors concentrate upon areas of a work that raise artistic problems; editors concentrate upon areas of a work that raise editorial problems, because of accidents of transmission that have corrupted the work or fortuitous changes in the prevailing system of signs that have rendered the work unintelligible. Authors can be spontaneous; editors must be deliberate.

> The thing to do was to be prepared—as my grandfather had been when it was demanded that he quote the entire United States Constitution as a test of his fitness to vote. He had confounded them all by passing the test, although they still refused him the ballot.

But however deliberate, however prepared, the editor will always fall short. The kind of work an editor does on a work will always differ from the kind of work the author did, even when the editor's results successfully duplicate those of the author. Hence, even when—or perhaps especially when—the editor successfully represents the author, the editor will be despised for the disparity between the editor's attributes and those of the author. The author, after all, was a great creator, a founder; the editor is a mere tinker.

> Though invisible, I am in the great American tradition of tinkers. That makes me kin to Ford, Edison, and Franklin.

And yet, we know the qualities of the creator only through the efforts of the tinker. The tinker transmits to us the image of the creator and preserves for us the magnitude of the maker's achievement. Moreover, the magnitude of the maker is always established partly by contrast with the minitude of the editor, even though it is the editor who conveys the magnitude of the maker. The more idealized the maker, the more demonized the editors of that maker will be. Witness the abuse heaped upon editors of the Bible, Shakespeare, and Joyce.

Witness also the abuse heaped upon politicians in our most idealized political system.

POLITICIANS

Editors and American politicians have one thing in common: their only function is to represent other people.

Editors are sacrificed on the altars of representation, as politicians are sacrificed on the altars of representative democracy. A single delegate representing many thousands of different persons will not be able to represent all of their differing interests simultaneously. Inevitably, therefore, many of the constituents of a politician will feel, at any given moment, that he is not properly representing them. The politician, we say, has "forgotten" the people he is supposed to be standing in for.

But the American politician's problem is even greater than this observation suggests, for public servants are supposed to remember and represent the intentions not only of a living constituency but also of the dead Founding Fathers. Every new president takes the place of the first president.

Has not your present leader become his living agent?

How can the contemporary politician live up to that duty? The authors of the U.S. Constitution (the first successful text of representative democracy) expected representatives to differ from the populace they represented. James Madison wrote in 1787 one of the most famous defenses of the new and still unratified Constitution. In *The Federalist* 10, Madison explained that the purpose of a representative democracy was "to *refine* and enlarge the public views, *by passing them through the medium* of a chosen body of citizens, whose wisdom may best discern the true interest of their country, and whose patriotism and love of justice, will be least likely to sacrifice it to temporary or partial considerations" (my editorial emphasis). In other words, Madison—whose authorship of this *Federalist* essay has been established by modern editors—presupposes that representatives will sometimes be torn between the immediate desires of their constituents and the long-term interests of those same constituents. When they remember the short-term interests of their constituents, politicians are accused of forgetting the long-term vision of the Founders; when they remember the long-term vision of the Founders, they are accused of forgetting the short-term interests of their constituents. Either way, the politician is doomed to a failure of representation, and that failure magnifies, by contrast, the achievement of the Founding Fathers.

Editors are, of course, in much the same situation. They must represent the many competing, often contradictory, interests of an artist. To begin with, many, perhaps most, artistic works are produced collaboratively. They incorporate the intentions not only of the acknowledged artist or artists but also of friends, relatives, publishers, actors, censors. Even when editing a single, never revised work—a text like the German poet Rainer Maria Rilke's *Sonnets to Orpheus*, "written down in a single breathless act of obedience"—what may have been a unified compound of authorial intentions will, over time, inevitably disintegrate into incompatible parts. The artist must use a particular system of signs to communicate to a particular audience, but the system of signs changes, the original audience dies, and the new audience will not understand the old signs in the old way. Editing an author's "Complete Works" is even more perilous, for the editor must represent simultaneously decades of separate intentions. An author at one time may intend to suppress his own intentions at an earlier time. Editors, like politicians, cannot avoid misrepresenting some of the intentions of their constituency; they cannot serve equally well the dead past and the living present. Editing, like politics, is the art of the impossible.

The U.S. Constitution, like *Las Meninas*, is a classic "representation of representation." As we know from James Madison's record of the deliberations of the Constitutional Convention, the collective authors of the United States of America realized that all systems of representation are inadequate. The history of Western political life had demonstrated that built-in weaknesses and instabilities plagued every known system. Every system of representation (like every memory) was partial, passionate, artful. The Founders constructed a new system, a new representation, a collective memory, by an act of synthesis. (All representations are actively constructed. All representations are acts of combination.) But because they realized that, however carefully it was constructed, their new system of representation would also be inadequate, the Founders made explicit provision for it to be altered. Unlike *Las Meninas*, the Constitution represents its own amendment by the future. The Founders knew that successful representation—enduring collective memory—depends upon editors, who stand in the place of the original artist and transform the original work.

But what could prevent those future representatives, those unborn politicians, from usurping total power and utterly destroying the system of representations that the Founders had created? The Founders constrained American politicians by turning them quite explicitly into mere editors. Editors do have power, but they never have legitimacy. Their lack of legitimacy is the chief mechanism for circumscribing their power. After all, the constituency an editor represents—the artist—is always already dead, and cannot recall or depose them. An editor, by definition, is a survivor, and creators are ghosts. (As Marx said, "They cannot represent themselves; they must be represented.") In the government of texts, the author would be powerless, and the editor all-powerful, if the editor's power were ever legitimate. But the editor's power is never legitimate. The power of the living editor can always be successfully denounced and resisted by appeal to the authority of the original, for only the authority of the original legitimates the power of the editor. Likewise, the authority of the Constitution is the only thing that legitimates the power of an American politician. And because, like the editor, the politician can never fully live up to the imperative to represent that authoritative memory, the power of the politician can always be denounced and resisted. In the formula articulated by *The Federalist* 51, "Ambition must be made to counteract ambition." The more important an author, the more editors will rush to represent her, and each will compete for the right to represent the author by denigrating the claims and abilities of the other suitors. Politicians, likewise, ambitiously compete to represent both the Constitution and their constituents. And since their representations will always, in one way or another, fail, their power is always circumscribed.

The success of a *system* of representation depends upon an awareness of the inevitable failure of each *individual* representation. American representative democracy will collapse only if the American people lose faith in the original system and put their faith instead in an individual. Our system will fail if we are persuaded that our problems can be solved only by abandoning the collective memory constructed by the Constitution and entrusting our fate to one heroic individual, a representative who claims not to suffer from the inherent weaknesses of all representation—a man, for instance, like Ross Perot.

MEDIUMS

Wait a minute. How did we get from a seventeenth-century Spanish painting to American politics in the 1990s?

We got there through a medium. Politicians are mediums, and so are the many different kinds of people I have called editors. Collective memory depends upon mediums, upon representatives. Both the politician and the editor are expected to preserve our most cherished traditions; each is, in the words of the novel I have been quoting throughout this chapter,

> a trustee of consciousness.

The nameless hero of Ralph Ellison's *Invisible Man* wants to become a teacher, wants to follow in the footsteps of "the Founder" and become, like him, a "black Aristotle," but these plans are derailed by the unfortunate fact that the college created by the Founder is located next door to an insane asylum and run by a cynical politician who is interested only in preserving his own power. Having failed as a transmitter of the past—as an editor—the narrator becomes instead a politician, an orator, "a voice for his race." But his political career is aborted by the inescapable failures of representation. He cannot satisfy the conflicting demands of all those he is meant to represent. He retreats to a room in a basement, flooded with stolen light, and writes his memoir, *Invisible Man*, in which he represents his people by recording a series of failures to represent his people.

When Roger Kimball, the author of *Tenured Radicals*, complains of "how politics has corrupted higher education," he is—like anyone who complains of "political correctness"—trying to separate culture from politics. It can't be done. The politician is an editor, and the editor is a politician; our collective memories always depend upon systems of intermediaries. It may not surprise us that an author such as George Orwell, who wrote so often and so powerfully about politics, should be subjected to what John Rodden calls "the politics of literary reputation." But the same mechanisms and mediums go to work upon makers less openly polemical than Orwell. If you have heard of Shakespeare's play *Othello*, it is because many mediums between the early seventeenth century and the late twentieth century chose to reproduce and circulate that representation of a seemingly civilized, Christian black man who collapses in the end back into his natural state of barbarism, a barbarism epitomized by sexual violence against a white woman. If you have heard of D. W. Griffith's silent film *Birth of a Nation*, it is because many mediums chose to reproduce and circulate that representation of the rise of the Ku Klux Klan as the heroic instrument of a just southern white resistance to Reconstruction. Of course, *Othello* and *Birth of a Nation* are, by all sorts of criteria, great works of art; Shakespeare and Griffith each created a powerful cultural stimulus. But those stimuli could be created only in a racist cultural niche; they could be perpetuated in collective memory only by editors, by mediums, who were at least tolerant of racist representations of the world.

By choosing these examples, I am myself engaging in cultural politics. By quoting Ellison, I am making a choice; by that choice, I am trying to influence our collective memory of the past. For I, too, am a medium. I have myself edited Shakespeare's works (including *Othello*). And my own memories are dependent upon choices made by other mediums, other transmitters of the past. I am a teacher, but before I became a teacher, I was a student, and I was taught to read

Ellison's novel, in my first year of college, by Professor Margaret Arnold (the teacher who also recommended that I read Northrop Frye's *Anatomy of Criticism*).

These are my personal memories; they probably mean nothing to you. But you and I do share collective memories that are, like my personal memories of the distant past, dependent upon mediums, upon editors who are hard to distinguish from politicians. The European Renaissance was a sustained editorial attempt to recover the authority of the Greek and Roman past. The Protestant Reformation was an editorial dispute about the proper text, translation, and interpretation of a single ancient anthology. The challenges to royal power by English Parliaments in the seventeenth century were legitimated by the archival research of editors like John Selden, research that undermined the historical authority of absolutism. The American Civil War resulted from an editorial dispute about the Constitution and led to further editorial changes to the Constitution. Every case decided by the Supreme Court is an editorial decision. Even the contemporary debate about a line-item veto is an editorial argument: should the president be limited to approving or vetoing legislation, or should he have the right to edit congressional texts? Culture cannot escape from politics because neither culture nor politics can escape from the need for mediums who transmit collective memories.

I have been using the word *mediums* for these editors, but the word *medium* usually takes the plural form *media*. What I have said about editors applies also to the cultural intermediaries we call "the media"—newspapers, periodicals, books, radio, television, movies. These media are epitomized by that triumvirate of "tinkers" identified by Ellison: Ford (transportation), Edison (communication), and Franklin (information). These cultural industries create collective memories by reproducing and circulating representations. In the process of reproducing and circulating those representations, they—like all editors—inevitably transform them. If we like the representations they reproduce, then the media seem transparent, apolitical, invisible, an impersonal mirror accurately reflecting the reality of the world. If we do not like the representations they reproduce, then we attack the media for distorting reality. We "see" the mirror only if it is flawed. We "see" the transmitter only as a failure of transmission.

We tend to separate "editors" (restorers, curators, emenders of the past) from "politicians" (representatives of the present) and "the media" (retailers of the present). But the four kinds of transformation performed by editors—recontextualizing, reproducing, restoring, and resituating—do not, in fact, depend upon the passage of time; they can result just as well from movement in space. Politicians, like museum curators, bring representations from many scattered sites and concentrate them in one place (city hall, the state capital, Washington, D.C., the United Nations). In that place, their representations are valid for a particular period, fixed by a constitution or treaty; during that historical instant, each political representative embodies the collective memory of a constituency. The modern mass media work to eliminate time altogether by moving representations as quickly as possible over the largest possible area. Like editors, they create collective memory by giving the same selection of representations to large numbers of separated persons.

All memory depends upon a system of representation; collective memory depends as well upon a system of representatives who, in our attempts to abolish the geographical and mental distance between members of a social group, are entrusted with the reproduction and circulation of representations. Collective memory, then, the memory of culture, depends upon systems of representation and systems of representatives.

But those systems are never stable. They change, too.

7.

Time Present
and Time Past.

If we ask ourselves why we measure music in time in the first place, we can only answer: because we would not otherwise bring it into being. We measure time to make it conform to ourselves.

ARNOLD SCHOENBERG

I am listening to *Le Sacre du printemps.* When this music premiered in Paris, my grandfather was four years old, playing in the dirt in a small town in Kansas, half a world away geographically, arguably even further away socially. That was 1913; I was not born until forty years later. More than another forty years have passed since my birth; my grandfather and the people who first performed this ballet music are all dead now. How can I be listening to this long-ago faraway music?

I can listen, first of all, because *Le Sacre du printemps* was a strong stimulus in a strong niche. It was produced by the collaborating talents of three great makers: the composer Igor Stravinsky, the choreographer Vaslav Nijinksy, and the impresario Sergey Diaghilev. Its first performance, on May 29, 1913, occasioned a riot and a scandal. Within a year, the music had been given triumphant concert performances in Moscow, Saint Petersburg, and Paris; it became a landmark of modernism. By every external measurement, it was the most powerful new ballet produced by the Ballets Russes at the very moment when ballet was at its most influential as an art form, Russia was at its most influential in the culture of western Europe, and western Europe was globally the most influential of cultures. Such a strong stimulus in such a strong cultural niche is especially likely to be remembered.

The cultural niche that produced *Le Sacre* was very different from the cultural niche that *Le Sacre* represents, and the work is powerfully aware of the distance between those two niches. The ballet dramatizes an act of ritual human sacrifice in pagan Russia; Jean Cocteau called it "the georgics of prehistory" (itself an allusion to the *Georgics* of Virgil, written almost two thousand years before). But this representation of the ancient past was designed to be heard and witnessed by the most culturally sophisticated of modern audiences. Musically, choreographically, scenically, the ballet insisted upon the epochal passage of time between *then* and *now*.

Le Sacre remembers and represents human prehistory, but such a representation could not have been produced before the twentieth century. Debussy, recognizing this paradox, characterized the work as "primitivism with every modern convenience." The music was composed on a modern piano, and the full score can be played only by an orchestra of typically modern European size and character; indeed, the ballet requires a larger orchestra than any other work by Stravinsky (not to mention forty-six dancers). Its musical organization, particularly its rejection of traditional melodic development, owes a great deal to the experiments of Modest Mussorgsky and Claude Debussy. It also incorporates—sometimes consciously and sometimes probably not—many small fragments of specific Russian folksongs and, more generally, folksong techniques; those musical memories were available to the composer only through the labors of editors like Nikolay Rimsky-Korsakov (Stravinsky's teacher), who transcribed and published anthologies of Russian folk tunes. And Russians were not the only composers interested in folk music and folk memory: the same enthusiasm was shaping the work of Béla Bartók in Hungary, Antonín Dvorák in Czechoslovakia, Gheorghe Enescu in Romania, Edvard Grieg in Norway, and Ralph Vaughan Williams in England. These musical excavations and re-creations belonged to a much larger nineteenth-century ethnographic effort to identify and preserve vanishing folk traditions. Nicolay Roerich, for instance, who designed the scenery for the ballet and to whom Stravinsky dedicated the score, had devoted much of his life to the restoration and celebration of early Slav culture. This interest in early Europe was reinforced and influenced by a fascination with Amerindian culture, which was put on display by touring entertainments like Buffalo Bill's Wild West Show; indeed, some reviewers mistook the dancers in *Le Sacre*, in their authentically Slav costumes, for Amerindians.

Le Sacre, like every other work of art, originated in a niche created by a unique combination of circumstances. Those circumstances had never before existed, and the niche in which they coexisted soon disintegrated. Thirteen months after the premiere, an assassination in Sarajevo precipitated events that disrupted the international ballet circuit, exiled Stravinsky from his homeland, separated Russia from western Europe, and weakened western Europe's global dominance. The time that made *Le Sacre* possible came, and then went.

Nevertheless, despite the decay of its original niche, I can still listen to *Le Sacre* anytime I want; collectively, we have remembered it. The power of the stimulus explains *why* we have wanted to do so, but it does not explain *how* we have done it.

We remember it—as we saw in chapter 6—because it has been transmitted by editors, who have mediated between the original and ourselves. One of the effects of making a memory collective is making it less vulnerable to destruction: the greater the number of individual memories that recall an event, the safer it is. But even if a representation is widely distributed within a single generation, that generation will eventually die. The representation will survive only if it can be transmitted not only across space but also through time.

Psychologists conventionally divide memory into short-term and long-term, and as we have already seen, that distinction has some relevance to cultural memory: a representation, like Coleridge's "Kubla Khan" or Ben Jonson's *Henry V*, can fail to cross the threshold between short-term and long-term. But both kinds of memory, short and long, are framed by the lifetime of a single organism. *Le Sacre* may have been retained in Stravinsky's long-term memory, but Stravinsky is dead. Nevertheless, I can still listen to his music. Since culture does not end but actually begins with the death of a creator, it depends upon memories that are not bounded by biology. Culture labors to create "no-term" memories: representations as immortal as we are mortal, as eternal as we are ephemeral. Such memories cannot be human; they are designed never to decay, and human beings, alas, disintegrate soon enough. Consequently, the most enduring memories of human culture are inhuman.

What makes us human? Our ability to supplement ourselves. *Our human essence is to supplement our essence, inhumanly.* This paradox, which defines us as a tool-making species, afflicts us as individuals: how do I distinguish my self from my tools?

Henry David Thoreau, seeking to sublime life to its quintessence by retreating to the solitude and simplicity of Walden Pond, nevertheless packed tools and books, paper and ink. He brought, inside him, a language. He carried with him artificial memories of the Greek Gospels and the Hindu *Bhagavadgita*. Like Stravinsky and Roerich and Nijinsky, he pursued primitivism in a way possible only for a nonprimitive. Thoreau could isolate his essence only by supplementing it. Even the idea of an essence was a supplement. That idea added philosophical density and dignity to the naked routines of biology.

Parts of my own biology—the fingers keyboarding these letters, for instance—can come to seem tools, prosthetic appliances; indeed, the whole body may be no more than a tool for the mind, or self, or soul. And if I can regard my own body as a tool, why shouldn't other people treat me as a tool? Whole persons and classes of persons— slaves, prostitutes, untouchables, the "human resources" of a modern nation or a postmodern multinational corporation—can be reduced to conveniences, mere supplements to the essence of some other more important whole. In *Le Sacre du printemps*, a young girl becomes a tool, an expendable sacrificial victim. Her community can preserve its essence only by treating part of itself as a supplement.

But it is the victim we remember, the Chosen Virgin that *Le Sacre* commemorates. What the pagan Russians treated as a supplement has become for us the essence of what they were. Likewise, I cannot visit Walden Pond—it is only a few miles from where I sit writing this, writing as I listen to *Le Sacre du printemps*—without carrying with me a memory of Thoreau. It is now impossible to separate the essence of that place from the supplement given it by that person. That supplement does not inhere in the geographical site; it has been added by texts, by edited texts, by memories of edited texts, which I and all the other tourists bring along in our mental luggage and append anew to the place. We know of Thoreau's encounter with nature and essence only by virtue of the artificial supplement provided by his synthetic textual representation of that encounter. And we remember the ritual human sacrifice, the propitiation of nature by natural man, only by virtue of edited artificial representations like the performance of *Le Sacre du printemps* that I am hearing as I write.

INHUMAN MEMORY

Le Sacre du printemps is usually translated "The Rite of Spring," but it is not a rite, and it does not have to be performed in the spring. It does not depend upon, or anticipate, ritual repetition. It was never designed to be remembered by an institutionalized community of priests devoting themselves to the conservative reproduction of a sequence of actions believed to have magical consequences. It represents such a rite, but it is not one, and at the level of its own practice, it does not believe in them. It believes in, depends upon, is perpetuated by, entrepreneurial initiative. It was commissioned by Diaghilev for the touring seasons of his commercial Ballets Russes in Paris and London; it opened in the Théâtre des Champs-Élysées, which Gabriel Astruc made profitable by attracting subscription audiences to such shows. The success of Diaghilev and Astruc within the social system of twentieth-century western Europe depended upon the very newness of the products they marketed. Indeed, Diaghilev said that the riot on opening night was "exactly what I wanted." The fierce reactions to the ballet confirmed the newness of the company's work—and therefore its value in a society obsessed with the new. The scandal also increased curiosity within a society committed to the importance of individual judgment: if opinions were so divided, then one must simply see and decide for oneself. One must also be sure to subscribe to the next season, because there was no telling what novelties such a company might offer next. Cultural capitalism depends upon the novel best-seller—that is, upon the something new that you buy because everyone else is buying it.

Of course, *The Rite of Spring* is no longer new. But it continues to be marketed in a succession of newnesses. I can choose from several different compact disc recordings of the music, each offering a distinctive new interpretation of the work. The compact disc itself is a new format that replaces cassette tape, which replaced stereo records, which replaced hi-fi records, which replaced 78rpm records. The continuing reproduction of Stravinsky's music depends not on ritual repetition but on commercial variation. Every repetition prides itself upon its differences from its predecessors; even an editorial attempt to reproduce as exactly as possible the original ballet, such as Millicent Hodson's 1987 production based on meticulous reconstruction of Nijinksy's choreography and Roerich's sets, is advertised as a renovation—new, and therefore valuable, because it differs from all intervening versions.

I can listen to *The Rite of Spring* today because of technological developments that are themselves intimately related to social and economic forces that have dominated the twentieth century. But those technological developments cannot in themselves explain the survival of *The Rite of Spring*. The first performances of the ballet were not electronically recorded, and neither were the early concerts. Eric Walter White, who has written three books on Stravinsky, was only a schoolboy in 1923 when he first encountered the composer's work. At that time, a decade after the premiere of *The Rite of Spring*, opportunities to hear Stravinsky's music played live "were comparatively few" and almost entirely confined to metropolitan venues:

For a provincial amateur like myself, such performances were difficult to attend. Few of his works had been recorded for gramophone;
and broadcasts on the sound radio, which was still in its infancy,
were rare occurrences and had the disadvantage that, apart from the
quality of the actual performance—and some of these performances left a lot to be desired—the sound that emerged through
earphones or amplifiers was apt to be crude and distorted.

White satisfied his curiosity by reading the published scores.
The full orchestral score for *The Rite of Spring* was not published
until 1921; all our electronically recorded performances derive from
that score or from revisions of it published later in the composer's
lifetime. What if the score had not survived? The music could have
been reproduced only by bringing together the ninety-seven members of the original orchestra and asking them all to play their parts
from memory. Any such reconstruction through the medium of
purely human memories would be defeated not only by the complexity of the music, but by the fact that modern musicians do not
expect to have to play old parts from memory; they had no incentive to memorize, for life, each note of their contribution to *The Rite
of Spring*.

Without an inhuman memory, without a score, *The Rite of
Spring* would not have survived into the electronic age. Indeed,
given the complexity and unfamiliarity of the music, even the first
performances were dependent upon a score: each member of the
orchestra had a scored part to play, and a conductor coordinated
their playing by referring to his score. To communicate his musical
intentions to the many performers, Stravinsky had to write them
down. Doing so was not always easy. For instance, Stravinsky composed the climactic episode of the work, "The Sacrificial Dance," on
the piano; he could play it, but initially he did not know how to
write it down.

For Stravinsky, sounds were the essence of the work; the score
was a mere supplement, an afterbirth. For us, though, the score preserves the only representation of sounds that have vanished. Without it, Stravinsky's private memory of those sounds could never

have become collective. Our memory depends—even when we do not know how to read music—upon the score. Actual performances are judged by the abstract standard it sets. Real sounds become supplements to the score, and the score, once the supplement, becomes the essence. The human maker is dead; the inhuman score survives.

And the score that we read is not even in Stravinsky's handwriting. It is a printed book, published by Édition Russe de Musique or Boosey & Hawkes. Various handwritten papers do survive, but such relics are kept in archives or private collections. They may be consulted by editors, but our collective memory of the whole of *The Rite of Spring*, even among professional musicians, depends upon printed copies.

The score of *The Rite of Spring*, the foundation of our collective memory of Stravinsky's work, is a function of three interlocking factors: a system of signs (musical notation), an editorial institution (music publishing), and a technology of representation (print). In different periods, for different kinds of cultural work, the factors will vary, but these three are always present at the making of a collective memory. For example:

WORK	SIGNS	INSTITUTIONS	TECHNOLOGIES
Ecclesiastes	Hebrew language	Priesthood	Writing
Las Meninas	Perspective	Monarchy	Paint, canvas
Invisible Man	English language	Publishing	Print
Casablanca	Film conventions	Studios	Recording

As you can immediately see, this schematic diagram is too simple. In complex societies and complex art forms, more than one system of signs, more than one institution, and more than one technology are inevitably involved. The sign system used in the score of *The Rite of Spring* contains more than musical notes: it also records verbal instructions for the playing of musical notes, the title, and the titles of the various sections of the work. The score combines musical and verbal signs, and the verbal signs belong to more than one language (French, English, Italian). Likewise, although the score most obviously depends upon the institution of music publishing, that institution itself depends upon symbiotic relationships with music schools, orchestras, ballet companies, instrument makers, and text publishers. The technology we call "print" is a synthesis of paper, ink, type-casting, and machine-making technologies; by the early twentieth century, print had also adapted and incorporated various technologies for the manipulation of electrical energy. Moreover, although for analytical purposes we can separate signs from institutions and both from technologies, in practice all three are complexly related to one another. Particular technologies are associated with particular kinds of editorial community; different sign systems create different institutional and technological problems. Because they are so intimately interrelated, any significant change in one factor will affect the other two, and those changes in turn feed back to the first.

These three elements of collective memory interrelate dynamically; thus, the system they create is inherently unstable. But that isn't saying much. To misquote Tolstoy: all stable systems are alike; all unstable systems are unstable in their own way. Culture is neither random nor deterministic, but chaotic; that is, it is disorderly in orderly ways. That messy neatness may be exemplified by the score of *The Rite of Spring*. The score is a text. It therefore belongs to the history of texts. Stravinsky's personal difficulties in scoring *The Rite of Spring* are emblematic of a longer, larger, harder human struggle: to find an artificial supplement that will preserve something essential but mortal, to find a way of representing sounds in order to transmit the memory of music. How did the system of human culture evolve in such a way as to make possible a text, an inhuman memory, like the score of *The Rite of Spring*?

A complete answer to that question would be a comprehensive history of the human species. Because you and I are both busy and have other things to do, I will offer instead only an abbreviated scenario.

A BRIEF HISTORY OF TEXT

A writing or a painting is a mark upon a surface. To write or paint, one must have a marker and a surface to mark. I am writing this text on a personal computer, which governs an electrically powered desktop printer that will make ink marks on machine-made paper. But this word processor was preceded by the typewriter, which was preceded by the pen, which was preceded by the stylus; the stylus is a kind of knife. Machine-made paper was preceded by hand-made paper, which was preceded by parchment, made from processed animal hide. Human signs began with knives marking the skins of animals. And since we, too, are animals, we made marks upon our own skins. Human art probably began with painting, tattooing, and branding the human body. Art begins with makeup and costume, which are ways of turning bodies into representations (and turning persons into supplemental surfaces).

But the marked body will die and rot. To preserve its signs, you must learn to preserve the body. Egyptian mummies. Pagan sacrificial victims preserved in Irish peat bogs. The monumental Soviet conservation of Lenin's corpse. The individually embalmed cadavers prepared to order by American funeral homes. You can preserve these supplemented body-texts only by putting them in a supplementary body-place, a burial ground, which is almost inevitably in some way holy (sacred, and at the same time forbidden), and it is certainly marked in some way to distinguish it from other places. Arlington National Cemetery. The *Titanic*.

So the marking of bodies cannot be divorced from the marking of the earth itself. The earth was a textured surface before we marked it: we learned to interpret the meaning of its signs, and then we made new signs of our own upon it. The skin of Mother Earth is more durable than human skin. Other animals mark the earth; our family dog, Pepper, wants to sign every bush with his own urine flourish. But humans mark the earth in nonbiological ways. Upper Paleolithic cave paintings. Early Christian catacombs. Mount Rushmore. Graffiti. The flag planted on the South Pole, on the moon.

Sometimes the place is naturally conspicuous and can itself be interpreted as a reminder, a string around the earth's finger, a knot in her handkerchief. Mount Olympus. The Grand Canyon. Victoria Falls. But sometimes the place is unusual only because something human happened there. If we want to remember what happened, or remind others of what happened, or remind others of what we did and what they should do, then we must supplement the landscape by building a human structure on it. Stonehenge. Funeral monuments. The pyramids. Such structures mark a point on the earth. But we also draw lines on the earth. Hadrian's Wall. The great stone wall of China. The great earthen walls of Nigeria. The Maginot Line. The Berlin Wall. Frontiers. And sometimes we draw lines around points, points defined not by single structures but by collections of structures. Walled cities. Troy. York. And sometimes we sign those structures with a human name: China, Constantinople, Washington, Leningrad.

I have gotten ahead of myself. You can mark bodies, or mark the earth, without language. But you need language to name the marks you have made or to name the persons whom those marks commemorate. You do not need writing, but you need speech. Places have names long before those names are written down. The human ability to make sounds is biologically transmitted, but the organization of those sounds into speech depends upon the invention and transmission of specific artificial languages. Languages are culturally transmitted; they depend upon memory. If we want to remember something, we give it a name; to speak a name, we must remember a language.

But speech by itself is transient: it marks only the air, and only for an instant, and its mark on the air is erased by the briefest movement of time's hand. And so with language, as with the earth, we try to ensure endurance by making points or lines. Points: oracle, commandment, proverb, cliché, slogan, verbal formula, scientific law, advertising trademark, television sound-bite; pre-Socratic philosophy, Zen Buddhism, $E = mc^2$, a chicken in every pot. Lines: rhythm, repetition, song, verse, meter, rhyme, incantation, charm, lyric, hymn, national anthem, advertising jingle; Homer, Sappho, Billie Holiday.

A verbal point is small enough to be portable; it can be repeated easily, innumerable times. A verbal line, by contrast, must take us with it: it has a structure that will help us remember how to get from point A to point B to . . . point N. Such a map is most easily provided by musicalizing language, often by providing musical accompaniment, always by emphasizing the fact that speech is, like music, a temporal succession of sounds.

Both methods for increasing the memorability of speech depend upon repetition: either the unstructured external repetitions of a single portable formula or the internal repetitions of a musically structured line. Oral memory is repetitive, repetitive, repetitive; repetitive is oral memory.

But I have gotten ahead of myself again. Of course, I am not speaking these words to you, and you are not hearing them; I am writing, you are reading. My words have been translated out of sound into space, and the repetitivity of oral poetry isn't at all necessary in these circumstances. Written language applies to language the far more ancient human penchant for marking surfaces, and all the surfaces that humans learned long ago to mark have been marked, more recently, with language. The serial numbers tattooed on prisoners in Nazi concentration camps. T-shirts with team names, city names, college names, jokes. Epitaphs on gravestones. The stele commemorating the three hundred Spartans who died at the battle of Thermopylae. The Lincoln Memorial. And all the characteristics and examples of oral art I have mentioned can be, and have been, preserved in written representations. That is why I can allude to them and you can recognize them; that is how they have been kept in collective memory.

Nevertheless, writing transforms the memory of speech.

- *Writing changes which elements of language are remembered.* Writing is a representation, and all representations are partial.

Writing represents primarily the semantic content of language; it represents poorly, if at all, sound, rhythm, and intonation. It divorces the memory of semantics (preserved) from the memory of music (lost). Writing makes possible dead languages— languages we can read, though no one speaks them anymore.

- *In freeing memory from dependence upon the rhythm, repeatability, and musicality of the words themselves, writing changes which specimens of language can be remembered.* Initially, writing seems most often to have been used for tax records and legal documents and other sorts of lists that, with items in essentially random sequences, are very difficult to memorize orally. Writing makes bureaucracy possible. (A bureau is, after all, a desk.)

- *Writing changes the social character of memory.* Every functional human adult can remember and use language, orally or gesturally; biological memory and unwritten language thus tend to unify the collective memory of human communities. But not every human adult can write or read. Writing therefore tends to divide collective memory. Indeed, for most of the history of literacy, the ability to write and read has been confined to a small minority who are specially trained to use written language. The invention of writing required a writing class. Script creates and sustains a powerful secret domain of language, a grammatological priesthood. Writing makes possible the Bible, the *Mahabbarata*, the Tao.

- *Writing changes the perception of memorability.* The separation of music from meaning, combined as it is with the separation of those who use writing from those who do not, leads to different social evaluations and social uses of sound and sense. Plato banned poets from his *Republic* because they manipulated the emotive music of language in ways that enabled them to make the bad "sound" as though it were the good. Aristotle's *Poetics* ignored the music and spectacle of tragedy and concentrated instead upon the plot. In both cases, the philosophers objected to the false memorability that music could lend to language; to determine the true value of an ethical proposition or a play (and hence determine whether it was important enough to remember), you first had to strip away everything but the bare semantic content. But this rejection of the music of language coexisted with a cultivation of it. In the study of rhetoric, a staple of education in the West from ancient Greece to twentieth-century America, writing is used to train students to produce more effective speech—that is, speech that is effective whether its object is good or bad. I spent most of my waking hours in high school preparing for debate tournaments in which we argued alternately for opposite sides of the same issue. "Resolved, that Congress should prohibit unilateral United States military intervention in foreign countries." At 10:00 A.M., I was passionately defending this resolution; at 11:00 A.M., I was passionately opposing it. Debate is still considered great training for law school, which is considered great training for a career in politics. But the written study of rhetoric has not simply affected speech. Rhetoric is also designed to teach its practitioners, from the Athenian Sophists to Harvard Law School students, how to make writing as effective as speech, how to compensate for the deficiencies of the written by charging it with the repetitive emotive musicality of the spoken. Writing makes possible *The Aeneid, The Divine Comedy, Don Quixote,* the Gettysburg Address, "I Have a Dream."

Writing changes the mechanisms of memorability. By transmitting language optically, writing makes it possible for language to be remembered visually. Indeed, the first writing seems to have been wholly or partly pictographic. Calligraphy is cultivated in most scripted languages, and in China and Japan writing and painting were considered sister arts. The beauty of a classical poem was judged visually as well as semantically; indeed, much of the semantic context was specifically visual. But such effects are not limited to hieroglyphs and ideograms. The picture poems of George Herbert exploit the same potential, as do those of e. e. cummings. Written words can be displayed so that they

CATCH THE EYE

and having threaded the eye, they can more easily hook the memory. Moreover, all written languages have their own arbitrary internal principles of organization. Anyone able to use the written language will have internalized those principles, and a linguistic proposition can be made more memorable by linking it to those internalized memorial structures. For example,

Alphabetical

Bodies

Can

Defy

Entropy

Such mnemonics do not depend upon the structure of spoken English, for in speech there is no reason why the sound "b" should follow the sound "a." To describe God as "the alpha and omega" is to appeal to memories of the written word.

But I have gotten ahead of myself again. Written languages, after all, need not be alphabetic. The alphabet seems to have been invented only once in human history; all modern alphabets derive from a Semitic prototype. To speak of alphabets is to move from a panhuman history of text to a specifically Western one. But this is the road we must take to arrive at *The Rite of Spring*.

We must follow the alphabet because it leads to a revolutionary transformation of textual memory: the invention of the printing press. Print technology depends upon (among other things) movable type, which in turn depends upon the ability to construct all the words in a language by rearranging a very small number of tokens;

thousands of durable, interchangeable copies of each letter could be made from a single mold. Using such alphabetic types, the printing press could produce thousands of interchangeable copies of an alphabetic text.

Print geometrically accelerated the reproduction of texts. Representations began to multiply at an unprecedented rate. As a result, the same memory could be transmitted more cheaply, more uniformly, and more rapidly to more minds than ever before. Print made it much easier to create and alter collective memories in enlarged collectivities. And such changes were not limited to linguistic memory. The printing press could, with relatively simple adjustments, also rapidly reproduce visual representations, from woodcuts to an increasingly sophisticated succession of different forms of engraving. It was also possible to produce, in place of types representing letters, types representing musical notes. It took only a quarter-century to go from the printing of books (the Gutenberg Bible) to the printing of music (the Constance Gradual).

But before you can print music, you must first be able to write it. Stravinsky had to imagine what the music of "pagan Russia" might have sounded like, because the pagan Russians themselves could not write music. Neither could the ancient Egyptians or Sumerians or Indo-Europeans; neither could the Aztecs, the Incas, the Indians of the Great Plains, the peoples of Africa or the Pacific. Archbishop Isidore of Seville was speaking for forty thousand generations of human musicians when he declared that, "unless sounds are remembered by man, they perish, for they cannot be written down."

Classical Greece did develop a rudimentary system for transcribing music (which musicologists may or may not know how to read); in China, the Han emperor Wudi established a bureau of music, and music notation was well developed by the time of the Tang dynasty. But Stravinsky's score depends upon a system of notation slowly developed in Christian western Europe, beginning with neumes, which were used to suggest changes of pitch in medieval plainchant. These were eventually organized in a vertical pattern, with notes placed higher on the page indicating a "higher" pitch (that is, a mathematically greater frequency of sound vibration per second); signs were also introduced for distinguishing flats, sharps, and naturals. Two centuries later, note-ligature conventions for the first time clearly identified rhythmic patterns. This development led in turn to a codification of the forms of notes and rests. The rise of instrumental music in the Renaissance was accompanied by the extensive introduction of ties, slurs, tempo markings, and indications of volume; the five-line staff became standard. During the Baroque period, the function of bar lines was precisely defined and stabilized. Romantic composers and theorists developed score layouts to accommodate more complicated orchestration; ornamentation, which in earlier periods had been left for the performer to supply, was increasingly regulated.

Hence, by March 8, 1913, when Stravinsky completed and dated the full score of *The Rite of Spring*, it was possible for a composer to notate with extraordinary precision an extraordinarily complicated score. The music can be performed (as it is on my CD) in 32 minutes and 34 seconds, but the 201 bars of the score occupy 153 folio pages—almost 5 folio pages per minute of music.

. . .

But I have gotten ahead of myself again. The date written on the score, the length of the performance recorded on the cover of the CD, the sequence of bar and page numbers in the printed book—these are also artificial texts, each with a history of its own.

Oral memories are not broken down into numbered segments. If you want a Serbian tale-singer, or a griot in Mali, to repeat for you one particular part of a native epic tale, you do not specify a page or line or bar number; instead, you identify a narrative episode. In different tellings by different tellers, that episode might occupy a different position in the complete sequence. Even in written cultures, numbering is a late addition. Classical manuscripts, written on scrolls, did not have page numbers because they did not have pages; the text unrolled continuously, without division into arbitrary artificial units. Even when scrolls were replaced by codices (collections of separate pages bound together on one side, like the book you are reading now), the pages normally were not numbered, and different manuscript copies of the same work would not normally have the same pagination. By contrast, every copy of an edition of an early printed book places the same section of text on the same page. Such books were produced by a system of imprinting separately the two sides of a sheet of paper, which was then folded into anywhere from two to thirty-two pages; these sheets were usually identified by a "signature" (usually a letter) to ensure that they were bound together in the order in which they were to be read (not necessarily the order in which they were printed). These signatures, arranged in alphabetical order, divided a printed book into artificial but regular units. Page numbering, which eventually replaced signatures, carried this process of textual subdivision even further. Page numbers, unlike signatures, are purely for the convenience of readers; they were added initially to facilitate immediate reference to particular sections of the work, identified in tables of contents or indexes. Bar numbers in books of music—like line numbers in books of poetry—came even later and enabled ever more precise cross-referencing.

The pagan Russian rite represented in the ballet took place in "spring": an unidentified day in an unidentified year. Stravinsky's score was also completed in spring, but the modern Russian writer wrote down the day and year: March 8, 1913, on the old Russian (Julian) calendar—the same day as March 21, 1913, on the Western (Gregorian) calendar, which was not adopted in Russia until after the Bolshevik Revolution. Stravinsky recorded the fact that he completed his score on the first day of spring. He could do so thanks to the ready availability of printed calendars, owing to the evolution of calendrical measurement (itself dependent on the history of astronomy) supplemented by print technology. The technology of mechanical time-keeping—which makes it possible to measure precisely the length of a modern performance—was developed in western Europe in the Middle Ages. Initially a civic mechanism for dividing public time into hours, the timepiece was gradually miniaturized in both the size of the instrument and the size of the units of time it measured. (The watch on my wrist tells me that it is now 12:29:04.)

The clock and the printing press together created modern society, in part by transforming our collective perception of the past. As the philosopher Ernst Cassirer noticed, in oral cultures the perception of time is qualitative and concrete: the passage of time is marked by an uneven succession of particular remarkable events (the reign of the Han emperor Wudi; the invention of the printing press). In modern culture, by contrast, we perceive time as a continuum that is quantitative and abstract (seconds to minutes to hours to days to years to centuries to millennia). This is, of course, a willfully inhuman way to mark the passage of time. Our biological memories do not metronomically note and record the ticking of atomic clocks. I know what day and time it is only because I surround myself with artificial memento-makers: the calendar hanging on the kitchen wall, the appointment book in my briefcase, the seven clocks scattered throughout the house, the date/time prompt on my computer screen. Despite these proliferating supplements, our personal memories remain stubbornly qualitative and concrete, but beside the concrete events that seem to us qualitatively worth remembering we can now append a memorandum, locating each on a temporal continuum that is inhumanly linear and uniform.

28000 B.C. (?): Human language

c. 3500 B.C.: Sumerian cuneiform

c. 1500 B.C.: Semitic alphabet

c. 320 B.C.: Greek musical notation

c. 550: Earliest surviving musical notation in China

c. 1000: First marking of pitch in Latin plainchant texts

c. 1300: First mechanical clock

c. 1455: Gutenberg Bible (first printed book)

c. 1473: Constance Gradual (first printed music book)

1913: *The Rite of Spring*

Thus we can now construct a brief history of text, within which we can locate the precise position of Stravinsky's score.

Stravinsky's score does what I have just done: it turns time (the thirty-two minutes or so of a performance) into space (153 pages of notation). All systems of inhuman memory, or artificial representation, spatialize time. This should not be surprising: the making of texts began with the marking of places on the earth or our bodies, and we still think of remembering as the return to a place (losing, searching, finding, tracing a memory trail). The mnemonic systems of Simonides and Ricci and Shereskevskii all constructed a virtual "place" in the mind, a sequence of linked sites to which particular memories could be attached. Less systematically, most of us organize our thoughts by filing information, mentally, under certain topics; for years I have been collecting and sorting memories on the topic of memory. But *topic* comes from the Greek *topos* ("place"), which also gives us the word *topography*; I think of my memories of studies of memory being filed in different drawers, different places. And when I remember a particularly famous or influential expression of an idea, I am returning to what literary critics for centuries have called a *locus classicus*, a first-class locale.

To remember a time, therefore, we turn it into a space, a text. But some experiences are intrinsically easier to textualize than others. The earliest surviving artificial memory systems are cave paintings: visual representations of visual space. Music, dance, and speech probably originated long before painting—unlike painting, they require little if any technology. But speech, music, and dance were much harder to translate into artificial memories. Of the three, speech was the first to develop a spatial representation (writing), followed by music (notation), then dance (dance notation). Written scripts arise, apparently, from pictograms: since most individual words refer to an external spatial reality, most words can overlap with visual representations, and this overlap permits the evolution of a spatialized representation of words, which can then be developed into an increasingly independent and sophisticated system of signs.

Music notation always arises later than writing because music has no obvious spatial referent; in music, time itself is primary. Music notation is a kind of writing that originates when writing itself has reached a certain level of sophistication. Once writing is regarded as a representation of human sounds (rather than as a representation of things that humans make sounds about), then it is possible to imagine that writing should represent other, nonsemantic aspects of the sounds human voices make: rhythm, pitch, tone. Musical notation arises, initially, as a more comprehensive way of describing words that are sung (Greek or Chinese songs, Latin plainchant). In Greek mythology, the archetypal poet, Orpheus, is also the archetypal musician, and Apollo is the god of both poetry and song. Music is regarded as a supplement to language, and music notation is simply an extension of the spatial representation of vocalized language. Of course, once an independent system of notation exists, it can be extended to represent nonvocal music.

As music accompanies language, dance accompanies music, and dance notation is always developed after music notation. If the motion of a dancer is frozen, the position of parts of the body can be captured in a visual medium, as can be seen from Greek vases and Egyptian wall paintings. But the continuing action of a dancer's body can only be captured by a sign system that can spatialize movement through time. Systems for representing musical tempo and rhythm can eventually be adapted to represent the corresponding elements of dance, but those systems will have to be supplemented with new systems for representing multidimensional movement of multiple body parts and multiple bodies. Not surprisingly, given the difficulties of the task, even as late as the eighteenth century the most sophisticated choreographical description relied on bird's-eye-view drawings, with a verbal surround, to illustrate a strictly limited repertory of dance steps. The first true notational system was not published until 1852. Nijinsky's choreography for *The Rite of Spring* was never recorded. Stravinsky could preserve his work with a score, but Nijinsky could not; the original dances for the ballet are lost. Less than a decade after the first performance, a new choreography had to be commissioned.

The Rite of Spring was not particularly modern in combining dance and music; that combination is ancient. Classical Greek drama had fused language, music, and dance. Only the words of those plays have survived, not because the words were more important or more memorable, but simply because an artificial system for remembering language already existed. To the first audiences for *The Rite of Spring*, Nijinsky's choreography was as revolutionary or revolting as Stravinsky's score; the music has survived not because it was better or more important but simply because a sophisticated artificial system for remembering music already existed. For thirty thousand years, the memory of culture has been distorted by the uneven development of technologies for making artificial representations of the past.

Nevertheless, the direction of this development is clear enough. The memorial conquest of time by space has become increasingly comprehensive: from language to language-and-music to language-and-music-and-movement. This drive toward comprehensiveness has been inward as well as outward: not only to record more, but to record more precisely. The first alphabets had no vowels. The earliest texts in the voweled Greek alphabet did not contain punctuation marks, did not indicate accents, did not divide words, did not distinguish miniscules from majuscules: they consisted of undivided runs of capital letters. Songs were not displayed in line units that reflected the metrical structure but were written out continuously, like modern prose. The manuscripts of Greek tragedy, written in this way, separated speeches by different speakers but did not indicate which speaker spoke which speeches; nor did they include stage directions to describe the movement of bodies in space and time. By the late sixteenth century, English dramatists were routinely identifying speakers and supplying a few (usually formulaic) stage directions; by the eighteenth century, editions of those Renaissance plays began systematically sorting out ambiguities about the assignment of speeches and adding many more stage directions. By the twentieth century, English dramatists such as George Bernard Shaw and Harley Granville-Barker were writing texts in which stage directions occupied more of the text than speeches. Filmscripts have taken the process even further: direction dwarfs dialogue.

Texts have also become more and more comprehensively accessible. Representations multiply increasingly rapidly: from pictograph to alphabet, from script to print to electronic pulse. The rising speed of reproduction and transmission has been accompanied by a lowering of barriers to comprehension. It takes much longer to learn the tens of thousands of characters of a logographic language like Sumerian or Chinese than it does to learn the twenty-six letters of the Western alphabet. Handwriting is harder to decode than printing. (Compare the printed part of your prescription form with *the part filled by your physician*.) Printing is harder to decode than a cassette book, by means of which an author, or an actor, reads the text aloud. Shakespeare's plays are hard to read (ask any high school student); Kenneth Branagh's film of *Much Ado about Nothing* is easy to watch. Stravinsky's score of *The Rite of Spring* is, by virtue of its very comprehensiveness, extraordinarily difficult for most people to decipher; anyone listening to a CD performance can immediately effortlessly hear what the complicated notation labors to describe.

The technological evolution of texts has given us representations that are progressively easier to decode. But these easier to decode representations are much harder to encode. The compact disc I am playing now requires little effort or expertise on my part, but it requires an enormous amount of both from other people: musicologists, conductors, orchestra members, orchestra administrators, talent agents, inventors, engineers, technicians, industrial workers, copyright lawyers, transporters, retailers. A CD may be, at the point of consumption, the simplest and most direct way to recover the music of the past; but it is, of course, fantastically more complicated for society to produce. It requires an enormous interlocking infrastructure of invisible "editors."

Moreover, the more comprehensively expansive, specific, and accessible such artificial systems are, the less they resemble human memory. A CD can record any sequence of sounds; film can record any sequence of sounds and actions. By virtue of such mechanisms, works of art no longer need to be intrinsically "memorable" to be artificially remembered. Technology has made art easier for the culture to preserve, but technology does not make the art itself any easier for an individual memory like mine or yours to internalize. *The Rite of Spring* is not very hummable. Individual rhythmical phrases are strikingly powerful, but there is—quite deliberately—no melodic development. Like Eliot's *The Waste Land*, Stravinsky's *The Rite of Spring* is a collage of ancient, evocative rhythmical shards ("These fragments I have shored against my ruins"). In each work, the semblance of a logical sequence is provided by supplemental notes (the titles of sections of *The Rite of Spring*, the notes to *The Waste Land*), but essentially, neither work has any plot. Without a plot, without a map that gives us a sense of directed movement, it is extraordinarily difficult to remember how to get from one point to the next, or what comes after which.

As in all communications systems, information density is a function of unpredictability. But the unpredictability that makes such texts so rich in meanings also defies and defeats biological memory. Artificial memory makes it possible to record, preserve, and transmit denser communications, but the very density of such representations will limit their potential audience. In the late nineteenth century, poets such as Tennyson and Browning, composers such as Tchaikovsky, were admired by fellow specialists but were also enormously popular with the nonspecialist public. Stravinsky and Eliot, by contrast, never became popular. Their work appealed, instead, to memory specialists: other artists, critics, reviewers, teachers, scholars, people who make a profession of remembering a certain fraction of the cultural past. The work of such makers was aimed at, and sustained by, a small population of "editors."

As the artificial memory of the past becomes more complete, the social memory of the past becomes more fragmented. Artificial memory remembers more than persons can; that is its function. There is just too much for a body to remember. The gap between human and artificial memory continually widens. So humans have come to rely increasingly on memory specialists. The number of such specialists has multiplied as a function of the division of labor—including the divisions of labor that sustain the proliferating infrastructures required by the evolving technologies of representation. Critics remember the history of art; lawyers remember the history of law; engineers remember the history of technology. Or rather, this critic remembers for us the history of English drama from 1580 to 1640; that critic remembers the eighteenth-century novel. This lawyer remembers divorce law; that lawyer remembers patent law. We rely upon these specialists, and at the same time we despise them for the narrow pedantry of their memories and resent them for the power that their specialist memories give them and for the arrogance that power breeds.

Artificial memories turn time into space. The more comprehensively they conquer time, the more textual space they create. The more textual space they create, the more social energy is required to survey and govern that space. As the expanding past becomes more and more ungovernable, it has to be broken down into more and more, smaller and smaller, administrative districts. The larger the empire, the smaller the village. The more comprehensive and multi-dimensional artificial memory becomes, the more it fragments and belittles our biological memories. Thoreau wakes to find himself surrounded on every side for farther than any human eye can see by an army of importunate supplements.

FANTASIA

Why did I keep getting ahead of myself in narrating my brief history of text? Because, in human culture, more than one thing is happening at the same time, but human prose can only describe one thing at a time. While I am telling the story of A, the story of B is taking place somewhere else, and the story of A is eventually affected by that story of B, and so before I can finish telling the story of A, I have to stop and go back to tell the story of B, but while I am telling the story of B, the story of C is taking place somewhere else—and so on.

Stravinsky does not have the same problem. What distinguishes music from poetry is polyphony: the ability to sound, and hear, many notes at once. Plainchant needed to develop a notation in order to regulate the interaction of many separate voices. Stravinsky's score can represent different sounds made by different instruments at once, in many different relationships of harmony and dissonance; those participants and their relationships shift from moment to moment. A musical score could represent the polyphonic temporality of human history much more accurately than my sentences do. One word at a time, one after another—how can such a linear system of monodic signs represent the multidimensional disorderly order of civilization? One system of artificial memory may be invented before another, but the appearance of the second seldom completely, and never immediately, displaces the first. The alphabet was invented thirty-five hundred years ago, but in the twentieth century the world's most commonly spoken language still uses a nonalphabetic script (although it will not do so for much longer if the linguistic reforms of the Chinese government succeed). For at least forty-five hundred years after the invention of writing separated language from speech, reading remained an aural activity; people read aloud, even when alone, and silent reading did not become the norm until the Renaissance. People still read aloud. I have spent many hours of my life reading to my wife or my children and listening to others read to me. Older artificial memory systems survive even after more advanced artificial memory systems have become dominant. If this is true of technology, it is even more insistently true of biology. Like the regular and unbroken ostinato that underlies all the rhythmical variations of the "Dance of the Earth," biological memory persists alongside the most sophisticated mechanical systems. Our inhuman supplements evolve rapidly, but the biochemical mechanisms that enable our brains to remember stay the same. Most human memory is still oral memory. The most sophisticated and literate professors of English still speak and listen at conferences, still teach (as they were taught) orally, and still gossip. The proliferation of artificial memory has not made culture mechanical but polyphonic.

Our brains were produced by a similar evolutionary process and, as a result, have a similar structure. Just as collective memory employs many different systems of representation, so individually we each have many different kinds of memory: somatic memory, recognition memory, linguistic memory, eidetic memory, narrative memory. Just as old and new artificial memory systems coexist in a single culture, so the earliest structures of the brain were not replaced but supplemented by successive additions; a reptilian brain, a mammalian brain, a primate brain, a hominid brain, a human brain. This means that the brain of a modern human being consists of different *parts*, which themselves represent different *times*.

This is not just a fact of anatomy—it is a fact of daily experience. Every adult human carries in her head the memories of a child, sometimes without knowing it. My friend Barbara had always, as an adult, been powerfully moved by parts of *The Rite of Spring* without knowing why. Then she had children, and one day she watched with them the Walt Disney movie *Fantasia*, which she had not seen since she was a child. Seeing it, hearing Stravinsky's music accompany its concluding history of the dinosaurs, she remembered what had been haunting her, and why: she associated the music with her deep emotional reaction as a child to that frightening final sequence. The connection between Stravinsky's music and a cartoon for children is not as fortuitous as it might seem. According to the composer himself, the inspiration for *The Rite of Spring* was "the violent Russian spring that seemed to begin in an hour and was like the whole earth cracking. That was the most wonderful event of every year of my childhood." More than one musicologist has described the music in terms of a translation into music of childlike gestures and mentalities; the critic Theodor Adorno analyzed the "infantilism" of Stravinsky's complex technique.

This memory of childhood is also, deliberately, a memory of the distant human past. Stravinsky was not the only composer to link child memory with folk memory. Mussorgsky filled *The Nursery* with fierce folk music; Debussy put "Golliwog's Cake-Walk" into *The Children's Corner*. But the childhood being recovered here is not the idyllic golden wholeness that people find so appealing in Wordsworth or Tchaikovsky. One critic saw in *The Rite of Spring* "the unconscious, childish frenzy of primitive tribes." So conceived, childhood is a violently disordered spring: not the Garden of Eden but the *Lord of the Flies*. Our feelings about that childhood may be similarly violent. Stravinsky said that he wrote *The Rite of Spring* "to send everyone" in his early life "to hell."

Whatever it was like—Wordsworth or Stravinsky, Paradise or *Fantasia*, dream or nightmare—we have all packed memories of our childhoods somewhere in our heads. But we can carry those packages around forever without opening them; we can store them in the attic and then forget where in the attic to find them, and then forget that we put them in the attic at all, and then forget that they ever existed. The fact that a stimulus has been represented *in* memory does not mean that it will ever be recalled *from* memory. What happens when we recall a memory? And why do we recall some and not others?

PART III

Recollect.

8.

Humpty Dumpty's Resurrection.

> *He dived his arm down to the bottom of the chest, and brought up a small wooden box, with a sliding lid, such as children's toys are kept in. From within he produced a crumpled piece of paper, an old-fashioned brass key, a peg of wood with a ball of string attached to it, and three rusty old discs of metal.*
>
> ARTHUR CONAN DOYLE

EXHIBIT A

My own earliest memory is of a museum. I am vaguely aware of having traveled, in a car, in darkness, of turning off a smooth road onto a bumpy one. I am very sharply aware of standing in daylight in the entranceway of a house, not our own but someone else's—the room is so BIG and has such a *shiny* floor. In a separate instant, I am standing outside with my dad and another man (he seems to me very old), and there is a long low building, with LOTS of stalls like they use for horses and cows, only in each of these stalls there is a *shiny* odd car, and one of the cars is out of its stall so we can look at it and pet it. I am sure that these three impressions are connected.

There are no family photographs of this occasion, and my mother is surprised that I remember it. We saw this place and met

173

these people only once. She tells me that I was not quite three years old, that we were traveling cross-country, that we stopped to visit my dad's aunt and her rich husband, that we stayed less than twenty-four hours, that the aunt taught Mom how to bake pecan rolls (presumably while the males were out gaping at cars), that they owned the biggest, grandest house she's ever been in, that the spare bedroom was equipped with the softest feather bed she's ever slept on. The rich uncle, as a hobby, collected antique automobiles; he personally conducted us, that sunny morning, on a tour of his private collection. But all I remember is turning onto a different kind of road, the vast bright entrance, all those strange machines.

I was three years old, and I did not have a word to describe how these events electrified my mind and body. I recognize the feeling now, though: wonder. I have encountered many wonders since, but the same stilled hypersensitivity is threaded through my memories of them all, and the thread begins, with a tight knot, here.

FIRST LESSON: There are special places you can visit where huge and strange and beautiful creations are collected.

SECOND LESSON: It takes plenty to purchase the past.

EXHIBIT B

The incident I have just described dates from the summer of 1956. I am remembering it now in the summer of 1994. In fact, I am writing these words on July 4, 1994. My anecdotal recollections of 1956 are obviously private; by contrast, my recollections of the Fourth of July, on this year or any other, clearly belong to what the French sociologist Maurice Halbwachs first described as "the collective memory."

The Fourth of July celebrates the signing more than two centuries ago of a short text. The Declaration of Independence was a gathering of signatures that defined a new "us" (a collection of representatives from thirteen American colonies), partly by defining a "them" (the monarchy and parliament of Great Britain—and the Native American "savages" to whom they were militarily allied). We were united initially by an act of division. We are reunited now by dividing this day, July 4, from all the other days of this year, separating it from its immediate temporal context and uniting it instead with another July day, last year, and another the year before that, and so on in an artificial thread that leads back to July 4, 1776. We separate July 4 from the rest of the calendar by not doing, today, the things we normally do, like going to work. Instead, we devote the day to reunions—with family, with friends, with hundreds of known and unknown neighbors gathered in a field beside the high school to watch the town fireworks. We display flags: a collection of stars and stripes, originally designed by Betsy Ross, that unites one people by distinguishing it from other peoples. We collect in groups to recollect our collective history.

Lewis Mumford, describing the relation between technology and civilization, wrote, "The clock is not merely a means of keeping track of the hours, but of synchronizing the actions of men." But every human method of marking time serves the same purpose. The rhythms of music synchronize labor in the innumerable work songs of tribal cultures. In every part of the globe, the onset of centralized civilizations was attended by the development of calendars. The calendar enables people separated by space to be united in time. Throughout the 3,679,245 square miles of the United States of America, everyone knows that today is July 4. The clock simply extends the time discipline of the calendar to smaller units of time, breaking down the day into segments, as the calendar breaks down the year. Along thousands of miles of battlefront, the First World War ended at 11:00 A.M. on the eleventh day of the eleventh month of 1918. By marking time, human societies can synchronize not simply actions but *memories*. Whether or not we are gathered together physically, we can be gathered mentally.

As an individual, I am already gathered together physically, but I still need to gather myself mentally. An individual mind is a complex system made up of many disparate components. Marvin Minsky describes the human brain as "The Society of Mind." Nor is this idea limited to contemporary American theorists of artificial intelligence.

Four centuries ago in rural France, Michel de Montaigne was saying something very similar: "Whoever studies himself really attentively finds in himself, yes, even in his judgment, this gyration and discord. I have nothing to say about myself absolutely, simply, and solidly, without confusion and without mixture, or in one word." According to Montaigne, every individual human being is a patchwork, a fricassee, a farrago. Multiple personality disorders and less extreme forms of dissociation are now widely recognized by the medical community and are beginning to be recognized by the courts; such disorders are created by a rigid compartmentalization of memory. But such illnesses simply exaggerate tendencies that operate in normal minds. We all, to some degree, compartmentalize our memories and behaviors; notoriously, people are often very different at work than at home. Indeed, the multiplicity of the self, and particularly of the memory, is implicit even in Aristotle's descriptions of remembering. I know, for instance, that I have met someone before, but I can't remember his name; I therefore "hunt" through my memory to find the name. One part of "me" is, as Aristotle describes it and as we have all experienced it, rummaging through other parts of "me."

Again, personal memory is closer to collective memory than we suppose. As an individual, I do not "retrieve" memories; I literally recollect them. I put Humpty Dumpty together again. Biochemically, remembering is associated with complex, shifting, differentiated patterns of increased neural activity across the brain. The world is multidimensional, our perception of it many-sensual; every representation is a combination constructed within a system of representations. When we recall a memory, then, we call back together a combination of senses and perceptions. My own first memory, elementary as it is, entails movement, feeling, light, shape, dimension, recognition of persons, language, emotion. The most famous narrative of recollection in twentieth-century literature, Proust's *A la recherche du temps perdu*, begins with an account of waking up:

> I could not even be sure at first who I was; I had only the most rudimentary sense of existence, such as may lurk and flicker in the

depths of an animal's consciousness; I was more destitute than the cave-dweller; but then the memory—not yet of the place in which I was, but of various other places where I had lived and might now very possibly be—would come like a rope let down from heaven to draw me up out of the abyss of not-being, from which I could never have escaped by myself: in a flash, I would traverse centuries of civilization, and out of a blurred glimpse of oil-lamps, then of shirts with turned-down collars, would gradually piece together the original components of my ego.

The ego is pieced back together from memories of places, things, times. Normally, we are hardly conscious of this process, but on special occasions we deliberately recollect ourselves: on a birthday, a wedding anniversary, the anniversary of someone's death, the beginning of a new year, the Fourth of July. Whenever we cross an emotional frontier, we stop and examine our own identity papers. Our sense of coherence, as individuals and societies, has to be continually reconstructed, recollected.

Personal memories often seem involuntary: "a rope let down from heaven." But unlike Proust and most of the rest of us, people afflicted with Korsakov's syndrome or Alzheimer's disease will wake up and not remember where they are or what they did yesterday. Putting ourselves together again involves some complex brain activity that such disarticulated souls can no longer perform. Even in well-behaved minds, a pet memory doesn't always come when we call it. "It is labor in vain to attempt to recapture" the past, according to Proust. "All the efforts of our intellect must prove futile. The past is hidden somewhere outside the realm, beyond the reach of intellect." No doubt, most of the more than 1,250,000 words of *A la recherche du temps perdu* must have lain within reach of his long-legged strong-armed intellect. Proust is being a bit coy: "gusts of memory" sounds more romantic than the endlessly spinning electric fan of a memory like his.

But you know what he means. We have all been enraged, knowing that a memory is in there somewhere but just refuses to come out; we have all been transfixed when one comes unbidden. "I feel something start within me, something that leaves its resting-place and attempts to rise, something that has been embedded like an anchor at a great depth; I do not know yet what it is, but I can feel it mounting slowly; I can measure the resistance, I can hear the echo of great spaces traversed." What appeals to us here is the sense of reunion, of someone familiar returning from a great distance; what frustrates us on other occasions is the sense of separation, of someone familiar refusing to cross a very short distance. Our own minds seem to us—as indeed they are—social and physical. When we remember, normally separated elements of that internal society are collected together—like people on the Fourth of July.

FIRST LESSON: Identity, personal and social, depends upon memory.

SECOND LESSON: Memory works by re-collection.

THIRD LESSON: Recollections presuppose, and create, separations.

EXHIBIT C

One of the places where people assemble on the Fourth of July is the Vietnam Veterans Memorial. That memorial was dedicated on November 11, 1982—Veterans Day, another national holiday. A public monument is to space what a public holiday is to time: a part marked and set apart for collective remembrance. Holidays and monuments create what the contemporary French historian Pierre Nora calls *les lieux de mémoire*, "the places of memory." In and through such charged points of reference, millions of individual rememberings intersect to form a shared sense of national identity. A point of reference can be provided by flags, museums, maps, national anthems, dictionaries; it does not even need to be native to the people whose identity it anchors. For instance, for innumerable Americans what it means to be an American is epitomized by the Statue of Liberty. Relatively few Americans recall that the quintessential American symbol is a French creation—just as few Americans recall that the independence declared on July 4, 1776, was eventually realized militarily and politically only because of massive French support for the Yankee rebellion.

The Statue of Liberty is probably still America's favorite memory, but it is no longer our favorite memorial. Commemorating the most unpopular of American wars, the Vietnam Veterans Memorial is now the most popular of American monuments. An extraordinarily strong stimulus in a strong niche, it is still visited by more than two and a half million people a year. The memorial collects people. Each year it is the site of between eleven hundred and fifteen hundred organized reunions. It also collects things. People leave flowers, small American flags, military uniforms, dog tags, identification bracelets, medals, awards, certificates, letters, poems, memos, photographs; each day government employees collect the imperishable mementos and transfer them to the Museum and Archaeological Regional Storage Facility.

Why does this site collect so many people, so many things, so many feelings? The initial structure has been and will probably continue to be supplemented by various additions, but visitors are always most deeply affected by the two black walls sloping into the earth. The walls, designed by Maya Ying Lin, are composed of granite panels on which are inscribed the names of 57,939 American soldiers who died in the war. The memorial is primarily a collection of the names of the dead. It resembles, in that respect, a cemetery, like those in Normandy that recollect the human carnage of D-Day. But a cemetery collects bodies as well as names, and as a result, the names themselves are individualized and dispersed in space, surrounded and separated by lawns and life. Because the Vietnam Veterans Memorial collects names without bodies, it can compress them into a much smaller space. It thus creates not only a sense of intricate, ramifying intimacy among the dead, but also an overwhelming sense of memorial density. Too much grief, too much memory, has been collected and impacted in this place; there is more knotted here than anyone can unpick. However hard we try, we just cannot multiply our feelings for one person by 57,939; emotion defies quantitative manipulations. But we can sense intellectually what we cannot feel, and our inability to close the distance between thought and feeling becomes itself part of what we think and feel. The very structure of the memorial reminds us not only that we are inadequate but that the memorial is inadequate—even *this* memorial, so powerful, cannot be powerful enough. Every representation is inadequate. Although the collection of names is meant to be complete, that collection is also inevitably only a selection. Every name is the smallest possible fraction of a whole complex life—which has not been collected, which is uncollectible.

Every building sits in a literal niche, an existing site with which it interacts. Romanesque Durham Cathedral commands a sandstone bluff on the neck of a peninsula craning out into the River Wear; Gothic Notre Dame is an island of medieval sanctity in the river that flows through hectic Paris. The Vietnam Veterans Memorial was placed in a collection of memorials, the Washington Mall. The two granite walls are joined to form an open 125-degree angle; the two rays of that angle point, respectively, at the Washington Monument and the Lincoln Memorial. (Every representation belongs to a system of representations.) The meaning of this memorial depends, in part, upon its relationships to the other items in the collection to which it belongs. Some of those relationships are formal: black/white, depressed/elevated, small/large, open/closed, cleared/wooded, acoustically dispersed/echoing, tens of thousands of names/one name, eloquence/silence. Other relationships are historical supplements to the architecture itself: local/foreign, then/now, victory/defeat, popular/unpopular, and, for many visitors, legitimate/illegitimate, right/wrong. As the collections of written responses to the Vietnam Veterans Memorial demonstrate, these formal and historical relationships between the three monuments can be grouped and interpreted in many different ways.

By means of its content and its form and its relation to other inhabitants of the same geographical and generic niche, the memorial collects meanings. Nevertheless, it does not collect *all* meanings. The list of names may be comprehensive, but the list of memories is deliberately selective. These walls do not make room for foreign fatalities, or for wounded Americans, or for American veterans who have committed suicide since the war—though these categories contain many more names than the category recorded by the memorial. The walls do not identify the dead by rank, age, race, or class; they do not remind us that the war was fought by a rigidly hierarchical military establishment; they do not recall how many of the fatalities were young, black, poor enlisted men. They do not distinguish those who volunteered from those who were drafted. They record nothing about the war itself, its purposes, its outcome, or the controversies surrounding it.

Nor do the walls record the complicated circumstances of the memorial's own creation. Like other war monuments, like funerary sculptures and elegies and epitaphs, this selection of memories was made by and for survivors. When the memorial was dedicated, the roll call of the dead was read aloud by the living; it took fifty-six hours. The dead do not speak to us; instead, the living address us in the name of the dead. The very collection and arrangement of those names, moreover, depended upon a technological editorial apparatus. Only a sophisticated modern military bureaucracy could keep track not only of all 57,939 fatalities but of the death date of each, in a war fought for twelve years across more than two hundred thousand square miles of jungle terrain half a world away. But the collection of that data did not ensure, and was not directed toward, its reproduction in granite on the Mall. The decision to build a memorial was initiated by veterans, formalized by the creation of the Vietnam Veterans Memorial Fund, widely debated in the mass media, and finally authorized by Congress. Lin's design was selected by the Commission of Fine Arts from more than fourteen hundred entries. Her design was subsequently editorially altered, by order of Interior Secretary James Watt, to incorporate a minimal statement about the war, an American flag, and a statue of three American soldiers (white, black, Hispanic). The walls were also reproduced and transported in a "moving" memorial that has toured the country, and the design has been imitated in various local monuments. The Lin design has collected all these supplements in order to satisfy various conflicting editorial constituencies. But these editors, as usual, are not represented in the memorial itself; they remain invisible.

What the Vietnam Veterans Memorial collects, above all, is memories. It is a memory trap, designed to attract, stimulate, focus, and reproduce recollection. Proust's epic memoirs were precipitated by the taste of crumbs of madeleine cake soaked in lime-blossom tea; out of "the tiny and almost impalpable drop of their essence" comes, involuntarily, "the vast structure of recollection." Proust denies that we can deliberately hunt out and find that impalpable drop that will resurrect the past for us; "it depends on chance whether or not we come upon this object before we ourselves must die." But societies do not leave such resurrections to chance. Societies decide which moments to commemorate and what kind of commemoration to bankroll. Maya Lin's design for the Vietnam Veterans Memorial was controversial, but no more so than many other memorials. The official committee that had commissioned Rodin's monument to *The Burghers of Calais* was appalled by the sculptor's design. "This is not the way we envisaged our glorious cititzens," they complained; Rodin's masterpiece irresistibly stimulated their imaginations, but not in a direction they anticipated or approved. The initial anger over Lin's design, or Rodin's, arose because public monuments create a material object that is made to order for the sole purpose of releasing specific memories of the past: a memory jar, inhabited by a powerful (but domesticated) genie. Some material objects do this much more successfully than others. (Some stimuli are stronger than others.) What a madeleine cake soaked in lime-blossom tea may do for one individual's memory, the Vietnam Veterans Memorial tries to do for collective memory; the walls of that memorial have succeeded where other parts of the memorial, and other memorials, have failed.

The way in which monuments and holidays deliberately structure group memory and identity was first analyzed by the French founder of sociology, Émile Durkheim. According to Durkheim, commemorative rites and symbols "serve to sustain the vitality of [traditional] beliefs, to keep them from being effaced from memory." For Durkheim, such commemorations were always celebratory; through them, "the group periodically renews the sentiment which it has of itself and of its unity." But more recent scholars have challenged this model. Robin Wagner-Pacifici and Barry Sullivan, for example, have argued that the Vietnam Veterans Memorial demonstrates the possibility of "commemoration without consensus, or without pride." The collective American anxiety about Vietnam, moreover, is not unique: similar problems are faced by, for example, Southerners (the Civil War), Israelis (the Lebanon War), Germans (World War II), and Russians (Afghanistan). In each case, commemorations separate the dead (whom we remember) from the cause (which we would rather forget).

Pride may bring people together, but so may grief, self-doubt, regret, repentance. Individuals have all these feelings and memories—why shouldn't collections of individuals? After all, a person whose identity is defined solely by self-praise is insufferable. A society so defined is equally insufferable. Collective memory need not be conceited.

Durkheim did not address such cases because he insisted upon the moral unity of societies, and upon self-approval as a condition of that unity. But societies are no more monolithic than individuals. Depending on our view of the war, the dead commemorated by the Vietnam Veterans Memorial may be interpreted as heroes, victims, heroic victims, victimized heroes, or a number of victims mixed with a number of heroes; the memorial collects and permits all these different kinds of memory. The war itself was controversial precisely because it divided national memory against itself. Was it most important to remember that we are Americans (and therefore should support American soldiers and the American government), or was it most important to remember that America was itself once a little country created by a war of national liberation against a great faraway imperial power (and therefore should not be acting the part of a great imperial power suppressing a national liberation movement in a faraway little country)? The memorial perpetuates those conflicting factions of memory. For some, it serves as a reminder that we should never again let our soldiers down; for others, it is a reminder that we should never again betray our own political first principles.

All enduring memorials stimulate conflicting memories and emotions. In Christian memory, the crucifixion has inspired more art and more devotion than the resurrection. In American memory,

Lincoln has surpassed Washington as the most revered of national heroes, even though he was assassinated after presiding over the bloodiest and most divisive war in our history; the larger-than-life statue in the Lincoln Memorial is bent and sad. Memory, by definition, is a recollection of the past, and our sense of the very pastness of that past complicates any other emotions we may feel about it. The dead are dead. We cannot bring back any heroes; we cannot save any victims. My name is not on that wall. Neither is yours.

This conflictedness of personal and public memory prevents any single interpretation or intention from controlling future recollections. Many left-wing historians and cultural critics have emphasized the political manipulation of "invented traditions" by powerful elites, and the political intentions of commemoration are often demonstrably manipulative. Every collection is selective, and the selection of public collections is always politically biased. But it is worth remembering the Austrian novelist Robert Musil's remark that "there is nothing in this world as invisible as a monument." A powerful person or group may erect a monument, but they cannot force future generations to collect there; regimes may force people to visit places or attend festivals or perform rites, but they cannot compel particular memories or feelings. (The mind of Leopold Bloom wanders as the priest approaches him with the communion wafer.) The original sponsors of the Vietnam Veterans Memorial never anticipated the strength and range of responses that would be generated by an Asian-American woman's commemorative vision of America's most recent Asian war.

FIRST LESSON: Every collection is a selection.

SECOND LESSON: Every collection is supplemented by every interpreter in ways that partly determine its meaning.

THIRD LESSON: Every recollection produces a collection of emotions.

FOURTH LESSON: No collection can compel or control its own future recollection.

EXHIBIT D

"Is there no way to make the past the present?" I am quoting from Murasaki Shikibu's *Genji Monogatori*—or rather, from Edward Seidensticker's English translation, *The Tale of Genji*. Completed early in the eleventh century, *The Tale of Genji* is the greatest work of Japanese literature, and Lady Murasaki herself enjoys a supremacy as unchallenged as Homer's, Virgil's, and Dante's in their respective languages. But unlike their epics, unlike the Declaration of Independence and political architecture, *The Tale of Genji* represents private, not public, life. Making the past the present would consist here simply of the return to a more intimate relationship between a man and a woman.

Nevertheless, this quotation from *The Tale of Genji*, though seemingly private, is fundamentally public, for the question I have quoted is itself quoted from another work, the anonymous *Tales of Ise*, compiled early in the previous century. The protagonist, Genji, has written a letter to Princess Asagao; the letter consists of a short poem of his own, followed by this fragment of a poem from *Tales of Ise*. He expects the princess to recognize the quotation and supply its missing second half ("To wind and unwind it like a ball of yarn?"). Genji and Asagao are privately connected by their shared knowledge of a public text. Texts, unlike time, can be wound and unwound at pleasure.

Remembered texts connect Genji to others; they also connect Genji to the world. When he is sent into exile, he takes (like Thoreau) "only the simplest essentials," but those few indispensables include "a book chest" and "selected writings of Po Chü-i and other poets." Snow cascading from the branches of a pine tree reminds him of a poem. After the death of his first wife, shaken and unable to sleep, he whispers to himself, "What would we have to remember her by?" This little soliloquy is another quotation, taken from the *Gosenshū*, the second official anthology of Japanese poetry, compiled perhaps fifty years earlier. Genji interprets his own life in terms he remembers from texts. (Identity, personal and social, depends upon memory.)

Genji is not alone in this penchant for quotation. A command of poetry is an accomplishment necessary for advancement at court, for "both the emperor and the crown prince were connoisseurs of poetry, and it was a time when superior poets were numerous." People are judged socially by how quickly, aptly, and originally they connect present events to past poems. The irresistible cultural supremacy of "the shining Genji" is established, in part, by the range and delicacy of his literary allusions; those with less rigorous standards produce instead "a misquoted poem for every occasion." And those unable to quote at all are simply incomprehensible: to the courtiers, village fisherfolk are "as noisy and impossible to communicate with as a flock of birds." They may speak the same language, but they are disconnected from the network of literary memory that unites the elite. As the modern French sociologist Pierre Bourdieu has demonstrated, shared artificial memories create a kind of "cultural capital" that distinguishes social classes far more effectively than lineage or income. (Recollections create separations.)

The Tale of Genji contains 795 poems by Lady Murasaki herself; her characters compose and exchange poems continually as a formal social ritual. By contrast, although quotations from other writers are even more numerous than original poems, those quotations are almost invariably incomplete. The reciprocal ability to "fill in the blank" connects characters to one another, while also creating a relationship between the author and the reader. As readers, we can grasp the full richness of the story only if we recognize the literary allusions and reconnect each to its missing part. (Memory works by recollection.) The text asks to be connected to another text. When the grieving Genji asks, "What would we have to remember her by?" we are supposed to recall an earlier text, from the *Gosenshū*, that reads:

> *What would we have to remember our lady by*
> *Were it not for this keepsake, this child she left behind?*

Only then do we realize why the text that Genji remembers at this moment comforts him: it turns the living child into a textual memento of the dead mother. And if we remember this moment, we can connect it to other moments in the text. Another child will later be defined as "a memento" of Genji's affair with the Akashi lady, and a faithful servant will be "a sort of memento" of her dead mistress (a memento that Genji rereads sexually). Genji connects to his own experience by connecting it to a remembered text; he connects to his personal past by reading a present body as the textual reminder of an absent person. People are memorials of other people.

In this way, the continual recycling of past poems resembles and intertwines with the recycling of past lives. Exorcists call from a woman's body "spirits which had been with the family for generations." Sexually or tragically attracted to each other, people wonder, "What might it have been in other lives that had brought them together?" Inexplicable events, inexplicable talent and grace, are attributed to "a legacy from former lives." This Buddhist belief in reincarnation is expressed in the ritual repetition of old religious texts. Genji's lover, Murasaki, puts scriveners to work for years making a thousand copies of the Lotus Sutra. Genji reads the sixty Tendai fascicles and asks the priests for explanations of difficult passages. But this holy reading is preceded by exchanges of determinedly secular letters and followed by the emperor asking Genji "about certain puzzling Chinese texts," after which the talk naturally turns "to little poems they had sent and received."

Texts connected to past texts, lives to past lives, lives to texts—everything is connected. The most pervasive connections are sexual, and the novel recognizes no limits to the possibilities of combination. Both the story and Genji's own life begin with an outrageous union between the reigning emperor and a woman of impossibly low rank. Genji himself connects sexually with innumerable beautiful women of varied social status, with a boy, with his own father's consort, with an old crone, with a woman in the emperor's harem, with his wife's servants, with his lover's sister; he abducts a ten-year-old girl and soon makes her his consort; he entertains thoughts of corrupting a nun. Most women consent or invite, but resistance does not deter him; it just introduces an interesting variation. ("In a curious way, her hostility made her memorable.") His life is complicated by the fact that "each of his ladies had something to recommend her." Every connection has its merits.

And every sexual connection is also textual. Women are, in this polygamous society, systematically separated from men. Messages—poems and poetic allusions—are delivered by carefully chosen intermediaries or exchanged from either side of an opaque screen. Unseeable, untouchable, a person is epitomized by his or her hand—not the actual hand, which is unavailable, but the handwriting, which can venture into the world, embodying in its calligraphy an entire physical and social self. After Murasaki dies, Genji destroys all her letters. Doing so, he is blinded by tears—"The handwriting of the dead always has the power to move us, and these were not ordinary letters"—but he does not want others to see what only he was meant to see. Having sequestered her body during life, he now destroys her poems after death, so that no one else can glimpse even her "hand."

But we, of course, have already read those poems and poetic allusions: the author collected and preserved the textual memories that Genji collects and destroys. She did not preserve all of them; sometimes she explicitly tells us that it would have been too much trouble to collect all the relevant stories and poems, or that she collected them but did not find them all worth reproducing. (Every collection is a selection.) *The Tale of Genji* could be described as a carefully selected collection of poems connected by a prose narrative. Given the brevity of Japanese poems, poetry anthologies—beginning with the first official collection, the *Kokinshū*, a century before—always prefaced each poem with a prose explanation of its author and context. (Every collection is supplemented by every interpreter in ways that partly determine its meaning.) Prose supplements poetry; context supplements text. Lady Murasaki inverts this hierarchy, turning poetry into a supplement of prose. Still, they remain connected, just as Japanese literature remains connected to Chinese literature. Poetry and the Chinese language were dominated by men, who left prose and the Japanese language (both inferior) to their women. *The Tale of Genji* and its characters often allude to Chinese poets and poems, which Lady Murasaki knew well; indeed, she mastered Chinese more quickly than her brother, leading her father to wish she had been born male. *The Tale of Genji* contextualizes and legitimates its own original vernacular prosaic (female) structure by connecting it to a foreign poetic (male) tradition.

The connecting never ends. Present lives recapitulate past lives and anticipate future ones; the text cannot be bounded by a single physical existence. Genji dies (offstage) between the end of one chapter and the beginning of the next, but *The Tale of Genji* continues, following the life of his supposed son. Murasaki Shikibu dies, and her text, too, passes into the hands of survivors. (No collection can compel or control its future recollection.) Other writers attempt to continue the story where she left off, or to alter aspects of her story that they dislike. The elliptical quality of the writing encourages readers to imagine parts of the story that the narrator withholds. Later authors supplement the surviving manuscripts by supplying lost or unwritten chapters. Editors, too, begin to supplement the text, identifying literary and historical allusions, providing names for the characters, constructing chronologies of events and genealogies of persons, connecting one part of the story to another, connecting readings in one manuscript to readings in other manuscripts, connecting *The Tale of Genji* to Lady Murasaki's *Diary* and her collected poems, translating Heian Japanese into modern Japanese, into English and French and German and (ironically) Chinese, connecting, connecting, endlessly connecting.

This active editorial desire to supplement and reconnect *The Tale of Genji* is supplemented by an authorial desire: authors actively supplement and legitimate their own work by connecting it to Lady Murasaki's. The influential twelfth-century critic and poet Fujiwara Shunzei insists that anyone who expects to be taken seriously as a poet must read *Genji*. Its luxuriant amplitude is boiled down to more economical portions: the poems are separately collected, and digests, plot summaries, and lists of chapters proliferate. *Genji* becomes the mother lode of literary allusion, unavoidable model for Japanese fiction, fertile source of episodes for playwrights and images for paintings. To understand the meaning of *Genji* (or other *lieux de mémoire*) we must understand not only its moment of origin but also its successive transformations. "The book," as the literary historian Gustave Lanson declared in 1904, "is a social phenomenon that evolves." That phenomenon results from a "connection that is established between the work and the public, which continually modifies, reshapes, enriches, or impoverishes the work." For centuries, Japanese people have interpreted their lives by connecting them, directly or indirectly, to memories of *The Tale of Genji*. They quote Genji, even as Genji quotes others. Consequently, everywhere you look in Japanese culture, public and private, you see reminders of *The Tale of Genji*. ("He tried not to remember, but everything his eye fell on brought such trains of memory.")

But what is it precisely that we are being reminded of? A collection of separate memories—54 chapters, 57,939 names. What does it all mean? Like Sherlock Holmes or Arthur Gordon Pym, we collect clues and then connect them by interpreting each clue as a sign. We could decode the clues' message if we could grasp how they are related, how they were once connected—and can now be reconnected—into a single coherent system. In the detective genre, an extraordinary imagination reconnects the signs and thereby delivers the true past. Imagination re-produces fact. But imagination can just as easily reproduce fiction. Sherlock Holmes's rediscoveries of indisputable singular fact are themselves fictions.

The Tale of Genji, too, remembers a historical past that is, in fact, unhistorical. Devout Buddhists believed that Murasaki Shikibu was burning in hell because she devoted her life to creating frivolous fictions. Worse, she made fictive frivolity seem more real than life, more important than the truths of religious texts. *The Tale of Genji* juxtaposes its fictional past with the reader's real present, and the past consistently proves more satisfying. Although the past that *Genji* represents is a fiction, *Genji* itself—the text, the novel, the representation—is a fact. Genji's own gifts as a calligrapher, poet, and lover may be illusory, but Murasaki Shikibu's achievement is not fictional. It is a real part of the Japanese past. But again, that past reality is more powerful and satisfying than the representations of the present. The fictional tale of a fictional Genji and the real *Tale of Genji* reinforce each other: both provide a remembered standard of past value by which we interpret and judge the present.

FIRST LESSON: Lives are connected by memorial representations, and memorial representations are connected by lives.

SECOND LESSON: The more often and widely a memorial representation is circulated, the more new connections it forms.

THIRD LESSON: The number and character of those new connections is dependent upon editors and technologies.

FOURTH LESSON: The more connected a memory, the more easily recollected it is.

FIFTH LESSON: National and personal identity can be constructed upon memories of fictions.

EXHIBIT E

> *You, when your body life shall leave,*
> *Must drop entire into the grave;*
> *Unheeded, unregarded lie,*
> *And all of you together die;*
> *Must hide that fleeting charm, that face, in dust,*
> *Or to some painted cloth the slighted image trust—*
> *Whilst my famed works shall through all times surprise,*
> *My polished thought, my bright ideas, rise*
> *And to new men be known, still talking to their eyes.*

The eighteenth-century English aristocrat Anne Finch is here translating into English a poem written in Greek by Sappho twenty-three hundred years before. One woman poet remembers another woman poet, who addressed other women and predicted (correctly) that men would be remembering her long after she was dead. But very little of Sappho's poetry was available to Finch. This translation is based upon "a fragment of Sappho's"; for more than two millennia, Sappho survived in collective memory as no more than a handful of fragments. And most of Finch's poems—including this one—remained unpublished for almost two centuries after they were written, utterly unknown to any "new men."

Finch cannot equal Sappho; she cannot equal the most powerful poets of her own time, and people turned off by the conventions of Augustan verse will find it hard to appreciate her. Sappho, like Murasaki Shikibu, belonged to an island literary culture (Lesbos, seventh century B.C.) dominated at the time by educated women. Finch, by contrast, belonged to an island culture (England, 1661–1720) dominated by men. Strong stimuli cluster in dominant niches, and Finch knew it. Nevertheless, she struggled to find or make a place for herself in an inhospitable environment.

> But I write ill, and therefore should forbear.
> Does Flavia cease now at her fortieth year
> In every place to let that face be seen
> Which all the town rejected at fifteen?
> Each woman has her weakness; mine, indeed,
> Is still to write, though hopeless to succeed.
> Nor to the men is this so easy found.
> Ev'n in most works with which the wits abound
> (So weak are all, since our first breach with heaven)
> There's less to be applauded than forgiven.

All representations are inadequate. Someone determined to find fault will therefore always be able to find it. And the men of her time were particularly determined to find fault in the writing of any woman.

> They tell us we mistake our sex and way;
> Good breeding, fashion, dancing, dressing, play
> Are the accomplishments we should desire.
> To write, or read, or think, or to inquire
> Would cloud our beauty and exhaust our time
> And interrupt the conquests of our prime—
> Whilst the dull manage of a servile house
> Is held by some our utmost art and use.

Women in this society are "to be dull, expected and designed"; such prejudices make them "Education's, more than Nature's, fools." To prove that women are capable of more, Finch cites various biblical precedents, including particularly the Old Testament judge and poet Deborah. Finch self-consciously links her own work to a legitimate and venerable tradition—translating Greek and French poems. Her iambic pentameter couplets connect her verses to the dominant poetic form of her time; her use of the name Flavia connects them to Augustan satire and its English derivatives; her allusion to Genesis connects her to the Christian tradition and, more specifically, to its Protestant interpretation. Finch labors to connect herself to the memories of her culture.

Such connections are not easily made. With the exception of Deborah, the biblical precedents prove illusory or marginal. Sappho's frankly lesbian love poems make her an uncomfortable model; closer to her own time, Aphra Behn is also disqualified by her salacious heterosexuality. (Of course, Behn was no more salacious than her contemporary John Wilmot, Earl of Rochester; but he, after all, was a man.) Wishing to write a poem, Finch sends to the Muses on Parnassus for help; the divine sisters promise to assist her ("no female's voice below They sooner would obey"), until they discover that the proposed subject of her poem is "a husband's praise."

> *A husband! echoed all around—*
> *And to Parnassus sure that sound*
> *   Had never yet been sent.*
> *Amazement in each face was read;*
> *In haste th'affrighted sisters fled*
> *   And unto council went.*

The Muses refuse to assist her, excusing themselves by explaining how overworked and busy they are. Only a woman could write a poem in praise of a husband; consequently, there are no such poems. It's a man's niche.

Heian Japan was a man's world, but within its literary culture a group of powerful women managed to create a niche of their own, a niche in which *The Tale of Genji* could be brought to life. Through the subsequent efforts of male editors, authors, anthologizers, summarizers, illustrators, and printers, Murasaki Shikibu's work has been continually reproduced for ten centuries. It has been circulated into niches of time and space the author could not have imagined. In each new niche, it has stimulated powerful responses. We can collect the responses from all those niches and use them as a measurement of the stimulus. That measurement guarantees *The Tale of Genji* a place in any collection of the world's greatest texts. The other items in that collection—the works of Homer, Virgil, Dante, Rabelais, Shakespeare, Goethe, Darwin, and others—have been measured by similar criteria. Such measurements of collective memory are the foundation for the great tradition, the canon, whatever we wish to call the selective collection of the brightest and the best. Such works deserve to be recollected, because they have been recollected.

On the other hand, we can measure those responses to *The Tale of Genji* only because so many people were given the chance to respond to it. They were, in fact, actively encouraged to respond to it—and encouraged to respond favorably. To be a cultured person, to be a good poet or fiction writer, demanded familiarity with and appreciation of *The Tale of Genji*, which fundamentally reshaped the very niche that was used to measure it. Within that niche, people were encouraged and expected to "quote" *Genji*, to connect their own lives to memories of its text. Not surprisingly, people who interpreted life in terms that *Genji* gave them found *Genji* to be a remarkably fertile and accurate representation of life. And as the culture to which *Genji* belongs has become in our own century more and more powerful, the new power of that niche has created a new interest in *Genji*. It has been translated into new niches. It has been given another chance to make connections. We can measure the power of *Genji* across time and space only because it has been repeatedly reproduced across time and space. What is true of Lady Murasaki is also and equally true of any other artist who has become the standard of value in a particular culture or genre. Recent studies of the history of great reputations—William Stafford's *The Mozart*

Myths, A. Richard Turner's *Inventing Leonardo,* my own *Reinventing Shakespeare*—tell parallel tales of cultural saturation, appropriation, reinterpretation. What began by being compelling becomes compulsive and compulsory. Such makers keep being recollected, in part, just because they have already been recollected so powerfully often.

Anne Finch has not pleased many or pleased long. Most of her poetry remained in a private manuscript from her death in 1720 until 1903, when Myra Reynolds of the Department of English at the University of Chicago published a collected edition of *The Poems of Anne, Countess of Winchelsea.* The manuscripts of the poems survived primarily because of Finch's aristocratic rank; their preservation did not reflect any high appreciation of her literary achievement. Reynolds, Finch's first editor, was at pains to emphasize not Finch's own talent but her links with other talented people— Matthew Prior, Nicholas Rowe, Jonathan Swift, Alexander Pope, John Gay, William Wordsworth. Finch entered scholarly memory through her connections to already remembered men. Having once been recovered, however, Finch slowly began to be connected to other lives and texts. Since the 1970s, she has become a regular presence in anthologies of women writers and from there has made her way into integrated anthologies as well.

The recollection of Finch after a long period of oblivion was made possible by two things: changes in the niche, and the longevity of artificial texts. The gradual extension to women in England and America of rights described as "universal" but initially limited to white men, revolutionary technologies of birth control, the rise of university departments devoted to the study of English literature, the preponderance of women students in those literature programs, the slow evolution of a female professorate, the growth of university presses committed to the routine publication of academic monographs on obscure topics—these changes to Anglo-American cultural life created a niche in which Finch's texts might be reproduced. And they created a body of readers who would find connections between Finch's texts, other texts, and their own lives. For those readers, Finch belonged to what the French postmodernist Michel

Foucault calls "counter-memory," a collection of recollections that the dominant culture ignores or disparages or persecutes but cannot successfully abolish. Potentially, any such counter-memory could someday come out of opposition and ascend into prominence, or even dominance.

Sometimes what seems forever lost is, improbably, found again. The coelacanth, a fish that flourished in the Devonian and Cretaceous periods, between four hundred and ninety million years ago, was long assumed to be extinct—until one was caught by fishermen off the coast of South Africa in 1938. The work of Menander—the leading playwright of fourth-century Athens, author of one hundred plays, the most important single influence upon Roman comedy, which was in turn the foundation of Renaissance comedy—was long assumed to be permanently lost, until the discovery in the twentieth century of papyrus fragments preserved in the sands of Egypt. We can now read one whole play, *Dyskolos*, and substantial fragments of others. The female literary tradition, through which Finch tried to legitimate herself, has become far more visible since her death. Twentieth-century archaeologists have recovered papyrus texts of Sappho, who is now represented by perhaps a dozen complete poems and by more and fuller fragments than before. Closer to home, Finch's English foremothers have also been slowly recovered. Lucy Hutchinson's *Memoirs of the Life* of *her* husband was finally published in 1806, a century and a half after its composition. *The Book of Margery Kempe,* written in the early fifteenth century, and providing a model of female Christian spirituality, was rediscovered and published in 1936.

We can now recollect and reconnect with Menander, Sappho, Kempe, Hutchinson, and Finch because their work was written down. Texts make it possible for work to survive, unnoticed, in artificial memory even when it has disappeared from every intervening human memory. Finch herself wrote a poem "In Praise of the Invention of Writing Letters":

> Blest be the man!—his memory, at least—
> Who found the art thus to unfold his breast,

> *And taught succeeding times an easy way*
> *Their secret thoughts by letters to convey*
> *To baffle absence . . .*

She then proceeds to prophesy, correctly, a future technology of cultural reproduction:

> *Oh! might I live to see an art arise,*
> *As this to thoughts, indulgent to the eyes,*
> *That the dark pow'rs of distance could subdue*
> *And make me see, as well as talk to, you—*

Her visionary fiction has become, of course, our photographic fact. And from here she leaps into a genre that women have found particularly congenial from the seventeenth century to the present—science fiction:

> *Yet were it granted, such unbounded things*
> *Are wand'ring wishes borne on fancy's wings,*
> *They'd stretch themselves beyond this happy case*
> *And ask an art to help us to embrace.*

Artificial memory may not yet enable us physically to embrace the absent or the dead, but it does permit us, across centuries of indifference or oblivion, to recollect them—to reconnect them to a future from which they seemed to have been forever exiled.

FIRST LESSON: An intelligence in a hostile niche will try to solidify its identity by establishing connections outside that niche.

SECOND LESSON: Each recollection transports the original stimulus into a new niche.

THIRD LESSON: Each new niche creates a new opportunity to measure the force of the stimulus.

FOURTH LESSON: Every recollection of a stimulus enhances its ability to transform its niche to its own advantage.

FIFTH LESSON: Recollections condition expectations, which then confirm the authority of recollections.

SIXTH LESSON: The desire for reconnection and recollection defies all boundaries.

9.

Memory Work.

"I did this," says my Memory. "I cannot have done this," says my Pride, and remains inexorable. In the end—Memory yields.

At the end of the nineteenth century, a German philologist reinterpreted a Greek play written more than twenty-three centuries before. The philologist was Sigmund Freud; the play was Sophocles' *Oedipus*; the reinterpretation has influenced more people more profoundly and variously than any other piece of literary criticism in modern times.

Sophocles had dramatized the myth of Oedipus, a man who murdered his father and married his mother. How, Freud asked, are we to account for this ancient play's "profound and universal power to move us"? This is a question other critics had asked, but Freud answered it in a new way. "His destiny moves us only because it might have been ours. . . . It is the fate of all of us, perhaps, to direct our first sexual impulse towards our mothers and our first hatred and our first murderous wish against our fathers." Here, in *The Interpretation of Dreams*, Freud supplemented the assertive comprehensiveness of "It is the fate of all of us" with a cautious little "perhaps," but as he reiterated this interpretation of the play, he insisted more and more emphatically upon its "universal validity." In the incestuous and murderous desires of what he would eventually call "the Oedipus complex" lay the foundation of all individual psychological

199

development; there also "the beginnings of religion, morality, society, and art" converged.

But however extensive and complex its ramifications, Freud's account of the Oedipus complex began as a recollection of a single ancient text. Freud, the living survivor, set out to link the remembered text of a dead author to the experiences of the living. Like other nineteenth-century Germans who excelled at gymnasium and university, his mind had been fed on the Greek and Latin classics, and years before he published these theories, he had clearly internalized this text in particular, quoting it to himself to make sense of his own behavior. In private letters, he linked his own early "infatuation with the mother and jealousy of the father" to "the gripping power of *Oedipus Rex*." He identified strongly with Oedipus and later nicknamed his daughter "Antigone." But Freud also postulated as early as 1897 that such feelings were "a general event in early childhood." In *The Interpretation of Dreams* and his many later publications, Freud worked to link that dearly remembered text to as many lives as possible, partly by linking it to as many other texts as possible—his own, and other people's.

Indeed, Freud's entire intellectual enterprise consisted of retrospectively reinterpreting texts: accounts of dreams, literary classics, jokes, slips of the tongue or the pen, biographies, scriptures. He compared his psychoanalytic work to paleography, translation, archaeological excavation, the decipherment of ancient languages; he likened the displacements of meaning in dreams to the effects of literary censorship; he compared memories to monuments. By now you will recognize this figure. Freud was an editor. He retransmitted and reinterpreted cultural representations.

Most of the representations Freud retransmitted have been preserved for us only in his own accounts of them. We do not have full transcripts or recordings of the sessions with his patients in which they recounted their dreams. Of those oral relations little remains beyond his own fragmentary recollections of their substance. In such cases, in the absence of independent evidence, we cannot analyze the process by which Freud himself recollected the past. But we can analyze that process in Freud's interpretation of the text of *Oedipus*, which exists outside of his interpretation. We can still read Sophocles' play, in Greek or German or English, and then compare the text Freud was recollecting with Freud's recollection of it.

What must strike anyone who comes to Sophocles after Freud—which is the usual order now, with the decline of classical literature and the rise of psychology—is that it has so little to do with incest or patricide. Both take place offstage; both happened before the play begins. Moreover, unlike other offstage or long-ago events, the incest and patricide are not even described in one of those long retrospective speeches so common in Greek tragedies. Oedipus and Jocasta are married, but we are not encouraged to imagine them having sex offstage during the action of the play—as we are, for instance, very pointedly encouraged to imagine black Othello and white Desdemona consummating their marriage offstage in act 2 of Shakespeare's tragedy. Relatively few of *Oedipus*'s words concern incest or patricide. Nor does the play pay much attention (as Freud does) to the desires of children. Oedipus, of course, is an adult. His two daughters are brought onstage at the very end of the play, but they say nothing; they appear not as active agents of any kind but as the pathetically innocent victims of adult actions.

How are we to account for the discrepancy between Sophocles' play and Freud's account of it? We might say that Freud was more interested in the Oedipus myth than in this particular incarnation of it; but Freud insisted more than once on referring quite specifically to the play, and he credited "the Attic dramatist" with perceiving the psychological truth of the myth. Besides, before Sophocles, the myth had not demonstrated much "profound and universal power to move" people. Homer disposes of Oedipus in a cursory list of names-in-the-phonebook-of-hell. What did Sophocles do to make this story resonate so long and powerfully in Western memory?

Oedipus is a play not about incest or patricide but about memory. In fact, memory is the subject to which Sophocles most often returned. Both *Antigone* and *Electra* dramatize conflicts about whether and how to remember the dead; in *Philoctetes*, the hero obsessively remembers how he has been forgotten by other people; *Oedipus at Colonus* negotiates the transition from tragic individual life to heroic collective memory. But *Oedipus* explores the psychological and social paradoxes of memory more fully than any other tragedy.

The play begins with the citizens of Thebes begging Oedipus to save them and remembering that he had saved them once before; Creon then enters, reporting that the oracle at Delphi has promised relief if Thebes will find and punish the murderers of Laius. In effect, the gods order Thebes to remember a crime that it has collectively forgotten. Oedipus knows nothing about the crime, which took place before he arrived in Thebes, but he immediately begins to collect as much information as he can about these past events. The puzzle is solved not by any single revelation but by the acquisition and bringing together of different isolated items: this is a tragedy, quite literally, of re-collection. When Oedipus, Jocasta, and the Messenger all come together onstage, Jocasta can connect the dots; when Oedipus, the Messenger, and the Herdsman come together, Oedipus can connect them, too. In fact, Oedipus, the Messenger, and the Herdsman had all come together once before, when the Herdsman passed the infant Oedipus to the Messenger; when these characters are re-collected, the past can finally, horribly, be reconstructed. That past is a history of fatal re-collections. At a place where three roads came together, Oedipus (unknowingly) came together again with the father who had expelled him; when Oedipus entered Thebes and Jocasta, he was (unknowingly) reunited with his home and his mother.

What torments Oedipus? Killing an aggressive man at an intersection was, at the time, not painful; making love to his royal wife was, at the time, not painful. What is painful now, what is "more than man can bear," is the memory of what he has done. But he had had memories of those events before, and those earlier memories were not painful. What makes the memory painful now is that he has reinterpreted its meaning. He has many of the same memories, but now he connects those memories in new ways. That process of memorial reconnection is enacted onstage at the same time Oedipus is enacting the reconnection internally. At first, the old Herdsman does not remember the Messenger, but the Messenger refreshes his memory by connecting their earlier encounter to a whole series of other memories of times, places, and events. Once the Herdsman reconnects those memories, he can connect the shepherd he once knew to the Messenger now standing before him; once he reconnects Messenger to shepherd, he must also connect the infant to Oedipus; the pity he felt for that infant is connected to the pity he, and we, must now feel for the grown man the infant has become. In Sophocles' play, people are forced to connect separated memories in a way that forces them to reinterpret their connections with other people. These lives were connected physically, but they had not been fully connected memorially. The unwanted reconnection (like the forced fusion of hydrogen atoms) produces not only a new composite, an altered identity (a helium atom), but an explosion of emotion. Reconnection generates horror.

The horror is ours as well as theirs. Or rather, the horror of the characters is only an illusion, a performance, the representation of a fiction; the only real horror generated by these reconnections occurs within us, as readers or spectators. This play about memory labors to construct memories in an audience. *Oedipus* was designed to be performed on the occasion of an annual public festival (like the Fourth of July) in a venerated public building in the capital city of an empire (like the Vietnam Veterans Memorial). Its performance was punctuated, its visual field dominated, by the singing and dancing of a chorus that represented the people of a Greek city, like the people of the city of Athens who assembled to witness the play. It told a story that, whether fictional or not, was already familiar. Although it represents individual memories, the play works to reconnect collective recollections.

Hence the play's famous relentless irony. Irony depends upon our memory of things that the characters do not remember. When Oedipus, near the beginning of the play, curses the murderer of

Laius, we know (as he does not) that he is cursing himself and that he will later realize that fact. How do we know? Because we remember this myth; we have already heard this story. Throughout the play, we make connections between the present speeches and actions of the characters and what we remember about the past or future of the story.

The past *or* future. Much of the play consists of the recounting of predictions about the future. Creon reports a prophecy from the oracle at Delphi; Tiresias prophesies onstage; Oedipus remembers another prophecy that persuaded him to exile himself from Phocis; Jocasta recalls a prophecy that persuaded her husband Laius to order their infant son killed. The play combines memories of prophecy with prophecies about what will be remembered. *Oedipus* represents, among other memories, the memory of prophecy. All prophecy depends upon memory. We must remember prophecies made in the past if we are to know later whether or not they have been fulfilled. Jocasta recalls a past prophecy to demonstrate that prophecy is bunk. She is wrong: without her knowledge, the prophecy has already been fulfilled. Our conviction that these events were destined, unavoidable, originates in our memory of a prophecy. The events themselves might be utterly fortuitous; they seem utterly determined only if we *remember* that someone said they would happen, just like this.

Of course, Jocasta is only a character, a fiction; what she or Oedipus thinks about prophecy is less important than what we, the audience, think about prophecy as a result of experiencing this play. *Oedipus* was performed as part of a religious festival. All ancient religions—not just Greek paganism but Judaism, Christianity, and all the rest—derived their authority from prophecy. The power of prophecy as a social and psychological reality depends upon our connecting a memory of the past with a present reality. *Oedipus* forces us to make exactly those connections. It can do so with such extraordinary effectiveness because our collective memory of the myth confirms the validity of the prophecies in the play. *Oedipus* creates a feedback loop in which a social memory enhances the

affective and intellectual power of the play, which in turn strengthens the social memory of the myth, and so on. Every recollection of
this representation strengthens its equation between memories of the
past and predictions of the future. Of course, both the myth and
the prophecy may be fictions. But as we have already seen, being fictional does not diminish the power of a memory to shape our individual and collective identities.

Freud's recollection of the play forgets all of this.

What does Freud remember? The "secret meaning and content
of the myth." As Freud explains in *Introductory Lectures on Psychoanalysis*, the spectator recognizes "the Oedipus complex in himself"
and "remembers in himself the wish to do away with his father and
in his place to wed his mother"; the poet's words tell him, "In vain
do you deny that you are accountable, in vain do you proclaim how
you have striven against these evil designs. You are guilty, nevertheless; for you could not stifle them; they still survive unconsciously in
you."

What Freud wants us to remember is that Oedipus is guilty. Is
that what Sophocles wanted us to remember? Apparently not. As an
adult, Oedipus leaves Phocis, beginning the sequence of actions that
leads to his patricide and incest, because someone questions the
validity of his memories of the past. Specifically, someone suggests
to Oedipus that the man he regards as his father did not, in fact,
father him. Oedipus has, in the nature of things, no way of knowing
whether this story is true or false; to know, he would have had to be
a present, conscious witness at his own conception. To be confident
of his father's identity, he would have to know what happened
before he was born.

What is the first, most important thing a human child learns to
remember? Who its parents are. Nevertheless, Sophocles reminds
us, the child may be misled about the identity of its parents. This
always was, and still is, true. I did not discover the identity of my
own biological father until I was thirty-four; two of my four children are adopted. As children, we have a parent-in-the-present who
raises us, but this person may bear no relation at all to the parent-

in-the-past who gave us life. Oedipus built his identity upon a memory that turned out to be a fiction.

To survive, the child must learn to remember, but what the child remembers may be false or unhelpful. Why? Because most of a child's foundational memories come from other people. Deliberately or unwittingly, sometimes or often, those other people may conceal the truth from the child.

Oedipus faithfully remembers what he has been told, that his parents are the king and queen of Phocis. But he has been misled about his parentage; he has been given, and has internalized, a misleading account of the past.

Oedipus is destroyed by false memories.

FALSE MEMORIES

Freud, of course, had a lot to say about false memories. By 1895 he had an explanation of what nineteenth-century medicine called "hysteria," a collection of symptoms that we would now define as post-traumatic stress. Freud believed that this syndrome was a reaction to sexual "seduction" in childhood—what we would call adult "sexual abuse" of a child. But in 1897 Freud abandoned his revolutionary hypothesis, in part because he had found too much evidence for it. Freud could not believe that so many of his patients had actually suffered such abuse; if they had, then sexual abuse permeated the social and familial structures of his entire culture. To defend society, he rejected his patients. He did so by deciding that they must all have imagined the abuse. Why would they imagine it? Because they secretly desired it. Rather than admit their forbidden desire, they projected it into a fabricated memory of the consummation of that desire, a consummation actively initiated not by themselves but by the adult of their dreams. According to Freud, what had seemed historical was only psychical; what had seemed a true memory was a false one. This accusation of falsehood is the founding gesture of psychoanalysis. Even more specifically, this accusation laid the foundation for Freud's story of a universal Oedipus complex. To explain all those false memories, Freud had to postulate that many—or most, or all—young children secretly sexually desire one or both of their parents.

Both Freud and Sophocles emphasize the problem of false memory; false memory stands at the very beginning of the stories both are telling. But they tell radically different stories. In Sophocles, memory is essentially social; in Freud, memory is essentially personal. Therefore, in Sophocles false memories are socially constructed. Human individuals cannot personally experience everything that might be relevant to their survival or happiness; our memories are inevitably dependent, in crucial particulars, upon what others have told us to remember ("You must remember this"). In Freud, false memories originate inside the patient's own head; they *pretend* to be social, but they are *actually* just personal. There is no necessary connection, memorial or physical, with other people. Sophocles gives us a dramatic theory of memory, a theory founded upon intercourse, sexual and social; in Freud, by contrast, memory is masturbatory. Incest happens in our heads, not in our beds.

At the very outset of his career, Freud insisted that "a psychological theory deserving of any consideration must furnish an explanation of memory." Just as Aristotle and Velázquez offer different representations of representation, so Freud and Sophocles ask us to remember different explanations of false memory. But there is an important difference between these two pairs. Aristotle did not claim to be interpreting a specific painting by Velázquez; after all, Velázquez was in Aristotle's future, not his past. But Freud does claim to be interpreting a specific play by Sophocles. The text of *Oedipus* is not just in Freud's head; *Oedipus* belongs to the past, a real past that existed—and still exists—outside of Freud's representations of it. Aristotle is a maker (of philosophy); Freud is only an editor, a philologist, an interpreter of texts.

In particular, and centrally, Freud remembers this text by Sophocles. When Freud remembers the memories recounted to him by his patients, we lack any reliable way of comparing his memory with the past reality it represents. Were those women sexually

CULTURAL SELECTION

abused? Were they just imagining it? We may guess, but we cannot know, and across that disputed gap psychoanalysts and feminists fight battles that cannot be won or lost. Even when all the parties are still alive, it can be extraordinarily difficult to prove whether or not a child was sexually abused by a parent, and the cases Freud considered occurred more than a century ago. But Freud's account of *Oedipus* can be compared with *Oedipus* itself because *Oedipus* survives in artificial memory, outside of time, outside of Freud; Freud knew *Oedipus* only because it survived in artificial memory, and it is as available to us now as it was to him then. In the play, intercourse, physical and memorial, does take place. Incest happens in the parent's bed, not in the child's head. Indeed, it never happens in the child's head at all: Oedipus did not know that he was doing anything wrong. Here, and in almost every other particular, when we reconnect Sophocles' play with Freud's interpretation, it is evident that Freud's account of *Oedipus* radically distorts the text it purports to describe.

Freud propagates a false memory of Sophocles.

Of course, Freud is not the only literary critic to have misrepresented a text, or even the only one to have misrepresented this text by Sophocles. Interpretations of *Oedipus* have come and gone, without transforming our culture. Why should so many people have cared so much about Freud's interpretation of a play that was over twenty-three hundred years old?

They cared, and still care, because Freud was offering not just an interpretation of one play but a whole new theory of memory. *Oedipus*, he proclaimed, "portrays the gradual discovery of the deed of Oedipus, long since accomplished, and brings it slowly to light by skilfully prolonged enquiry, constantly fed by new evidence; it has thus a certain resemblance to the course of a psycho-analysis." In Freud's interpretation, *Oedipus* the play resembles, and justifies, psychoanalysis. And psychoanalysis is not only a theory about memory but a mnemonic practice. Freud invented a new technology of recollection, one that promised a recovery of the past more comprehensive and accurate than had ever before been possible.

The key to this new technology was the postulate, articulated in *The Interpretation of Dreams*, that "in the unconscious nothing can be brought to an end, nothing is past or forgotten." Thirty years later, in *Civilization and Its Discontents*, Freud was still promising "that in mental life nothing which has once been formed can perish—that everything is somehow preserved and that in suitable circumstances . . . it can once more be brought to light." If our representations of the past have been successfully and indestructibly made, then all we need is a method for recollecting them. The method was psychoanalysis. By its means, Freud first "brought to light" memories of the earliest childhoods of his neurotic patients; then he revealed that the same developments were recapitulated in all our childhoods. Soon he declared that the Oedipus complex and other neuroses "bear witness to the history of the mental development of mankind." Applying the same methods he had used to psychoanalyze individuals, he psychoanalyzed "primitive" tribal rituals, thereby uncovering "memory-traces" of the early history of civilization. Like *The Rite of Spring*—and at virtually the same moment— *Totem and Taboo* linked childhood and the distant past. Freud recollected our very origins as individuals and as a species.

Many of these recollections were, of course, false memories. *Totem and Taboo*, almost from the beginning, embarrassed Freud's admirers, based as it was on minimal and dubious anthropological evidence; even that evidence was soon comprehensively undermined. More fundamentally, Freud's history of the species invoked Lamarckian biological theories (that the acquired experience of an individual organism is somehow genetically transmitted to its offspring), which were generally discredited at the time and have been even more thoroughly discredited since.

Similar difficulties pervade his account of childhood. Freud treats childhood memory as though it were, from birth, identical to adult memory: the content may differ (or not), but the process of memory formation is the same. Between 1925 and 1934, however, L. S. Vygotsky and a group of Russian researchers designed a series of experiments that demonstrated "the development of mediated remembering" in children between the ages of three and thirteen. The gradually acquired ability to internalize and then manipulate signs—or as we might say, artificial memories, socially transmitted—"changes the psychological structure of the memory process." These conclusions were confirmed by the very different work of the Swiss psychologist Jean Piaget on the development of mental processes in children; one of Piaget's more famous experiments, the "mountain" test, showed that young children find it impossible to describe how something (a model of mountains, for instance) would look from the point of view of another person in a different location. Both Vygotsky and Piaget, in their different ways, insisted that the development of a child's mind is social; like Sophocles but unlike Freud, they offer dramatic models of memory. These foundational studies have been confirmed and expanded by many more specialized and sophisticated investigations of childhood development, language acquisition, and perceptual disorders like autism.

Though psychoanalysis depended upon a theory of memory, Freud never articulated or acknowledged a history of memory, at either the personal or the social level. Indeed, psychoanalysis depended upon the assumption that the mechanisms of human memory do not change over time. Freud reverted to *Oedipus* again and again for precisely that reason: the very ancientness of the play demonstrated that the human psyche, as interpreted by Freud, had not changed.

How could Freud, or anyone else—or many million elses—believe memories that were so obviously false? In part, they believed because psychoanalysis constructed a feedback loop as compelling as that which sustained (and still sustains) the collective belief in prophetic religions. Psychoanalysis predicted that an Oedipus complex would be found in every person. How was this prediction to be tested? By psychoanalysis. The practice inevitably confirmed the theory that lent authority to the practice; each clinical confirmation increased the authority of the theory, which lent authority to the practice, which lent authority to the theory, which. . . . This circularity was recognized by early critics who accused psychoanalysts of persuading suggestible patients that they had the complexes the analyst expected them to exhibit. "I can assert without boasting," Freud replied, "that an abuse of 'suggestion' has never occurred in my practice." But such a claim is contradicted by the example, from his own practice, with which Freud introduces his discussion of Oedipus in *The Interpretation of Dreams*. After describing the dream of a female patient, Freud continues, "I told her that this dream must mean. . . ." Freud was both oracle and priest: dispenser of predictions and cunning interpreter.

People believed, in short, precisely because—despite Freud's theory—memory is not masturbatory but dramatic. Psychoanalysis reconstructs memory through a social relationship between two persons, who themselves belong to a vast network of social relationships. The Oedipus complex may not apply very well to *Oedipus*, or to all cultures, but it evidently did prevail in Freud's own niche: in a heavily repressive, patriarchal culture, sons often do secretly hate their fathers. For Freud himself and many of his heterosexual male contemporaries, the theory not only fit their experience; it also legitimated their feelings by declaring them universal and unavoidable. Freud's interpretation was often accurate as a description of the present, however false it may have been as a memory of the past.

When the theory did not actually fit the present, it could nevertheless be imposed upon the present, precisely because present recollection was guided by an analytic relationship. Freud's theories of censorship, symbolism, condensation, displacement, recombination, secondary revision, conversion, transference, and the rest gave the analyst virtually unlimited freedom in interpreting the evidence delivered by a patient ("Whatever you say, it means something else"). As Karl Popper complained, psychoanalysis is not a scientific theory precisely because it is not falsifiable. But its very deficiencies as a scientific theory increased its effectiveness as a social practice. The (usually female) patient was impressed by the way her own testimony unexpectedly confirmed the analyst's authority; the (almost invariably male) analyst was exhilarated by the unlimited freedom of interpretation Freud had given him.

This freedom, of course, created its own problems. As a form of literary criticism, psychoanalysis creates, again and again, a very satisfying sense of closure: like Sherlock Holmes, or Oedipus, the superintelligent analyst begins with a jumble of oddities and leads us, by keen observation and relentless logic, to an authoritative reconstruction of the past. But as a form of social practice, analysis could seldom—perhaps never—achieve the closure of a cure. Limitless interpretation led to interminable analysis. Moreover, the seemingly infinite range of interpretive possibility opened up by the method had to be somehow constrained in practice to preserve the authority and coherence of the theory. Using similar methods, psychoanalysts like Carl Jung, Alfred Adler, and Otto Rank soon began reporting clinical results that apparently contradicted Freud's theories, particularly the theory of a universal Oedipus complex. The very flexibility of Freud's interpretive methods meant that such recollections could not be disqualified logically, so they were simply disqualified socially. If psychoanalysts recollected the wrong past, they were not psychoanalysts. The civil wars of psychoanalysis are not incidental but intrinsic to its method. Freud's recipe for reconstructing the past depended upon controlling the future, for only the future could confirm his prophecies. Hence Freud's obsession with finding an heir—first his "adopted . . . son" Carl Jung, later his own daughter Anna—a survivor who would perpetuate the right memories.

People believed because Freud created an intellectual and social mechanism, a genre, that simultaneously authored and authorized new recollections. But people also believed because psychoanalysis had made a great and genuine discovery: that memories can be deliberately repressed.

REPRESSED MEMORIES

The human mind's facility for repressing painful memories was discovered late in the nineteenth century by a group of physicians pursuing investigations begun by the great French neurologist Jean-Martin Charcot. Pierre Janet recognized that his patients' neuroses were caused by "subconscious fixed ideas," ideas fixed in the sub-conscious by memories of traumatic events. Freud himself collabo-rated with Joseph Breuer to reach the famous conclusion that "*Hys-terics suffer mainly from reminiscences*" (his emphasis). These studies "of pathological repression" led Freud to take seriously and scientif-ically the concept of "the unconscious," and indeed he declared, "The repressed is for us the prototype of the unconscious." In *The Psychopathology of Everyday Life*, Freud gave many ordinary exam-ples of the axiom that "forgetting is very often determined by an unconscious purpose." In *Inhibitions, Symptoms, and Anxiety*, he identified two particular unconscious mechanisms for repressing memories: "undoing" (what happened never happened) and "isolat-ing" (separating what happened from the emotions that properly belong to it). As Judith Lewis Herman shows in her book *Trauma and Recovery*, the reality and symptomology of repression have since been confirmed by many independent studies of war veterans and rape victims. One of the recognized symptoms of complex post-traumatic stress disorder is amnesia of traumatic events; amnesia is not inevitable, but it is common.

Most of the forgetting we do is routine and psychologically harmless. If a stimulus is not strong enough, it may not be repre-sented in memory at all; no amount of effort will permit us to rec-ollect such stimuli, because no representation is available for recall. But traumatic events—rape, torture, prolonged physical humilia-tion, witnessing violent death—clearly do produce strong stimuli. Such events threaten our biological integrity; our survival may depend upon recording such events so that we may recognize and avoid them in the future. In the case of trauma, then, forgetting—the belief that what happened never happened—cannot be due to a failure to stimulate or a failure to represent; it must result from some malfunction in the mechanisms of recollection. This hypoth-esis has been confirmed by innumerable demonstrations that trau-matic events, apparently forgotten, can indeed be recalled, usually in fragments of extraordinary vividness, even after the passage of years or decades.

The frequent failure to remember traumatic events therefore belongs to a larger category of forgetting that might be called misplacement. We have all experienced this effect: you know that you know something (a name, a date, the answer to a question on today's physics test), but you cannot immediately recollect it. It is like my knowing that a piece of paper is somewhere in this chaotic office of mine, but not being able to lay my hands on it just at this moment. The memory, the piece of paper, is there, but where? Traumatic memories, however, are not accidentally misplaced; they seem to be deliberately hidden. How can a memory be hidden? And why should it be?

These two questions are, not coincidentally, connected. Memory depends upon recollection; memories can therefore be hidden by making them difficult to re-collect. As we have already seen, if you want to make recollection easier, you increase the number of connections between that memory and other memories. The Vietnam Veterans Memorial was placed, spatially, inside a collection of uniquely familiar American monuments. Over time *The Tale of Genji* became connected with the whole of Japanese literary memory; if you followed virtually any string, it would lead you eventually to *Genji*. By contrast, most of the poetry of Anne Finch was isolated in two collections—two individual manuscripts—that were stored in places where no one was likely to see them; thus, they remained wholly disconnected from literary memory for almost two centuries. To prevent something from being recollected, you disconnect it.

Traumatic memories can thus be "forgotten" by being disconnected from the rest of an individual's mnemonic system. That is, in any case, precisely what a traumatized person wants to do. Experiences so painful cannot easily be integrated. They challenge or destroy a person's beliefs about the family, the world, themselves. Moreover, to integrate this disturbing new information, we would have to touch it. In fact, because it is so difficult to integrate, because it impacts upon so many areas of our lives and minds, to accommodate it we would have to keep touching it, again and again, making a whole complex series of connections, line by line, stitch by stitch, revising and reconnecting the circuitry of the entire mnemonic system. But every time we touch it, recollect it, it hurts us again. It may seem better not to touch it at all—just forget that it ever happened. Leave it completely uncollected; quarantine it. (Memory in more than one way resembles the immune system.)

But this strategy of isolation never works. It is defeated by a linguistic paradox: when a memory is deliberately repressed, one part of the mind tells another:

REMEMBER TO FORGET THIS!

You can forget only if you keep remembering the order to forget, and if you keep the part of the mind giving the order from the part of the mind receiving the order. Every reiterated act of deliberate disconnection depends upon, indeed creates, another connection. Moreover, the repression will work only if the offending memory is *systematically* disconnected from the *system* to which it belongs. Freud called one system consciousness, the other the unconscious, but he eventually realized that this simple distinction was misleading: to maintain relations between these two entities, parts of consciousness had to be unconscious. The forbidden-but-required interactions that destroyed Freud's tidy schematic diagrams also discombobulate the mind. The more systematic the forgetting, the more imparadoxed the whole system becomes. These paradoxes create, within a biological system designed for connection, malfunctional disassociation. Since the offending memory cannot be successfully isolated, it is dismembered, and its dissociated members are reassociated with memories to which they have no logical connection. The intense emotions connected to the original trauma are attached instead to some other representation for which they are desperately inappropriate: a woman reacts to being touched on the back of the head as though she were being raped. Fragments of horrific recollection pop, without warning, without explanation, into consciousness, like shards of a broken stained-glass window falling out of a desert sky; then the images disappear again and are often immediately re-repressed, leaving people utterly disoriented, unable to remember what caused the disorientation, uncertain of the distinction between reality and imagination, increasingly unsure of their own sanity.

The ineradicable persistence of these repressed memories was vividly described by Freud in a lecture on psychoanalysis he gave in 1909 at Clark University:

> What should we think of a Londoner who paused today in deep melancholy before the memorial to Queen Eleanor's funeral [at Charing Cross], instead of going about his business . . . ? Or again, what should we think of a Londoner who shed tears before the Monument that commemorates the reduction of his beloved metropolis to ashes . . . ? Every single hysteric and neurotic behaves like these two unpractical Londoners. Not only do they remember painful experiences of the remote past, but they still cling to them emotionally; they cannot get free of the past and for its sake they neglect what is real and immediate.

This description is impressive and true, but its very accuracy undermines some of Freud's own beliefs. In the first place, Queen Eleanor actually did die, and most of London actually was destroyed by fire in 1666; the monuments commemorate historical events, not mere fantasies. Second, not every event from the past is memorialized by a monument; the death of Queen Eleanor and the Great Fire of London were particularly traumatic national memories.

As these discrepancies illustrate, the problem with Freud's theory of repression is that it makes repression a universal response to fictional stimuli. In fact, the sustained repression of memory is a very particular response to an excessively real stimulus. What appeals to us and appalls us is not that the story of Oedipus is universal or fictional, but that it is so uniquely and horribly real—and at the same time so unlikely. There is only one Oedipus. Why should this have happened to him? Or as we are likely to say on other occasions, "Why me?" Sophocles confronts us—as Freud does not—with the recurring human problem of coping with statistical improbability, the problem of fortune, predestination, and quantum mechanics, the problem raised by *A Game at Chess*. Life is so unlikely.

The sexual abuse of children seemed to Freud so unlikely that he decided that it had not happened. At the end of *Oedipus*, he tells us, we learn the truth about our own incestuous and parricidal wishes, and "after their revelation we may all of us well seek to close our eyes to the scenes of our childhood." Certainly, Freud closed his eyes to some scenes of childhood. Incest is usually desired and initiated by parents, not children; it usually involves fathers and daughters (not mothers and sons); the father is not usually killed but survives and dominates. A much more realistic account of such relationships is given in *The Tale of Genji*. Genji sees and is attracted to a nine-year-old orphan girl and asks her guardians if he may take charge of her; they resist, suspecting him of having "improper" and indeed "outrageous" motives, so he simply kidnaps the girl and installs her in his home, where she is completely isolated from the outside world. He becomes her teacher and tells her to "think of me as your father." "It was as if he had brought home a daughter," and she causes him much less trouble than a grown woman would; she is "the perfect companion, a toy for him to play with." He occasionally makes amorous overtures, but she is too young to understand them, and he worries about being considered "a lecher and a child-thief" whose sexual tastes are "altogether too varied." Nevertheless, eventually he can restrain himself no longer, even though he realizes it will "be a shock, of course," to the girl. The line is crossed. Afterwards, she is sullen. "She had not dreamed he had anything of the sort on his mind. What a fool she had been, to repose her whole confidence in so gross and unscrupulous a man." He smiles at her childishness and finds "the stubbornness with which she refused to be comforted most charming." He continues to visit her sexually; she becomes one of his wives, but he is routinely unfaithful. She spends the rest of her life sequestered in his household. Later she wants to become a nun, but he will not allow it. He frustrates even her dying wishes.

This is not the story Freud tells, because Freud does not want to confront the realities of incestuous sexual terrorism. Nor does he want to face the realities of family violence. Violence between parents and children is usually directed *by* the father, not *at* him. Oedipus never initiates violence. When he defends himself at the place where three roads meet, he does not know that the old man he strikes is his father. By contrast, Laius had deliberately and consciously ordered his own infant son to be murdered. Moreover, although we and Freud routinely Latinize his name, the protagonist of Sophocles' play is named Oidipous; a proper English translation of the Greek word would be Swollen Foot. That name sounds like it belongs to a Native American myth, not an ancient Greek one, but the very name—reiterated over and over in the play—is a reminder that this child, soon after birth, had its feet pierced and bound together. The myth of Chief Swollen Foot is a story of the unexpected return of an abandoned and mutilated child to the home of its parents. A society that routinely leaves unwanted or defective children to die—as almost all early societies did—is haunted by dreams in which one of those abandoned children miraculously survives. In innumerable comedies, the lost child returns and is reunited happily with its family. In *Oidipous*, the lost child returns and is reunited horribly with his family, killing the father who ordered him killed, entering the womb that expelled him. Sophocles dramatizes the return of the repressed.

Oedipus reconstructs that repressed past by interrogating living witnesses: his is an oral culture. But we can recollect *Oedipus* because Sophocles could write, could leave behind an artificial memory of his play. Like Stravinsky, Sophocles was reconstructing a time earlier than his own. The cultivated primitivism of *The Rite of Spring* or *Oedipus* depends on a capacity to remember the primitive—specifically, to remember the difference between the primitive and the modern. Oral cultures cannot do that. In oral cultures, the only memories of the past are those handed down by tradition, which is embodied in living persons. The traditions of the living cannot be altered by direct appeal to the dead. In literate cultures, by contrast, "tradition" can be corrected by recourse to surviving ancient documents—like those used by Stravinsky, Roerich, and Nijinsky to create the music, costumes, and movements of *The Rite of Spring*, or those used by R. D. Dawe to create the 1982 Cambridge University Press edition of *Oidipous Tyrannos*.

This technological potential creates a conflict between two forms of memory: personal (which is always traditional, no more than a generation old) and artificial (in human texts, rocks, fossils, hundreds or thousands or even millions of years old). Print and electronic technology, universal education, and the increasing division of intellectual labor have geometrically accelerated our capacity to recover artificial memories of the past. But personal memory remains stubbornly "oral." The growing discrepancy between artificial and biological memory has created an increasing conflict between tradition and the editorial specialists who investigate artificial memories of the past. More and more often, more and more insistently, individuals in our culture are called upon to alter their memories of the past, as the traumatic memories our culture had chosen to forget have been recollected. We are inundated by the return of memories we had repressed.

What we have chosen to forget is always something painful or shameful or both. Though the Supreme Court desegregated the public schools in Topeka, in the 1960s my white teachers there never taught me that Langston Hughes had gone to school a few blocks away; indeed, I don't remember ever hearing of Langston Hughes, or of any other African American writer, while I was in school in Topeka. In 1992, in Massachusetts, my sixth-grade son Josh performed in a musical play based on the life of Christopher Columbus, but the play gave no hint of the genocide of native peoples that Columbus inaugurated. In the realm of specialists and artificial memory, our culture knows the truth about both Hughes and Columbus. But the biological memories of most people in our culture, the memories that are only a generation old, refuse to acknowledge these new memories. Such refusals depend upon what the German psychoanalyst Alice Miller calls a "poisonous pedagogy." Its first commandment is, "Thou shalt not be aware."

Remembering forgotten trauma is itself traumatic. And such "memory shock" is much harder to bear than the "future shock" popularized by Alvin Toffler. After all, our very ability to adapt to quickening change depends upon the stability and security of our sense of self. Memory shock undermines that foundational self. In the acute stages of traumatic remembering, an incest survivor no longer knows who she is, no longer recognizes who other people are, is no longer sure what is real. In effect, challenges to the traditional curriculum attack our memories of the happy childhood of our culture.

As a culture, we respond to the return of repressed memories about our collective past in many of the same ways an individual does. Like the chorus, we do not want to believe that this hero of our national past, Oedipus, could be guilty of horrible crimes. When he is first accused, Oedipus does not want to believe the new memories either. But how are these repressed memories to be resisted once they begin to resurface?

The most important ideological conflicts of the last five centuries—including the "culture wars" of the last fifteen years—have been driven by emotional resistance to the artificial recovery of repressed memories.

DEFENSE MECHANISMS

In the middle of a lovers' quarrel or a family argument, the raging urgency of the immediate issue makes it almost impossible to discern the logical structure of the conflict. But if someone videotaped all our quarrels and played them back for us years later, one right after the other, then we might begin to discern patterns of behavior that remained constant, whatever the particulars of a given argument. The artificial memory provided by the videotape would enable us to distance ourselves from the intensity of the quarrel. From that safe distance, what had once seemed axiomatic might come to seem instead merely symptomatic.

Unlike our private quarrels, unlike the nightly dreams and daily trivia that Freud psychoanalyzed, our public quarrels *have* been artificially recorded; we *can* review them; they *do* display recurring symptomatic patterns. From the Reformation to multiculturalism, from sixteenth-century philology to twentieth-century feminism, revisions to traditional collective memory have provoked firestorms of hostility so intense, so excessive, so immune to reason or the rules of evidence—and in their essential structure so very, very repetitive—that they can only be understood as the desperate defense mechanisms of an embattled psyche. The volume of these polemical battles is generated, in fact, by perhaps only a dozen simple reactions.

Reaction 1: Association

The old memories are familiar, as comfortable as old shoes; the new memories are painful. What causes pain is bad. Therefore, the mediums who are spreading the new memories must be bad people. Critics of Saint Jerome's revisionist edition of the Old Testament detected in it the baleful influence of Jerome's Jewish mentor, Bar Hanina. In the early sixteenth century, editors of the first printed polyglot Bible claimed that the original Hebrew and Greek texts of the Old Testament were tainted by association with the infidel Jews and schismatic Greek Christians; they therefore preferred the derivative traditional Latin Vulgate. Critics of the Revised Authorized Version of the English Bible were outraged by the presence of a Jewish scholar on the Old Testament committee. Albert Einstein's theories of relativity were condemned as "Jewish science." Edmund Burke nauseously reiterates that Dr. Richard Price's famous speech applauding the French Revolution was given "at the dissenting meeting-house" located in the "Old Jewry": Burke is soon describing the revolutionary's arguments as "Old Jewry doctrine."

A new memory is discredited by being linked not to the past but to a vilified minority in the present. That minority need not be Jewish, of course. Stravinsky was described as "a cave man of music," and *The Rite of Spring* compared to "the inarticulate refrain of a Zulu"; "the tom-tom melodies of the gentle Congo tribes seem super-sophisticated by comparison." (The Zulus recur: Pat Buchanan associates multiculturalism with the immigration of "a million Zulus to North Carolina.") Allan Bloom dismisses Margaret Mead, one of the most respected anthropologists of the twentieth century, as a "sexual adventurer." Critics of contemporary literary theory want you to remember that Michel Foucault was a sadistic homosexual, and Edward Said a PLO sympathizer; all the rest are Marxists. If the message is bad, it is because the medium is bad and has corrupted it.

Reaction 2: Fashion

Since the defenders of tradition deny that there is anything wrong with their own memories, they cannot recognize any basis in the real past for the newly emergent accusations. How then to explain the disconcerting power of these revisionist claims? In particular, how to explain the disconcerting fact that more than one person is challenging traditional memory? Usually, the existence of multiple witnesses confirms the validity of their testimony. But as far as the defenders are concerned, these independent witnesses cannot be right; therefore, they cannot be independent. Thus, when his own innocence is first contested, Oedipus immediately accuses Creon and Tiresias of conspiratorially inventing false memories to discredit him politically.

Revisionist memories are said to be false precisely because they are shared. What motivates and empowers the *Tenured Radicals* whose alarming rise was reported by Roger Kimball in 1990? All these individual revolutionaries could not have reached reasoned independent conclusions about the past as a result of arguments, evidence, and a lifetime of thought. No, their radical ideas have been so influential simply because they are "so exquisitely chic," so "in vogue"; "shallow intellectual fashion," "fashion," "fashion" is "aped," "aped," is "aped" in pursuit of a "modish" "conformity," "conformity," "conformity"; "imitators" "parrot" other "imitators" in repeating "fashionable clichés" like "verbal tics." A growing intellectual consensus is thus reduced to an infectious speech impediment.

But what spreads the infection? What transforms so many of

our best-educated minds into what Harold Bloom dismisses as a "rabblement of lemmings?" If only collusion can account for this collective challenge to traditional memory, only the power of rhetoric can explain the fact that so many people are joining the conspiracy. Oedipus attacks Tiresias for his "dark speech" and Creon for being "apt in speech": Tiresias owes his bogus authority to obscurity, while Creon cultivates greasy plausibility. Saul Bellow, introducing Allan Bloom's best-selling *The Closing of the American Mind*, boasts of his own ability "to detect the untreated sewage odors of a century of revolutionary rhetoric." According to Kimball, the new cultural revisionists make their pitch in a language of deliberately tangled, "jargon-laden" "opacity" designed to conceal weaknesses of evidence and logic. The radicals "seduce" with a "combative rhetoric"; they overwhelm us with "clotted academic rhetoric"; they inflame us with "overheated rhetoric." All this radical rhetoric is "intended not to further knowledge but to dazzle," to paralyze our mental faculties; we are stunned deer in the headlights of deconstruction; "rhetoric is all there is"; there is no one driving the car; there is no car; headlights is all there is.

Traditionalists claim to be defending the values and memories of a community. But when that community is fractured by the growth of alternative memories, the defenders of communal value are forced to attack the very idea of a community. A consensus, a common sensing, now becomes a cabal or a mob; grouped thought becomes the thoughtlessness of groupies. David Horowitz's satirical views-sheet *Heterodoxy* couples "animadversions on political correctness" with articles that dismiss the accumulating evidence of widespread sexual abuse as a mere "mass psychosis" engineered by a few demagogic leftists. What looks like confirmation is just a conspiracy of hypnotists.

Reaction 3: Hyperbole

Revisionist groups are not only alien, they are threatening. The more powerful they are, the more threatening they become. *Traditionalists exaggerate the actual power of revisionists.* By doing so, they increase the sense of threat, and an increased sense of threat will arouse and increase the vigilance of defenders. The *Wall Street Journal* warned its readers that "women are taking over" in corporate America—in 1949. In the 1980s, John Silber, president of Boston University, considered the English Department there a "damn matriarchy"—even though its chair was male and its faculty of twenty included only six women. Philosophy professor Michael Levin claims that feminists "have a lock-up on the media" and control the advertising industry. Hilton Kramer, in his journal *The New Criterion*, warns that a "barbarian element" of radical feminists and leftists "now commands an immense following in our mainstream institutions." Richard Bernstein warns of the "MLA Liberation Army" and the "MLA cult" that are working to impose a "dictatorship of virtue"—thus aligning multiculturalism with the worst excesses of the French Revolution.

Reaction 4: Inversion

The new power of these threatening aliens, defenders assure us, will have the direst consequences. In the sixteenth century, Maarten van Dorp feared that any criticism of the traditional Vulgate text of the Bible would erode faith in the integrity and validity of the scriptures. In the twentieth century, T. S. Eliot called the revised New English Bible "an active agent of decadence." Responding to the English revolution of the 1640s, Thomas Hobbes declared that those who pretended "to do no more than reform the Commonwealth shall find they do thereby destroy it." In our own time, defenders of the traditional family contend that women's liberation has enslaved women. Indeed, this argument is only one example of an axiom that, as the economist Albert O. Hirschman has shown, recurs again and again in the rhetoric of reaction: "Everything backfires." Every effort at improvement produces a deterioration. Therefore, *every effort to better recollect the past takes us, according to traditionalists, further from it.*

Reaction 5: Prophecy

Since these revisionist efforts will produce only disaster, traditionalists confidently predict that the future will reject them. Critics of Harley Granville-Barker's revolutionary productions of Shakespeare in the early twentieth century (which laid the practical and theoretical basis for all modern revivals) described his "frivolous and fantastic innovations" as a "craze," which like other "fads" had been "foolishly accepted by irrational persons who seek to run with every vagary of the hour"; these "mushroom votaries of reform" had sprung up overnight and would wither as quickly. In 1923 a London music critic claimed that "practically the whole lot" of Stravinsky's once-celebrated works (including *The Rite of Spring*) "are already on the shelf" and predicted that "they will remain there until a few jaded neurotics once more feel a desire to eat ashes and fill their belly with the east wind." In 1853 a Paris reviewer of *Rigoletto* was confident that "this opera has hardly any chance to be kept in the repertoire."

Such prophecies are as frequent as they are inaccurate. Oedipus, having been once accused of past crimes, predicts (wrongly) that whatever Tiresias says "will be in vain." *Defenders of traditional memory predict that it will be justified by the future.* They thereby attempt to focus attention not on an investigatable yesterday but on an utterly unknowable tomorrow. They defend the facticity of their own memories by an appeal to fictions.

Reaction 6: Arrogance

All these tactics, in fact, look away from the new memory itself toward something else: plots, rhetoric, Jews, Zulus, threats, futures. As with a sexual fetish, the intense emotions generated by the real stimulus, which is simply too powerful to confront, are redirected and focused upon something peripheral that is more manageable. Thus, rather than directly address the accusations that have been made about his own past, Oedipus ridicules the physical blindness of Tiresias and speculates about Creon's political ambitions. Freud, rather than expose to view an epidemic of "perverted acts against children," turned the glare of his attention onto the fantasies of the patients who had reported such crimes. Freud and Oedipus both attack the messenger who has brought an unbearable message. In the same way, other traditionalists focus upon the personal failings of a few individuals: the deconstructionist Paul de Man, who, as a young man, collaborated with the Nazis, or the Marxist philosopher Louis Althusser, who, as an old man, killed his wife. These are indeed contemptible actions, but they do not invalidate a lifetime of work.

Unfortunately, not every revisionist was a fascist or a wife murderer. But there is one sin of which they can all be accused: they are all theorists. Revisionists must always offer a new theory (which creates a new set of connections in memory) as an alternative to past practice (the set of familiar connections). As Edmund Burke complained, events in France in the years after 1789 constituted "a revolution of doctrine and theoretic dogma." Traditional practice is a "fact," whereas any proposed change in collective memory must be based on "mere theory." A revisionist, in other words, condemns some aspect of general behavior on the basis of a personal mental theory.

Accordingly, *revisionists are always accused of arrogance.* Oedipus calls Tiresias "brazen." In 1529 Franz Titelmans claimed that the driving force of Renaissance humanism was "base vanity, impious curiosity, and the urge to criticize and even to ridicule the scriptures." In 1546 the Council of Trent declared that the "ancient and Vulgate version" of the Bible had been "approved by the long use of so many centuries in the Church herself"; consequently, "no one may make bold or presume to reject it on any pretext." Stravinsky's music for *The Rite of Spring* was "presumptuous"; Brahms's First Symphony was "the apotheosis of arrogance." Against the arrogance of the revisionist individual, the traditionalist sets the collective authority of past behavior.

The accusation of arrogance is sometimes true, but it is made even when it is not true; it is made even when it is not immediately relevant. The "arrogance" of revisionists is not a personal attribute, and such accusations cannot be answered by an examination of individual cases because, in defensive rhetoric, revisions of memory are arrogant by definition. It is surely no accident that the first and most famous revolutionary, Lucifer, is the archetype of intellectual pride.

Reaction 7: Usurpation

Against this sin of pride, traditionalists set the virtue of obedience to authority. Not the authority of the distant past, of original documents or early historical evidence or repressed memory, but the authority of an intervening collective tradition. *In defensive rhetoric, the distinction between origin and tradition is elided into invisibility.* The editorial tradition perfectly recollects the original creation; thus, any attack on the intermediaries is interpreted as an attack on the maker. Lorenzo Valla's *Collatio novi testamenti,* the first humanist work to apply the new techniques of textual and philological criticism to the Vulgate text of the Bible, on occasion criticized both Saint Augustine and Saint Thomas Aquinas, and inevitably it often criticized the corrupt late medieval texts of the Vulgate. Valla's work was immediately attacked by Poggio Bracciolini, who accused Valla of "scorning the scriptures and slinging darts at Christ" and of deprecating the authority of Saint Jerome. The same criticisms were later leveled at Erasmus, and indeed, any revision of the reigning text or translation of the Bible has always been interpreted by traditionalists as an attack on the scriptures. The Ulster Unionist politician Dr. Ian Paisley, for instance, has written a pamphlet entitled *The New English Bible: Version or Perversion?* Paisley identifies 222 passages in which the new translation is "a corruption of the word of God"—that is, the New English Bible "corrupts" the word of God whenever it disagrees with the King James version.

Traditionalists attack a new edition of a canonical text—a revision of a collective memory—by claiming that its latest editors have displaced the original author and substituted themselves. The revisionist editor is visible and, like all editors, can only be visible by being defective. The new transmitter is accused of trying to displace the dead makers and usurp their authority. Sir Thomas More's reactionary *Confutation of Tyndale* complained that William Tyndale's revolutionary English translation of the Gospels was "not worthy to be called Christ's testament"; it was instead "Tyndale's own testament." The editor Tyndale had conspicuously intruded himself between God and the reader. This rhetorical tactic is not limited to reactionary Catholics. John Calvin, who in theological terms belonged to the revolutionary camp, was a reactionary when it came to sixteenth-century science: "Who," he asked, "will venture to place the authority of Copernicus above that of the Holy Spirit?" Whose word do you want, God's or Tyndale's? Who is the more credible witness, the Holy Spirit or Copernicus?

Reaction 8: Betrayal

The revisionist is a noisy intruder; traditional memory is unobtrusively embodied in venerable, impersonal institutions. But successful revisionists will at some point seize the editorial institutions entrusted with the preservation and reproduction of collective memory. That moment of seizure triggers an emotional crisis. The defenders of authority find themselves deserted by their own authorities. *Traditionalists respond by proclaiming that the institutions of authority have lost their authority.* They have been infected or infiltrated by some foreign element. The brilliant English biblical scholar Hugh Broughton—who was not invited to join the committees that prepared the "Authorized" King James version—declared that the 1611 translation had "barbarously perverted" the word of God. The reactionary French Cardinal Lefèvre, champion of an authoritarian Catholicism, denied the authority of the Second Vatican Council, and then of the pope himself. John Kidd accused the James Joyce estate (the legal guardians of Joyce's final testamentary intentions) of conspiring with Hans Walter Gabler to betray Joyce's intentions in our most admired modernist novel, *Ulysses*. Dinesh D'Souza warns Americans that Berkeley, Stanford, Harvard, Duke—indeed, all our most powerful and respected "enclaves" of intellect—have been invaded by "powerful and well-organized movements" of "Visigoths in tweed" who have installed intolerant new regimes of "illiberal education."

Reaction 9: Youth

Defenders of traditional memory describe their loss of institutional power in the language of betrayal. That sense of betrayal extends from institutions to generations. If a revolution succeeds, it will become the accepted worldview, the collective memory, of a new generation. That generation is, in any case, more willing to entertain revision, because it has less invested in the tradition; indeed, children often enjoy inflicting change upon their parents, biological or symbolic. As Thomas Kuhn observes, in the case of a scientific revolution, "Almost always the men who achieve these fundamental inventions of a new paradigm have been either very young or very new to the field whose paradigm they change." The hardcore defenders of the old paradigm are never converted; they just die out. Likewise in politics: for Burke, the French revolutionaries were "clubs of bold, presuming young persons."

Traditionalists perceive revisionists as young and inexperienced, as a gang of children who set their own arrogant theories against the accumulated ancient collective wisdom of their elders. But the youth of revolutionaries, like their arrogance, is at least partly metaphorical. Despite Goya's famous painting, a revolution devours its parents, not its children: it bites the hand that fed it. Revisionists are always the children of the culture they turn against and overturn.

Reaction 10: *Ressentiment*

Traditionalists see power being snatched away from them—by their own institutions, by their own children—and fear that in the long run there will be nothing they can do about it. This experience often gives rise to the emotional complex that Friedrich Nietzsche and Max Scheler described as *ressentiment*: a festering of impotent hatred, the anger of helplessness, which arises from reiterated humiliation. Such hatred will, by definition, only be redoubled— violently folded back upon itself again and again—by the succession of victories for a revisionist memory. Each new confirmation of the strength of the revisionist cause aggravates and intensifies the *ressentiment* of traditionalists. This hatred vents itself in the strident intensity of the defenders' attacks on individuals and groups. As more and more people accept the new memories, *traditionalists find themselves hating more and more of the society they claim to be defending.* Right-wing "patriots" bomb federal buildings.

Confronted with revisionist memories, Oedipus—the man who had saved Thebes, the man who, at the beginning of the play, even before he is petitioned, acts to defend the entire community— soon finds himself attacking the chief representatives of Theban religion (Tiresias) and politics (Creon). He is truculently suspicious of the chorus of Theban citizens when they urge reconciliation with Creon, and he eventually believes that even the family (Jocasta) is turning against him. Freud—healer, advocate for his patients, founder of psychoanalysis—accuses his patients of fabricating false memories, breaks bitterly with his friend William Fleiss, and indicts his fellow psychoanalysts for betraying him.

Reaction 11: Insanity

More is involved here than just another attack on the bearer of bad memories. *The embattled traditionalist can defend his sanity only by deciding that the rest of the world has lost its sanity.* Oedipus accuses Tiresias and Creon of "folly" and "madness." In 1596 Jean Bodin declared that "no one in his senses" (*nemo sano*) would accept the "absurdities" (*absurditates*) of Copernicus; in 1578 the French poet Seigneur du Bartas described those theories as an "absurd jest" propounded by "brainsicks." No sane person will treat theories so ridiculous as anything but a bad joke. Bishop Samuel Wilberforce, in a famous Oxford debate on Darwin's *Origin of Species*, chortled about "our unsuspected cousinship with mushrooms"; he wondered, facetiously, "if any one were willing to trace his descent through an ape as his grandfather, would he be willing to trace his descent similarly on the side of his grandmother?" An art critic described Paul Cézanne as "a madman" producing "a swarm of insane visions." A ballet critic imagined "four lunatics"— Stravinsky, Nijinsky, Diaghilev, and Roerich—conspiring to produce *The Rite of Spring.* A theater critic compared "the decadent followers and advocates" of Granville-Barker's avant-garde revivals of Shakespeare to the "unfortunate inmates of a large lunatic asylum."

Reaction 12: Loss

In all such cases, revisionism leads to the loss of reason. But more than reason is lost. Traditionalists do not need to create, because they are defending what has already been created; they claim to preserve what is. By defining their own task as preservation, *traditionalists define any revolution in terms of loss*. According to Edmund Burke in 1790, the French revolutionaries "destroy all traces of ancient establishments . . . totally abolishing . . . levelling all . . . breaking all . . . abolishing every. . . ." According to Allan Bloom in 1987, contemporary higher education impoverishes, destroys, deprives, lobotomizes, cripples, excises, strangles, dissolves; it bursts the mainspring of society; it makes the world meaningless; it culminates in cultural suicide. The tradition is lost, the fine art of comparison is lost, the practice and the taste for reading is lost; parental control is lost; the natural continuity between feeling and being is lost; modesty is lost; love is lost; country, religion, family—all lost, lost, lost.

But there is a paradox about such losses. Consider, for instance, Granville-Barker's revolutionary Savoy production of *A Midsummer Night's Dream*. Granville-Barker departed from tradition by performing *much more* of Shakespeare's text than ever before; nevertheless, many people felt cheated. One critic complained that "illusion was destroyed"; another lamented "the loss of all illusion." How can the provision of *more* Shakespeare be vilified as a *loss*? How can the restoration of more, and more accurate, memories of the past be described in terms of diminution and subtraction?

What traditionalists perceive is a loss not of memory but of value. William J. Bennett laments and resists what he calls "the devaluing of America." His opponents do not have alternative values; they have, he would have you believe, no values at all. Revolutions are always described as debasements. The Copernican revolution took away earth's status as the center of the cosmos and put in its place vastnesses of empty space; the French Revolution took away the elegant, beautiful, accomplished Marie Antoinette and put in her place what Burke called "monstrous savages," the dirty, howling, violent women of the Parisian mob; the Darwinian revolution erased the distinction between human beings and animals; the Russian Revolution took away the czar and made everyone dress in gray dungarees. Allan Bloom attributed a pervasive decline in American intellectual life partly to the influence of rock music, but he had been anticipated earlier in the century by similar reactions to jazz. For the Russian critic Maxim Gorky, "listening to this screaming music for a minute or two, one conjures up an orchestra of madmen, sexual maniacs, led by a man-stallion beating time with an enormous phallos." To the English critic Cyril Scott, "after the dissemination of jazz, which was definitely put through by the Dark Forces, a very marked decline in sexual morals became noticeable." In all these reactionary formulas, revolution is devaluation. Human beings are reduced to the status of madmen, savages, animals.

This sense of debasement has at least two causes. First, any revolution in collective memory will always revise the existing hierarchy of values; certain things that were valued greatly before the revolution will be valued less after it, and vice versa. The hero Christopher Columbus turns out to have initiated the greatest genocide in human history; the genius William Shakespeare turns out to have written sexist, racist, jingoistic plays; biblical astronomy and chronology are unreliable. People who adhere to the old value system see no value at all in the new system. Second, a revisionist movement can succeed in transforming collective memory only by attracting a large number of adherents, whom traditionalists must characterize as an unthinking, gullible mob. The triumph of revision is therefore inevitably seen as a triumph for the least respectable, least admirable subset of society—as the triumph of a debased humanity.

It would be tempting to generalize that traditionalists resent the loss of their illusions. But it would be more accurate to say that they resent the loss of their allusions. Thus, in the case of Barker's *Midsummer Night's Dream*, they resented, among other things, the fact that he deprived them of Mendelssohn's music for the play, a staple of Victorian and Edwardian productions. "To its rhythm our loyalties and beliefs have learned to move," said one reviewer. Barker took away the Romantic music, the archaeologically reconstructed classicism of the sets for the play's Athenian scenes, the elaborate pictorial forests to which regular playgoers had grown accustomed; he substituted what seemed instead "a world arbitrarily made." Frank Kermode proposes that editors should continue to print the traditional text of *Hamlet*, even if it does not represent Shakespeare's own intentions, simply because it is "our" *Hamlet*, the one recognized by our culture for three centuries. Critics of the *New English Bible* and the revised *Book of Common Prayer* complain that future generations of readers, raised on these new versions, will become deaf to the music of echo and allusion that plays through centuries of English discourse, written by authors who knew by heart the phrasing and imagery and rhythm of the old prayer book and the King James Bible. Students who have grown up in the universe of Copernicus and Newton do not recognize the cosmos that most previous literature—including the Bible—takes for granted.

In 1611 John Donne, reflecting upon the rise of modern science, complained that

> *new philosophy calls all in doubt.*
> *The element of fire is quite put out;*
> *The sun is lost, and th'earth, and no man's wit*
> *Can well direct him where to look for it.*
> *And freely men confess that this world's spent,*
> *When in the planets and the firmament*
> *They seek so many new; they see that this*
> *Is crumbled out again t'his atomies.*
> *'Tis all in pieces, all coherence gone,*
> *All just supply, and all relation.*

Donne's moving lament conveys, perhaps more powerfully than any other passage of English poetry, a sense of that reiterated "all" that has been "lost" and is now "gone." But what provoked this sense of loss, in part, was an addition to the cosmos: the discovery of "so many new" planets in the firmament. Donne was alluding to Galileo's discovery in 1609 of the moons of Jupiter. Galileo had found new "planets" and new stars; more generally, the new Copernican cosmology had vastly expanded the apparent size of the known universe by insisting upon the enormous distances between earth and the fixed stars. Paradoxically and paradigmatically, a revolutionary addition provokes a reactionary sense of loss.

What has been lost is what Donne describes as "coherence" and "relation": the addition of new worlds or new texts disrupts the existing structure of relations within a memorial universe. Without such a structure of relations, we do not know where to place the new objects, or even where the old objects now belong. We "lose" our way; we feel "lost." The sense of disorientation ("lost") easily leads to a sense of deprivation ("loss"): the etymological connection expresses an emotional one. Traditionalists yearn for and prophesy the restoration of memorial connection: the reunification of past and future, of editor and origin, of representation and what it represents.

Of course, what traditionalists are resisting is, precisely, new recollections, which create new memorial connections. For the traditionalist, as for Oedipus, rediscovery can mean only unbearable loss, and recollection—reconnection—can lead only to exile, to the end of all connections.

This may seem only a hyperbolic metaphor. But supporters of an old regime are often literally exiled from the new. And the logic of their position often compels an intellectual disconnection even more radical than the geographical one. From the traditionalist's perspective, the young betray the old, and the institutions of authority betray their function. In both cases, those who have been entrusted with the perpetuation of cultural memories subvert them. Editing is always about the transmission of a text, a set of instructions, from one person to another, one time to another; it therefore naturally lends itself to this imagery of corrupted transmission. But if the institutions that transmit cultural value can, in the present, be betrayed, seduced by a false rhetoric, corrupted from within by the accidental influence of a few personalities, then, of course, they also could have been corrupted in the past. By insisting that institutions and generations can be misled by rhetoric or foreign influence, traditionalists unintentionally and retrospectively undermine their defense of traditional memory: if old institutions and young people can be corrupted now, they could just as easily have been corrupted in the past. Such reasoning creates, for the defenders of memory, an unbearable paradox: how far back do traditionalists have to go to find the real "tradition" they are defending? Often very far indeed. For Allan Bloom, the malaise of contemporary American life must be traced, philosophically, back beyond the shallow rationalism of the Enlightenment, back beyond the founding of America, back to the academy of the Athenian philosophers. It has to be traced, in the end, back to Plato's *Republic*. Higher education may have failed democracy and impoverished the souls of today's students, but the only republic to which Bloom could pledge unqualified allegiance is an entirely fictional one, twenty-five centuries gone.

No doubt about it—the recollection of repressed memories is exquisitely painful. That is why we resist them so fiercely. And such defensiveness is not limited to the political right. The political left has been equally resistant to restored memories of, for instance, Communist and revolutionary atrocities, or the personal vices of John Fitzgerald Kennedy and Martin Luther King, Jr. Liberals can be nostalgic too: for a time before Republican landslides and fundamentalist activism and Supreme Courts dominated by conservative justices. Consequently, as the sociologist James Davison Hunter observes, in our culture wars the rhetoric of the left often mirrors that of the right, sometimes making it "nearly impossible to distinguish which of the two coalitions is speaking." We are all susceptible; the increasing gap between personal and artificial memory affects and afflicts us all. Oedipus, an unusually strong and capable man, is devastated by such recollections. Oedipus suffers, horribly; so does Jocasta; so do their children. Thebes is cured, and cursed. As anyone who has suffered the eruption of repressed memories knows, recollection of the past can utterly transform the future.

10.

Memories
of the Future.

*There was once a Lakota holy man, called Drinks
Water, who dreamed what was to be; and this was
long before the coming of the Wasichus. He
dreamed that the four-leggeds were going back
into the earth and that a strange race had woven
a spider's web all around the Lakotas. And he
said: "When this happens, you shall live in square
gray houses, in a barren land, and beside those
square gray houses you shall starve."*

BLACK ELK OF THE OGLALA SIOUX

Unlike the present, which becomes the past, the future cannot
stimulate us directly. We can imagine the future only by recollecting the past. We recollect, often, the dream of a nineteenth-century
Englishwoman. In her first novel, published before she was twenty,
Mary Wollstonecraft Shelley told the story of an abandoned child.
Like Swollen Foot of the Thebans, the child returns, destroys the
family that had rejected him, and then condemns himself to exile,
isolation, and death. In the novel, this child is never named, but he
has become so famous that we need a label for him; we usually call
him by the name of his father, Frankenstein.

We usually do not think of Frankenstein Jr. as an abandoned
child. But Mary Shelley did. At the moment of his birth, the person
who had given him life recoiled from him in horror, deserted him,

237

and later is deliriously pleased on returning to find him gone. The parent never for a moment considers how his behavior might have affected the child, but the child remembers; the child will never forget. ("I was alone. I remembered Adam's supplication to his Creator. But where was mine? He had abandoned me, and in the bitterness of my heart I cursed him.") Through no fault of his own, Frankenstein Jr. is disconnected from the human race. His benevolent and affectionate attempts to reconnect are, again and again, cruelly rejected. His creator refuses to provide him—as God provided Adam—with a partner. In human memory he can be connected only to images of horror and violence. So he connects in the only way left to him—by destroying.

> *Why do you complain that our young men have fired on your soldiers, and killed your cattle and your horses? You yourselves are the cause of this.*
>
> SHINGIS OF THE DELAWARE

Frankenstein represents the future.

Frankenstein Sr., the creator and narrator, tells his story to Robert Walton, an Englishman leading an expedition to the North Pole. Frankenstein's narrative is framed, literally and imaginatively, within a larger narrative of the Second Age of Exploration. In the First Age, the human species, apparently originating in Africa, slowly colonized the globe; the resulting widely separated human communities developed, in relative isolation from one another, an extraordinary diversity of cultural memory. In the Second Age, western European men—supplemented with new technologies of communication, transportation, and subjugation—colonized the globe once again, forcibly reuniting the human species. Frankenstein's friend Clerval has plans to visit India, in the hopes of "materially assisting the progress of European colonization and trade." Shelley's people are continually moving, traversing Europe from Italy to the Arctic, from Russia and Turkey to Ireland.

As the Europeans conquered geography, they also colonized

time. The ancient discipline of written history was reinvigorated, accelerated, and then supplemented by philology, ethnology, anthropology, archaeology, astronomy, and geology; the autobiographical past was extended back into childhood and then the unconscious. In traveling around the planet, explorers often felt that they were also traveling backwards in time: English colonists compared North American tribes to the ancient Picts who had once inhabited Britain. In the Second Age of Exploration, the future confronted the past, and the future won.

Biologically, memory enhances survival by enabling us to extrapolate from the past into the future. Historically, the multiplication of artificial memory made possible by the European colonization of space and time empowered an expanding collective engagement with the future. The profits of the emergent capitalist industries of the sixteenth and seventeenth centuries depended upon the ability to predict future markets for current investments. Since Francis Bacon, the authority of scientific theories has depended upon their ability to predict the outcome of repeated experiments. The appeal of Marxism depended upon its claim to predict scientifically the evolution of capitalist economies. These futures were not extrapolated from moral or theological postulates; they were secular and social, based upon analysis of an expanding database of artificial memories. Historicity made possible futuricity.

The developing futuricity of western European culture opened a new niche for literary creativity. In that new niche, *Frankenstein* was the first classic. The novel is technically set in the recent past, but it imagines the future. Such time shifts characterize the new genre of science fiction, which, paradoxically, recollects what has not yet happened. In *The Last Man*, published in 1826, Mary Shelley told a story set in 2073; the events of the film *Star Wars* are said to have happened "long, long ago." *Frankenstein* recalls the success of a scientific experiment that resembles experiments conducted by Shelley's contemporaries, but that success belongs to the future of the novel's readers (still). Science fiction reversed the direction of time, even before it began to imagine time travel.

Memory also, of course, reverses the direction of time. It transmits the past into what was, for the past, the future. It re-collects what has dissipated, as European exploration reunited dispersed human cultures. But what has long been separated from us may, when recollected, no longer seem familiar. It may seem instead horribly alien.

> *He is a different kind of man. . . . Nothing like that had ever been seen among the tribe, only animals were that way.*
> BAD HAWK OF THE ASSINIBOINE

What happens when we encounter an alien intelligence?

Every human who encounters Frankenstein Jr. recognizes at once his unrecognizability. He is not-human, but he is disturbingly like-human. Science fiction has often imagined future "close encounters" with a nonhuman culture, but Europeans had already experienced alien contact, repeatedly, in the Second Age of Exploration. Just before he describes the birth of his monstrous child, Father Frankenstein compares his own scientific obsessions to the passions of early European explorers: "If no man allowed any pursuit whatsoever to interfere with the tranquillity of his domestic affections . . . America would have been discovered more gradually, and the empires of Mexico and Peru had not been destroyed." Frankenstein Jr.'s first knowledge of human history comes from overhearing a man read aloud *Ruins of Empires*: "I heard of the discovery of the American hemisphere and wept . . . over the hapless fate of its original inhabitants."

Shelley also lets the alien tell his own story. In his final words, in the penultimate paragraph of the novel, he predicts his own death: "Soon these burning miseries will be extinct." Extinct—his death is the death of an entire species. European study of the geological and fossil record had already demonstrated that the earth was once inhabited by varieties of life that had since disappeared. And species death was coming to be seen as an inevitable extension of individual death. We can predict that we as individuals will die because we remember the deaths of other individuals; once we begin to remember the deaths of other species, we begin to realize that we as a species will also die. In *The Last Man*, Shelley would imagine the future extinction of the human race. In *Frankenstein*, the death of our species is averted, but only by ensuring the death of a rival species. Father Frankenstein refuses to provide his son with a mate because together male and female might propagate "a race" that would threaten "the very existence of the species of man."

> *Where today are the Pequot? Where are the Narragansett, the Mohican, the Pokanoket, and many other once powerful tribes of our people? They have vanished before the avarice and the oppression of the White Man, as snow before a summer sun.*
>
> TECUMSEH OF THE SHAWNEES

In *Frankenstein*, that threatening alien intelligence is a representation of human intelligence.

Father Frankenstein wants to reproduce humanity. He remembers, and editorially reenacts, God's creation of man by making an artificial representation of the human race. But representations are not equal to the realities they represent. Frankenstein's prototype representation of humanness conspicuously differs from the original on which it is modeled. For one thing, it is too big; science had not yet solved the problem of miniaturization. But since then, the developing technologies of representation have reduced the gap between reality and representation. In Philip K. Dick's *Do Androids Dream of Electric Sheep?* artificial "mentational entities" have become virtually impossible to distinguish from humans. They do not even realize that they themselves are androids; having been given "false memories" in an implanted "synthetic memory system," they think they're human. Since the androids believe they are human, any human might, without knowing it, be an android. "Do androids have souls?" (Do humans?) At what point does the tool become a slave? At what point does the supplement acquire an essence of its own?

What happens when the technological efficacy of representation exceeds the human perceptual ability to discriminate between the representation and the stimulus? Between forgery and original? Between virtual reality and reality? After all, the memories on which identities are constructed can be fictional. In Stanislaw Lem's *The Futurological Congress*, humans inhabit a world saturated with manipulative designer-hallucinogens; illusions are layered upon illusions. Like rats addicted to an electrical stimulus to the pleasure centers of the brain, Lem's humanity starves blissfully to death. Representations can be tailored to satisfy our desires more readily than reality.

But at some point the very distinction between representation and reality becomes obsolete. The future may be able to remember the past so comprehensively that memory becomes reproduction. In the film *Jurassic Park*, the future reconstructs the past; the past escapes from its prison and breaks into the future. It reenters the temporal continuum, with unpredictable and chaotically uncontrollable results. Doing so, it threatens—like Frankenstein Jr.—the survival of the species that re-created it.

> *It is not necessary for eagles to be crows.*
> SITTING BULL OF THE SIOUX

What happens when a representation surpasses its creator?

Frankenstein Jr. is bigger and better than his daddy—stronger, faster, stealthier. He does not murder his maker; he simply keeps running until he has exhausted his human pursuer to death. In Dick's novel, "androids equipped with the new Nexus-6 brain unit had from a sort of tough, pragmatic, no-nonsense standpoint evolved beyond a major . . . segment of mankind." One is an opera singer, performing brilliantly in *The Magic Flute*.

Our creations remember better than we do. All human technologies of artificial memory have been developed to supplement the deficiencies of biological remembrance; every new mnemonic mechanism reduces the need and the incentive for human efforts to remember. Why memorize anything when you can write it down? Why memorize what you can look up in a book, an index, a bibliography? Why memorize what you can access electronically? But electronic memories not only supplement our own; they seem, as books do not, to mimic our memories. Script and print merely "store" representations; computers both store and retrieve. They store more than we can, and they retrieve what they have stored more comprehensively, more accurately, more quickly.

There is too much to remember, and more to remember all the time. Unlike the machines, we cannot remember it all. The gap between what we feel we *should* know and what we *do* know increases constantly and exponentially. Alarming statistics demonstrate how little our children know about the world or the past— and those statistics join the endless multiplying list of things we *should* remember. Critics like E. D. Hirsch compile lists of what we should remember if we want to consider ourselves culturally literate. Every such list reminds us of something we don't remember. And every such list provokes complaints about what the list-maker has himself forgotten to include.

Our artificial memories of the past expand, but we cannot expand our biological capacity for memory, and we cannot increase the number of hours in a day. America is too busy to listen attentively to long, difficult, unfamiliar representations. Reading *Frankenstein* takes more time than watching any of the movies it has inspired; reading *Do Androids Dream of Electric Sheep?* takes more time than watching *Blade Runner*. Going to a play takes more time than going to a movie, which takes more time than renting and watching a video, which takes more time than watching whatever happens to be on TV. Even if we prefer the self-indulgent leisureliness of reading, we don't have time to read everything, and so must take time to find out which of the innumerable available books we *should* read. This is true not just of ordinary readers but of professionals as well. I teach and write about Shakespeare for a living, but even if I read nothing else, I could not read all the new essays and books on Shakespeare published in any given year. Every minute we spend reading the *New York Times Book Review* or the *Times Literary Supplement* is time we do not spend reading the books reviewed in them. Anyway, since it takes so much more time to read the book than to read the review, it is difficult to read even the books the reviewer tells us we should read. And these are just reviews of the new books. What about all the old ones? Which of those are still worth reading? Our increasing collective and individual dependence upon lists that tell us what to read explains the increasing visibility and bitterness of debates about the literary canon and the academic curriculum.

Most traditionalists blame the decline in humanities enrollments, the deterioration of collective memory, on radical university faculty and radical intellectual theories. But by the time students get to college, their most enduring memories and intellectual habits have already been formed. American eighteen-year-olds are full-grown consumers, and they judge a college education as they would any other consumer product. The real enemy of memory is not feminism or multiculturalism but capitalism. MTV molds more minds than deconstruction. The particular music being played, the particular product being advertised between songs, matters less than the ceaseless celebration of new sounds, new looks, new products. The actual events represented by the news media matter less than the fact that there is new news every day clamoring for our attention. Our entire economic system depends on production and consumption of a single good: newness. If Frankenstein Sr. were alive today, he would be CEO of a profitable bioengineering firm. How can the past—however taught, however theorized—compete against this multi-trillion-dollar global glorification of the new?

In her preface to the 1831 reprint of *Frankenstein*, Shelley remembered her own childhood, spent reading, writing, and day-dreaming. "It was beneath the trees of the grounds belonging to our house, or on the bleak sides of the woodless mountains near, that my true compositions, the airy flights of my imagination, were born and fostered." Our children have less time for airy flights of the imagination. The minds of most American children are invaded and occupied for sixty hours a week by television. Our local high school

expects children to spend three hours a night doing homework, and most parents in town supplement this with extracurricular lessons of one sort or another, educational camps over the summer, and private instruction to help students cram for the Scholastic Aptitude Test. In Japan—which we are told we should emulate—the educational regime consumes even more of childhood.

Nevertheless, this pressure-cooker educational system has little time for the humanities. Our children attend a junior high and high school that have both won presidential awards for educational excellence; many of the town's residents moved here, as we did, because of its excellent public schools. The math and science departments are superbly equipped and staffed, with a multitiered course system that separates children into ordinary, accelerated, and superaccelerated tracks. But my son Isaac was taught sophomore English from a textbook printed in 1951 (before I was born), by a man who bragged of using the same lesson plans for seventeen years. Although Isaac had already completed all his college preparatory requirements, counselors advised him not to take social science and humanities electives his senior year because such "soft" courses would not impress admissions officers at good colleges. Latin has just been dropped from the curriculum; it is not being replaced by an alternative language. For the last two years, voters have turned down school budget requests; next year, as a result, art and music will be eliminated from the grade school curriculum. The library budget continues to shrink.

While our collective commitment to the past keeps contracting, we keep demanding that our schools cram more and more into that diminishing box. Multiculturalism only intensifies the crisis, increasing the amount that needs to be remembered while simultaneously increasing the guilt over forgetting it. Awareness of the desperate inadequacy of our memories creates anxiety; anxiety increases the speed of our efforts to remember; speed reduces the time we can devote to any one memory. Anxiety and speed exhaust us, so that when we do have the leisure to slow down, we use it not to reflect upon our lives, not to connect the present to the past, not to question or reorganize our accumulated interlocking memory system, but simply to zone out. When we are picking a book to take to the beach, we don't want anything too taxing. We want to escape.

When I want to relax, I escape into the future.

> *And when the last Red Man shall have perished, and the memory of my tribe shall have become a myth among the White Men, these shores will swarm with the invisible dead of my tribe, and when your children's children think themselves alone in the field, the store, the shop, upon the highway, or in the silence of the pathless woods, they will not be alone. At night when the streets of your cities and villages are silent and you think them deserted, they will throng with the returning hosts that once filled and still love this beautiful land. The White Man will never be alone.*
>
> SEATTLE OF THE DWAHMI

All the futures of the past are inaccurate.

Frankenstein deliberately avoids describing the technology by which its horror is created, but any modern reader will find the process embarrassingly implausible. Shelley's artificial human, we are told, was created late in the eighteenth century by a college undergraduate working alone in an amateur laboratory in an upstairs room of his apartment. Late in the twentieth century, our huge, expensive collective laboratories still have not succeeded in creating an artificial human and show no signs of doing so anytime soon. Anyone who reads early science fiction or examines the past advertising of commercial engineers will find this mistake again and again. Future fictions almost invariably predict that we will get to (the moon, Mars, the outer planets, the stars) or that we will develop (robotics, commercial space flight, bioengineering, telecommunications, immortality, a new social system) much much faster than we do. We suffer more from future lag than future shock. The glorious futures we have been promised never arrive on time. The present, however amazing, always looks dreary when we remember the exciting future that should be here by now.

Imagination is faster than technology. But when I say "imagination," I am referring to an aspect of memory. "Invention, it must be humbly admitted, does not consist in creating out of void, but out of chaos," as Shelley explains in her preface. "Everything must have a beginning ... and that beginning must be linked to something that went before." If that is how Shelley the author creates, it is also how Frankenstein the scientist creates: he describes "collecting and arranging my materials," and Shelley refers to the result as "the thing he had put together." Invention, so described, is a process of linking and sorting images and ideas that already exist separately in the mind. Re-collection is not limited to restoring collections that already exist; the same process can recombine memories to produce entirely new configurations. In fact, every act of recollection, however accurate and disciplined, creates a new combination, because the memories recollected from the past are being combined with perceptions of the present. Each time a memory is recollected, it acquires new associations. Editors, for that reason, know that the least reliable textual traditions are those that have been most often copied; such texts become "sophisticated" and "contaminated" with their repeated passage through new networks of associations.

Imaginative activity consists of creative recombination; creativity is a form of retrieval error. The physicist Leopold Infeld, remembering Einstein, wrote, "There are no great achievements without error, and no great man was always correct." If we could not misremember, we could not invent; if we could not mis-recollect the past, we could not imagine not-yet-existent combinations. The very accuracy of machine memory, which makes it so useful and so daunting, prevents it from dreaming. The germ of *Frankenstein* came to Shelley in a dream. Dreams have midwifed many other imaginations and inventions precisely because, in dreams, the normal processes of memorial recombination are accelerated and disinhibited. But just as some stimuli are stronger than others, some dreamers are more creative than others. The fuller the memory—the more intricately interconnected and organized, the more skilled in manipulative recollection—the greater its imaginative powers.

"Originality" is a function of disciplined derivation.

Because we imagine a future by recombining memories into new compounds, we can imagine a future more quickly than we can create it. The obstacles to recombination in memory are psychological, not physical. One mind may imagine, by spontaneous fusion, a combination that may require days, decades, or centuries to achieve in the physical world. As the narrator of *Frankenstein* discovers, the desire to connect one place to another—so quickly accomplished in the mind—can be defeated by something as simple as ice.

> *You know our fathers had plenty of deer and skins, and our plains were full of game and turkeys, and our coves and rivers were full of fish. But, brothers, since these Englishmen have seized our country, they have cut down the grass with scythes, and the trees with axes. Their cows and horses eat up the grass, and their hogs spoil our bed of clams; and finally we shall starve to death.*
>
> MIANTUNNOMOH OF THE NARRAGANSETT

Memories connect, lawlessly.

The function of memory is to make links, and the human brain achieves this function by making links biochemically. By linking past to present, biological memory links one time to another, one representation to another. The evolution of artificial memory has increased our ability to link memories. I can link myself to Mary Shelley at any time by accessing an artificial printed memory of *Frankenstein*. Page and line numbers link textual memories to a reference grid; indexes link reference grids; bibliographies link indexes; computers link bibliographies; networks link computers. These interlocking artificial memory systems enable us to access any corner of collective memory relevant to our immediate utilitarian purposes. Using terminals connected to a library mainframe, we can rapidly identify artificial memories that fall within the parameters of our targeted area of inquiry. We no longer need to establish a long and intimate relationship with a subject or to linger and wander in order to familiarize ourselves with the terrain.

The totally accessible is totally vulnerable. Frankenstein Sr. has no privacy; wherever he goes, whatever he does, Frankenstein Jr. can reconnect with him at any moment. And every connection contains the potential for destruction. The more thoroughly connected, the easier to destroy. That is why the gates of Frankenstein's Geneva are closed at night. Humans encircle themselves with walls in an effort to protect themselves from intruders.

The imagination wants to extend memory's unlimited freedom of connection into the world. But the body that houses memory wants to preserve itself from destructive intrusions. Life is initially created not simply by recombining chemical elements into new organic compounds but by containing those new combinations within fortified compounds, fenced by membranes that regulate the interactions between inner and outer, organism and environment. Thebes was a walled city; Ellison's invisible man retreats to a secret basement; Genji contains his harem within the walls of a palace. If you want to keep a file or a computer safe, you isolate it.

Every increase in interconnectivity endangers the integrity of private memory and thereby redefines the boundaries between private and public, individual and collective recollection. Memories that are freely accessible to others can be destroyed, altered, stolen. In the future of William Gibson's *Neuromancer*, corporations and military establishments occupy heavily fortified enclaves of cyberspace. Within the warm oceans of the Net, there are islands of ice, guarded by hostile artificial intelligences—Frankensteins.

> *In these lands of Alabama, which have belonged to my fathers and where their bones lie buried, I see that the Indian fires are going out. Soon they will be cold.*
>
> EUFAULA OF THE CREEK

Every mind is an island.

While Frankenstein Sr. labors to create an artificial human, he isolates himself from the university and the world. He works in "a solitary chamber, or rather cell, at the top of the house, and separated from all the other apartments by a gallery and staircase." He grows "emaciated from confinement" and barely notices the passing seasons. To develop an artificial female, he exiles himself from family, friends, and country, retreating to one of the Orkney Islands, a barren, virtually uninhabited little rock surrounded by the violent North Sea.

Islands are good places for the genesis of new species. In astronomical terms, every planet is an island, and the futures of science fiction teem with planet-islands full of odd organisms. The eccentric biological diversity of the Galápagos Islands, which so stimulated the imagination of Charles Darwin, depended upon its very isolation from the mainland. In the relative protection of a disconnected niche, interbreeding multiplied the combination of recessive genes, thereby allowing the development of biological possibilities that would have been unlikely to occur or succeed in a more diversified and competitive environment. The same thing can happen in an isolated culture. The astonishing diversity of human cultures—which evolved extraordinarily quickly in geological terms—depended upon their relative isolation from one another before the age of European expansion forced them to reconnect.

Every mind is physically isolated from every other. Although every individual memory is a collection of collective memories, each memory is islanded, and an adult memory can continue to function and evolve in isolation. Physical solitude enables a memory (like Frankenstein Sr.'s) to construct chains of eccentric connections; one generation of recessive recombination may give birth to another and another, so that an uninterrupted, undistracted mind may, in a short time, evolve a new species of thought. That new thought is not unconnected to the past any more than a new species is unconnected to the gene pool from which it developed, but it may diverge rapidly and surprisingly from its archetype.

Although memorial isolation may be facilitated by physical solitude, solitude is not essential, because any human memory can create its own island. The configurations of biological memory depend, like other living boundaries, upon compounds within membranes. Membranes filter incoming stimuli: they do not prevent all interactions between one side and the other, but they do create a resistance to certain kinds of connection. In practice, no memory is equally open to every possible connection or equally responsive to every possible stimulus. Every organism and every machine has a default, which favors one set of actions and reactions over others. But a powerful stimulus can overcome the default and force the formation of new connections; if repeated often enough, or powerfully enough, the alien stimulus can create a new default. Within these membranes and defaults, memory constructs loosely interlocking compounds. The particular formation of each mnemonic cluster is partly motivated but partly random, as are a cluster's links to other clusters. Every adult human memory contains a more or less unique set of defaults, resistances, and compounds. Every mind is thus potentially, and partially, autistic.

Memory's ability to isolate itself is crucial to cultural evolution, because isolation accelerates diversification. The first age of human exploration, and much of the second, was driven by the desire not to join but to *escape* from other human beings. The Puritans who migrated to New England early in the seventeenth century did not come here to establish connections with the native Americans; they came to sever their connections with the government of England. In their old niche, they were a repressed and recessive cultural minority; in their new niche, they became a dominant cultural majority, free to develop in relative isolation their own emergent forms of collective memory.

On a continent and a planet now increasingly overpopulated and increasingly unified by technological media, physical isolation has become more difficult to achieve. The real threat to human culture in the next century is not "The Disuniting of America" but the homogenized Westernization of everything. The two words recognized by more human memories than any others in the history of the species are *okay* and *Coke*. Physically, there are no more islands. Tourists descend upon Galápagos, and the animals of Jurassic Park have already begun swimming to the mainland.

In this globalized niche, recessive cultural possibilities find it much harder to emerge, survive, and develop without being overwhelmed by the dominant culture. The cultural integrity of a minority community can now be sustained only by rigidly walling itself off from its surroundings, but that very act of enclavement attracts the suspicious attention of the dominant culture, committed as it is to pervasive connection. Moreover, the difficulty of cultural separation means that it can be initiated and sustained only by an extraordinary effort of collective will, which requires a correspondingly escalated vilification of the dominant community, which in turn almost inevitably justifies but also provokes violence. This dynamic has produced this century's succession of violently constructed and violently maintained ideological enclaves: the Soviet Union, Red China, North Korea, South Africa, Israel, Iran, Kampuchea, Jonestown, Waco.

Frankenstein Jr. wishes to create a minority culture for himself and his mate in the wilds of Argentina. Frankenstein Sr. at first agrees to this request but later decides that a little enclave of Frankensteins would eventually threaten human dominion over the earth. In the resulting struggle for the future, each side resorts to horrific preemptive violence against the other. But the minority, predictably, loses. Frankenstein Sr. dies, but the dominant human community survives, barely scratched by a struggle that completely destroys the minority.

But we only know of that minority at all because both Frankensteins transmit a memory of it into the future.

> In our every deliberation, we must consider the impact of our decisions on the next seven generations.
> THE GREAT LAW OF THE IROQUOIS CONFEDERACY

Forgetfulness imperils the human future.

Frankenstein Sr. creates a threat to human survival, in the first place, because he does not remember the future. He is so preoccupied with the task at hand that he does not consider what will happen when he finishes it. He remembers only the single part of the future that directly concerns himself: he will, he confidently predicts, be famous for his scientific achievement. He forgets that other people have futures, too, and that they may be affected by what he is doing. He forgets that his own creation will have a future. Having given it life, he abandons and forgets it, as though ignoring the past would make the future go away. Of course, ignoring the past makes the future worse. But Frankenstein Sr. succumbs, again and again, to "a kind of calm forgetfulness, of which the human mind is by its structure peculiarly susceptible."

Such calm forgetfulness has ravaged the planet. The characters of *Frankenstein* often pause, like Romantic poets, to remind us of the sublime natural scenery that surrounds them—the grandeur of the Alps, the "singularly variegated landscape" of the Rhine River Valley, "the distant inequalities" of Arctic ice caps—but they would be horrified by what the future has done to those places in less than two centuries. They would be equally horrified by our forgetfulness of the past. Frankenstein Jr. in his short violent life acquires a profound knowledge of human culture from just four books: Volney's *Ruins of Empires*, Goethe's *The Sorrows of Young Werther*, Plutarch's *Lives of the Noble Grecians and Romans*, and Milton's *Paradise Lost*. Most Americans have not read even one of these four. We are collectively worse educated than a figure characterized, in popular memory, as a mindless monster.

Our world has been built by obliterating past environments, natural and cultural. The pressure of human overpopulation is now destroying biological niches at a rate comparable to the great mass extinctions of the paleological record. Succumbing to the communicational and educational onslaught of the dominant technological culture, minor human languages—and the collective memories they preserve—are disappearing faster than linguists and anthropologists can record them.

Memory is the gene pool of culture. The future can be imagined only by creatively recombining memories of the past. The exuberance of future imagining depends upon the complex fertility of the decomposing memorial matter in which it grows. The smaller the memorial gene pool, the more restricted the possibilities of future cultural evolution. Whenever a memory of culture dies, a future dies with it.

Of course, though we can stop extinctions, we cannot prevent death. Death, as I said, is the foundation of culture. Culture is the gift of the survivor. It is bereaved, retrospective, at war with the present. Mary Shelley's mother, the feminist Mary Wollstonecraft, died within days of her daughter's birth; her father, the radical philosopher and novelist William Godwin, published a posthumous collection of her mother's writings, prefaced by his own account of her life. Shelley's husband, Percy Bysshe Shelley, wrote the preface to the first edition of *Frankenstein* (as she recalled in a later preface of her own); he died when she was twenty-five, and she edited a posthumous collection of his work. Creators and editors, makers and survivors, orphans and parents—the family of Mary Wollstonecraft Godwin Shelley epitomizes the interlocking mechanisms by which the memory of culture is created and recollected.

Death goes on. We cannot stop dying. But we can stop forgetting. The past, after all, does not suffer from our forgetfulness. The past is already dead; we cannot hurt it any more. No, the memory of culture, the memory of dead makers, has always been directed at the future. Culture is a gift from the past that the present gives to the future. What are *we* going to give the future?

> *The dead are not powerless. Dead, did I say? There is no death, only a change of worlds.*
>
> SEATTLE OF THE DWAHMI

PART IV

Judge.

11

The Birth of Culture.

It is with deep sadness that I announce officially the death of Richard Milhous Nixon.

BILL CLINTON (1994)

You won't have Nixon to kick around anymore.

RICHARD NIXON (1962)

Nixon is dead. We thought he had been laid to rest in 1962, and then again in 1974, but the irrepressible Houdini of American politics kept popping out of his coffin. This time, though, even he cannot engineer another resurrection. He has given his last press conference. He will never again make anything perfectly clear. You and I have survived him.

Death is the foundation of culture. From the impotent dignity of his grave, Nixon can no longer decide or do anything. The survivors now must decide what to do about Nixon. Is he worth remembering?

I remember him. He entered my life in 1960 in a schoolroom in El Paso, Texas, where my second-grade teacher conducted a mock presidential election; I raised my hand for Kennedy because Mom was voting for Kennedy, because Kennedy was Catholic and Nixon was not. Nixon lost. In 1972 in a voting booth in a schoolroom in Topeka, Kansas, I voted for the first time in a real election, and again I voted against Nixon. Nixon won. Like innumerable others whose lives and minds he altered, I never encountered Nixon in the flesh, though I could have: in December 1978 he traveled to England to speak at the Oxford Union, a few blocks from my office. I deliberately stayed away. But my righteous little boycott did not imperil his long march back to political respectability, any more than my idealistic little ballot had prevented him in 1972 from receiving more popular votes, and carrying more states, than any previous presidential candidate.

Other people remember him differently, and in greater detail. After all, his life was half over before mine began. He was born in 1913 (the year of the premiere of *The Rite of Spring*); by 1953 he had already won election to the House of Representatives and the Senate, ruined Alger Hiss, and become vice president. His contemporary, the playwright Arthur Miller, characterized Nixon as a man who "marched instinctively down the crooked path," but his daughter Julie described him as "the most moral person I know." Senator Bob Dole wept at his funeral, and as I write, some Republicans are wearing buttons with the slogan "Death Is No Excuse: Nixon in '96." Since the 1970s, oral historians and journalists have interviewed hundreds of people who, unlike me, did encounter Nixon in the flesh and who remember vividly some corner of his story.

I have interviewed only three people. One of my former graduate students was born in 1968, the year of Nixon's election to the presidency. When asked about him, she recalls that he resigned because of "a political scandal," and that he said, "I am not a crook"—a phrase she remembers not from the speech of November 1973 (when she was in kindergarten) but from the innumerable parodies it generated. Frankly, Nixon just does not interest her much, and she does not understand why he interests me. For a twenty-seven-year-old, Nixon is a rerun of irreverent routines on *Saturday Night Live*. My son Josh, born in 1980, recalls that "Tom Cruise got thrown out of the convention where Nixon was nominated for president, and then Nixon told Tom Hanks to stay in the Watergate Hotel, and that night Hanks noticed some burglars, and then Dustin Hoffman started investigating, and then Nixon had to resign."

Nixon, for a fifteen-year-old, is a collage of bit parts in hit movies (*Born on the Fourth of July, Forrest Gump, All the President's Men*). My son Michael, born in 1984, doesn't even recognize the name. For an eleven-year-old, Nixon does not yet exist.

Different human beings respond differently to the same stimulus. Late in the twentieth century, more people know and care about Nixon than about any of the other cultural objects analyzed elsewhere in this book, and anything I write about him could be contested by millions of readers. But for many other millions, Nixon is already just a face on a postage stamp, the subject of one twenty-page chapter in a high school American history textbook, an image in a television documentary, a character in an Oliver Stone film or a Robert Coover novel (whose fictions have now become indistinguishable from history). The millions in the firsthand category diminish as the millions in the secondhand category multiply. (That is why oral historians have rushed to extract memories from those who knew Nixon: before long, those who knew Nixon will all be as dead as Nixon himself.) What the millions in the secondhand category remember about Nixon will depend on the outcome of a continuing tug-of-war between the bitterly divided millions in the firsthand category. Culture is the story of a death, a survivor, and a struggle.

Nixon knew as much. The White House tape recording system, which destroyed his presidency, was originally installed to stockpile an "objective record" as ammunition against future "revisionist histories" of his administration. And just after Nixon's televised resignation speech, when Henry Kissinger told him that "historically this would rank as one of the great speeches" and that history would consider him "one of the great presidents," Nixon sardonically replied, "That depends, Henry, on who writes the history."

Who will write the history? We don't know yet. That is precisely why I have selected Nixon as my summary specimen. I could just as easily have picked any number of other lives or works to illustrate how stimulation, representation, and recollection complicatedly intertwine in the weaving of cultural memory. But Nixon, unlike the others, has just crossed the one-way threshold between biology and culture. The fact that anything I write about him will be contested is simply a reminder that culture is always contested, that (as I warned you at the start of this ride) comprehensive objectivity will not be found in this book because it cannot be found in this subject. Shakespeare, Ecclesiastes, Velázquez, Lady Murasaki, all my other examples, even *Casablanca* and *Invisible Man*—these have about them a comforting canonicity that can too easily lull us into thinking there is something cozily predictable about becoming a classic. There isn't. Cultural dominance does not just happen; it is fought for, tenaciously, ferociously. "This is a war," Nixon told his aides, describing not the conflict in Vietnam but the controversy over the Watergate break-in. One of his books is entitled *In the Arena*; he liked to imagine himself as a gladiator, fighting for his life. "That's the world of sports," he said; "that's the world of politics." It is also the world of cultural selection.

STIMULATE

Nixon is dead. He survives now only in memory—and therefore only insofar as he succeeded in stimulating the making of memories that would survive his own dissolution.

Richard Nixon was a strong stimulus in a strong niche. He is the only president to have resigned, and he resigned to avoid becoming the only president to be impeached, convicted, and removed from office for high crimes and misdemeanors. But he is also the only American twice elected vice president and twice elected president; only he and Franklin Roosevelt have been elected four times to national office. Moreover, Roosevelt's four elections were successive; Nixon's were separated by eight years, thus prolonging his prominence. Nixon's public life, partly because of its sheer length, contains a greater volume of "human stuff" than most other political careers; as always, the volume and variety of material increases the number of possible interpretations, making it, in turn, that much likelier that *some* aspect of Nixon's career will seem, to almost any observer, worth remembering. Commentators as different as the conservative Senator Dole and the liberal professor Joan Hoff have concluded that the second half of the twentieth century may come to be called "the Age of Nixon." Certainly, Nixon catalyzed American politics more pervasively than anyone else in the fifty years following the end of World War II.

During those fifty years, American politics dominated international politics. Nixon's life (1913–94) spanned most of what historians are already calling "the American century," a time when whoever moved America moved the globe. In his presidential diary, Nixon looked forward to "the opportunity to exert leadership, not only for America but on the world scene"; he realized that U.S. power had been "greater" immediately after World War II, "because of the monopoly of the bomb and the weakness of Europe and Japan as well as the weakness of China and Russia," but at that time the international agenda was still being shaped by other world leaders with powerful personalities (Churchill, de Gaulle, Stalin, Chiang Kai-shek). Now there was, in his diary, only Nixon—"an enormous responsibility but, of course, at the same time the greatest opportunity an individual could have." Fifty-five foreign countries are indexed in *RN: The Memoirs of Richard Nixon.* Nixon's decisions changed the history, most obviously, of the Soviet Union, China, Chile, Southeast Asia, and the Middle East. But the impact of a giant is not limited to the anthills he selects to step on; the anthills he leaves alone are also affected by his decisions. Nixon's almost complete neglect of black Africa, for instance, reflects America's planetary priorities just as much as his active intervention in Chile or Cambodia.

Memory is sensitive to change; we are particularly prone to remember stimuli associated with major changes in a niche. And Nixon's career depended upon, and helped create, major changes in American political life. Franklin Roosevelt's unprecedented election to four successive presidential terms prompted a change in the U.S. Constitution; the rules of the game were rewritten to prevent it from ever being successfully dominated by players like him again (just as the rules of basketball were rewritten in response to Wilt Chamberlain). The Twenty-second Amendment, ratified in 1951, limited future presidents to two terms. But this rule change also altered, in ways wholly unanticipated by its makers, the status of the vice presidency, to which Nixon was elected in 1952. Once a potential rival to the president, the vice president became his putative successor. In 1960 Nixon became the first vice president since Martin Van Buren (1836) to receive the nomination of his party for president, and the first since John Adams (1796) to serve *two* terms as vice president and then be nominated for the presidency. This pattern of succession, so rare before Nixon, has since become normal (Humphrey, Mondale, Bush).

Nixon's presidential progress depended upon a radical change in the vice-presidential niche, and his vice presidency depended upon an even more radical change in political culture: the rise of television. When Nixon's place on the 1952 Republican ticket was threatened by revelations about his fund-raising, he defused the crisis by making a nationally broadcast television speech. Just as Franklin Roosevelt's career was inextricably connected to the rise of radio, Nixon's was a function of TV. In 1952, for the first time, a political career was saved by a television appearance; the broadcast of the Kennedy–Nixon debates in 1960 was the first TV show to help determine the outcome of a presidential election; between 1965 and 1968, the first war televised in close-up created the national dissensus that made possible Nixon's comeback; in 1968 the marketing potential of commercials was first fully and consciously exploited in a process, now routine, that Joe McGinnis christened as *The Selling of the President*; the televised party conventions of 1968 and 1972 shaped voter attitudes more significantly than any conventions before or since, and in the Watergate hearings of 1973–74—part miniseries, part soap opera—television for the first time helped to destroy a presidency.

Of course, the impact of television extended beyond partisan politics. With other changes in communication and transportation, it helped homogenize America and the world. Nixon often bragged that he had met more world leaders than anyone else—a feat made possible by airplanes, and made desirable by the images broadcast back to his constituents of Nixon wrapped in the authority and dignity conferred by foreign leaders upon a representative of the world's most powerful nation. The achievement for which Nixon is best remembered was just such a technodrama, commemorated in the 1987 opera *Nixon in China* (music by John Adams, libretto by Alice Goodman). A huge jet taxis onto the stage, and Nixon emerges to sing, in baritone soliloquy:

> *When I shook hands with Chou En lai*
> *on this bare field outside Peking*
> *just now the whole world was listening*
> *and though we spoke quietly*
> *the eyes and ears of history*
> *caught every gesture every word*

"The eyes and ears of history! history!! history!!!" are, more prosaically, the cameras and microphones of "the three main networks":

> *It's prime time in the USA*
> *It's yesterday night*

Nixon's dramatic entrance was carefully timed to ensure maximum television coverage in the United States. The temporal paradox— "It's yesterday night," now is then, present is past—puts Nixon in his country's future, ahead of the temporal curve, leading where millions will follow. But it also reminds the audience that the opera is a representation of the past; what we are watching now happened "yesterday." *Nixon in China* charismatically offers us what theater can and TV cannot—physical presence, a musical emotion equal to the occasion (which the cool speeches to the cameras never articulated or conveyed), the unspoken thoughts of the participants. But live opera can stimulate only a few hundred wealthy spectators at a time; television electrifies millions of memories.

"No one is out of touch," Nixon sings. No one is beyond his

reach. American politicans can now travel anywhere, and American voters can now see what is going on anywhere—a new visual reality that made foreign policy the subject of much more immediate and visceral political interest than it had ever been before. And because the president is the primary maker of foreign policy, the world's new visual accessibility made presidents more visible and powerful than the framers of the Constitution had ever imagined. The new global simultaneity altered the American niche by altering its relation to other niches, thereby threatening the domestic balance of powers, which had been designed to ensure the stability of the republic. Nixon personified that threat.

He did not create the threat—he did not invent television—he just used what he found. Nixon was often called an opportunist— who is simply someone who seizes any opportunity given to him by circumstances beyond his control. Like other lives, his was shaped in part by sheer blind luck, good and bad. As Mary McCarthy noticed, much of the Watergate story depended "on accidents, as though offended reality were bent on showing its power—unpredictabil- ity—to the Nixon controllers and managers."

But if his fall owed something to the fortuitous, so did his rise. The assassinations of John and Robert Kennedy altered the niche to Nixon's advantage (just as the murder of Marlowe altered the niche to Shakespeare's advantage). And his rehabilitation owed a lot to the resurgence of the Republican Party, from the disaster of the 1974 midterm elections to the triumph of 1994.

But it was not all luck. Nixon flourished in the turbulence that disoriented and overwhelmed others. He survived in a niche where, by definition, those who *did* survive had to be in some way fit *to* sur- vive. Even people who hated him had to concede that he was a superb political problem-solver. Men as different as Henry Kissinger and Norman Mailer called Nixon a political genius—a genius being, in Mailer's definition, "a man who could break the fundamental rule of any mighty sport or discipline and not only survive but transcend all competitors, reveal the new possibility in the buried depth of the old injunction." Rule-breaking is a form of risk-taking, and throughout his life Nixon exemplified and celebrated a willingness to take chances. He launched his political career with money he had won playing poker. Of course, the more risks you take, the more likely that you will sometimes fail, but Nixon treated all failures as mere tactical obstructions, surmountable by someone with the appropriate strategic vision. To the extent that human beings are fascinated by characters who overcome obstacles, Nixon was the most fascinating politician of his time, winning again and again against seemingly insuperable odds. He overcame those obstacles partly by sheer stubborn perseverance. As California Governor Pete Wilson said in his funeral eulogy, the lesson Nixon taught was, "Never, never give up."

But this pit-bull determination cohabited with a chameleon versatility. The columnist and speechwriter William Safire said that Nixon could "don a personality by opening a door," and the biographer Stephen E. Ambrose concluded that "what Nixon did best, most consistently, through his career was to act . . . he was always an actor, observing the effect of his performance." But Nixon did more than act; he also directed. Successful competition depends upon cooperation, and he built his political base by working assiduously for the Republican party, managing in the process to secure and conduct the collaborative energies of thousands of Nixon loyalists.

Problem-solving, risk-taking, perseverance, versatility, cooperation, co-optation—these are the skills that lie behind all the greatest cultural reputations, from Aristotle to Michelangelo to Shakespeare. Nixon was the fittest American politician of his time.

Fittest for what? Fittest to flourish in a very particular niche, the niche of American politics in the fifty years after Hiroshima. A white male Christian niche in which no black, woman, or Jew could (to this day) successfully compete for the presidency. Nixon did not simply passively benefit from these exclusions; he consistently exploited them. In 1976 he privately advised President Gerald Ford, "The Negro vote's lost; don't let it lose you the white votes. The Democrats have the Negroes and the Jews, and let them have them—in fact, tie them around their necks." In 1950 Nixon first won statewide office by viciously maligning one of the few women in Congress, Helen Douglas, whom he characterized as "The Pink Lady" ("pink" being appropriate for females but also suspiciously close to "red" communism). At the other end of his career, he astutely hosted regular male-only dinner parties in New York as part of his campaign of self-rehabilitation. Political cartoonists sometimes portrayed President George Bush as a mincing grandmother, but such caricatures are unimaginable for the emphatically phallic Tricky Dick, he of the eternal five o'clock shadow. Nixon's niche seems, indeed, so wholly the testosterone domain that it is startling to be reminded, as we are by Robin Morgan's poem "On the Watergate Women," that the lives he ruined were not all male, that behind the succession of prickly witnesses before prickly tribunals lay that unrepresented other half of the human race.

But Nixon's fitness for the niche is more than a matter of gender, race, or religion; these he shared, after all, with virtually the entire governing class. A niche, a frame, is designed to enable us to measure particular attributes. And the niche of modern American politics measured—and found worth rewarding spectacularly—a paranoid, bigoted, lying lawyer who represented the prevailing business ethic who was seen and saw himself as "one of us." Our "Barbie doll President," as Hunter S. Thompson described him, "with his Barbie doll wife and his box-full of Barbie doll children," Nixon was the perfect plastic spokesman for "the silent majority"—or, as Thompson puts it, "the Werewolf in us." His most consistent and successful defense of his actions during Watergate was that there were precedents for all his dirty tricks. In defense of "the president," Nixon exposed the prevailing rottenness of the presidency and of the entire political elite to which he belonged. Some may be shocked to find, in *The Presidential Transcripts*, the president of the United States declaring, "Well, one hell of a lot of people don't give one damn about this issue of the suppression of the press," but here as so often elsewhere, he was accurately representing his constituency, including "one hell of a lot" of his fellow politicians. Nixon flourished in the niche of modern American politics because that niche is, as Nixon was, essentially amoral.

Nixon's career, his demonstrated ability to impress himself upon the memory of millions, reminds us of a fact about cultural stimuli that we would usually rather ignore: pain and pleasure both stimulate memory. Like Nixon himself, stimulation is about power, not propriety; it is concerned with "How much?" not "Should?" *Stimulus is amoral.*

REPRESENT

Nixon is dead. He survives now only insofar as he is represented in memories, human or artificial.

Every memory of Nixon—personal reminiscence, biography, autobiography, newspaper column, historical monograph, tape recording, photograph, film—is a representation subject to the laws that govern all representations. Take, for instance, a political cartoon by Paul Conrad, composed in May 1970, soon after Nixon ordered an attack on communist "sanctuaries" in Cambodia (figure 5). The main image in this cartoon is a seal, of the kind Aristotle had used as a metaphor for memory, but the cartoon itself, like Velázquez's *Las Meninas*, demonstrates that memory works very differently than Aristotle had imagined.

Memory actively constructs representations: Conrad drew this cartoon, indeed drew the seal itself, in a series of discrete successive actions, each requiring decisions and expenditures of energy. *Every representation is a combination*: Conrad combined two hands and a larger-than-life presidential seal, then combined both visual images with the caption "Speaking of Sanctuaries"—in the process combining the idea of Communist military sanctuaries with the idea that Nixon was using the authority of the presidency as a legal and moral hideout. *Representations are not equal to the realities they represent*: in the cartoon, neither the seal nor Nixon is three-dimensional, and Nixon is as inanimate as the seal. *Representations are always partial*: only Nixon's hands and wrists are shown at all. *Memories are emotive*: the cartoon expresses the outrage felt by most Americans at the time, and a contempt for the moral cowardice of the man who was demanding so much bravery from others. *The gap between represen-*

Speaking of Sanctuaries....

FIGURE 5
© 1970 Los Angeles Times Syndicate. Reprinted with permission.

tation and reality is filled with artifice, imagination, and feeling: Conrad's imaginative combination of hands and seal is entirely artificial, since it depends upon a grossly unrealistic distortion of scale and requires us to imagine the unshown face and body behind the seal; formally, the black smear across the bottom of the cartoon grounds the image and balances the hands above the seal, but the smear also conveys and elicits an emotional reaction to the sense of something dark, wet, staining, smudged, indeterminate, in contrast to the apparent moral clarity of seal and hands. *All representations are communications, and memory in particular is a representation that communicates across time*: Conrad's cartoon, printed in the editorial pages of a major newspaper, was distributed to hundreds of thousands of homes, and my reproduction of it communicates across time the same message originally communicated across space.

What is true of this cartoon is equally true of every other representation of Nixon. Certainly, Nixon's campaigns and books actively constructed memories (even when the memories were true) and required colossal expenditures of energy, personal and financial. Every representation of Nixon is a combination of elements and therefore represents a choice about which elements to select for combination. It is no accident that Nixon, in his *Memoirs,* makes Watergate seem "pygmy-sized" by juxtaposing it with his reception in Cairo—"perhaps the most tumultuous welcome any American President has ever received anywhere in the world"—just as Conrad juxtaposed Nixon's small hands with a huge seal. No representation of Nixon is equal to the reality it represents; the reality gap creates the continuing hunger for new representations and the continuing claims that the latest representation gives us "the real Nixon" (offered by the dust jacket of Ambrose's three-volume biography) or "the man himself" (offered by the dust jacket of the *Memoirs*). But, of course, these representations do not give us the man. They give us pieces of paper, and as Nixon's chief of staff, Bob Haldeman, brutally put it, "You can't ask questions of a piece of paper."

Every representation of Nixon is notoriously partial, from *The Presidential Transcripts* with their famous "expletives deleted" and "characterizations deleted" to the 1,080 pages of the published *Memoirs,* which contain only a fraction of the material Nixon dictated and reproduce only selected excerpts from his diaries and the five thousand hours of White House tapes available to him (but not to us). But the partisan partiality of representation is unavoidable; every representation is, to borrow another phrase from Bob Haldeman, only "a modified limited hang-out." And every memory is emotive, from Pablo Neruda's rage over Nixon's destruction of democracy in Chile to the fondness Nixon's grandchildren had for him, to the unqualified enthusiasm of what he himself called the four to five million "Nixon nutheads" who would cheer him whatever he did. Indeed, the very intensity of the emotions Nixon stimulated, positive or negative, accounts in part for his persistence in national and personal memory. The gap between Nixon reality and Nixon representations is filled with artifice (trickiness), imagination (fabrication), and feeling (usually hatred, either of Nixon or of Nixon's enemies). Andy Warhol did not expect anyone to believe that Nixon "really" had a blue-green face and yellow lips; instead, the imaginative artifice of his photo-silkscreen image was designed to elicit an antipathy strong enough to justify the message hand-printed across the bottom, "VOTE MCGOVERN." Warhol was communicating a message, as does every representation of Nixon, from his presidential speeches to his private diaries (which he fully expected the future to read).

Like all other communications, memory depends not only upon representation but upon *systems* of representation. Conrad's cartoon would be unintelligible without the sign system of the written English language ("Seal of the President of the United States," "Speaking of Sanctuaries"), and the text itself depends in part upon specific allusion to another text—Nixon's television speech with claims about "sanctuaries." Even the visual image depends upon sign systems. The hands are recognizable as a sign for "Nixon" only because readers were already familiar with countless photographs or films of him posed characteristically with both hands spread and raised, the forefinger and middle finger of each protruding in a "V" (for "Victory").

Conrad's representation belongs to the genre of the political cartoon, which is a system of its own. For instance, the slash lines on either side of the hands suggest, in cartoon convention, that the hands are waving—itself a gestural sign indicating surrender ("Don't shoot, I give up") or taunting ("Na-na, na-na-na, you can't get me"). More specifically, the intelligibility of political caricature depends upon the circulation of a few simple signs that "stand for" a public figure. Nixon became, for cartoonists, either the raised hands (figure 5) or a prominent nose, protruding jowls, shifty eyes, and receding hairline (figure 6).

Like the art of the haiku, the art of the political cartoon

depends upon achieving maximum meaning by minimal means: simplicity of line must be accompanied by complexity of reference, and complexity of reference can be achieved only by density of allusion. Thus, Edward Sorel's portrayal of Nixon and Ford in "Son of Frankenstein" (figure 7) not only alludes to the Frankenstein myth but also visually parodies old movie posters. Similarly, Ranan Lurie adapts the famous Iwo Jima image, substituting journalists for marines (figure 8). Pat Oliphant's "I Have Returned" (figure 9), alluding to Nixon's increasing visibility in the 1980s, deploys the familiar hands, eyes, and hairline but achieves most of its effect by inverting the black-lines-on-a-white-background transparency of the genre, creating an overpowering sense of darkness. The darkness, the absence of conventional connecting lines, also disturbingly

FIGURE 6
"TIM" (Louis Mitelberg), Cartoonists & Writers Syndicate.

dismembers hands and head, just as Nixon's resurrection depended upon severing past crimes from present respectability. Finally, the image also alludes to, and violates, the convention of the frame. In figures 5–8, as in almost all such caricatures, the complete image is contained within the frame; in figure 9, the frame cuts Nixon's face in half, thereby giving the impression that Nixon, midnight's eternal Peeking Dick, is peering over a wall or a window frame.

In collecting these five political cartoons (by a Frenchman, an Israeli, an Australian, and two Americans), I have fulfilled John Dean's prophecy that Watergate would be put "in the funny pages of the history books," but I have also done what every editor does: recontextualized, reproduced, restored, resituated. There are no

FIGURE 7
From *New York*, April 15, 1974. Reprinted by permission of the artist Edward Sorel.

unedited representations. History, memory, edits. As Nixon sings on the tarmac of the opera house:

> *the eyes and ears of history*
> *caught every gesture every word*
> *transforming us as we transfixed*
> *transforming us as we transfixed*
> *transforming us as we transfixed*
> *made history*

Nixon and Chou En-lai may have made history, but in another sense history made them: they are transformed and transfixed by it, altered and at the same time locked in place. Nixon cannot move in his grave; he has been pinned and cannot prevent the alterations performed by the editors, restorers, and curators of his memory.

The need to edit representations, and the impact of editorial interpretation, increase with distance. Sometimes the distance is

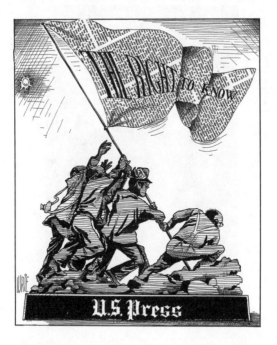

FIGURE 8
Ranan R. Lurie © Worldwide Copyright by Cartoonews International Syndicate.

spatial. Watergate was almost incomprehensible in the Soviet Union and China. In the context of a totalitarian regime, Nixon's "high crimes and misdemeanors" were just business-as-usual. Andrei Gromyko could reassure Nixon, "It's really about nothing." Nixon records this remark in his *Memoirs* precisely because he wants to recontextualize Watergate, to make American readers see it from the perspective of those "world leaders" who were dismayed by the fall of their admired buddy Dick Nixon.

But the distance that editing attempts to overcome may also be temporal. All these cartoons about Nixon or Watergate, once immediately comprehensible to millions, now have to be painstakingly explained. For a new generation of Americans, Watergate is not a personal memory but a representation that has to be provided with a context. That is why Nixon, in his campaign to rehabilitate his reputation, preferred to work with young journalists: not only were

I Have Returned

FIGURE 9
OLIPHANT © 1985 Universal Press Syndicate. Reprinted with permission. All rights reserved.

they more easily flattered by presidential attentions, but they had no context of their own to set against the context, the "background briefing," that Editor Nixon so willingly supplied.

Conrad's cartoon was first published in the *Los Angeles Times*; it belongs to that editing, communicating, representing system we call "the media"—or more simply, "the news." Nixon was fascinated by the news media; like every politician, he needed it, and better than most politicians, he exploited it. But he also notoriously hated the media, attacking the independence of the press more vehemently and successfully than any previous president. The logic of that hatred is articulated in one of his favorite quotations, taken from Teddy Roosevelt:

> It is not the critic who counts: not the man who points out how the strong man stumbles, or where the doer of deeds could have done them better. The credit belongs to the man who is actually in the arena . . . who at the best knows in the end the triumphs of high achievement and who at the worst, if he fails, at least fails while daring greatly, so that his place shall never be with those cold and timid souls who know neither victory nor defeat.

This is the familiar attack on representation. The critic is contemptible because he is not a doer; the aristocracy of champions is more important than the silent majority of editors; the representation is inevitably less than the real. Editing can be represented only as a failure of representation. Hence, "the record of the liberal left media on Vietnam is perhaps one of the most disgraceful in the whole history of communications in this country." But a good journalist, by this account, is simply one who reproduces accurately Nixon's words, Nixon's tone, Nixon's intentions—that is, the one who becomes an utterly transparent medium for Nixon's message.

When the media fails to satisfy this standard, it is guilty of misrepresentation, which is immoral; when Nixon becomes president, misrepresenting him becomes at worst treasonous and at best a despicable impediment to virtuous policies. Such misrepresentations must be stopped—by harassing journalists, ordering illegal surveillance of his own staff, launching a media counteroffensive. But because every representation falls short of reality, Nixon's attack on misrepresentation became, inevitably, a pathological attack on representation itself.

This very effort to eliminate (mis)interpretation led to Watergate. Once all representation is defined as misrepresentation, preventing misrepresentation can be achieved only by controlling all representation. But Nixon could not do that alone. Louis Mitelberg's image of the fifty stars of the American flag turned into a switchboard, enabling Nixon to bug the entire country (figure 6), represents the president's fantasy and the nation's nightmare, but it also represents an impossibility: no one person can listen to everyone else. The more you want to monitor and control representation, the more monitors and controllers you need; the more such intermediaries and editors you employ, the less personal control of their activities you retain. Nixon's desire for complete control of representation created a representational apparatus completely out of his control—an apparatus that, he would complain, did not accurately "represent" him. Nixon's ambition could have been satisfied only if the entire U.S. government had been reduced to so many obedient limbs of his own body.

The ideal medium of representation, for Nixon, is a prosthesis: a technological supplement that extends his essence, without independence, without interpretation, without threat. Television airtime let him step simultaneously into millions of living rooms; military airpower gave him muscle in Southeast Asia. Via satellite megaphones, his voice was thrown to the moon. Alexander Graham Bell's invention helped him undo the ostracism that followed his resignation: for the next twenty years, he "worked the phones" tirelessly. (Exile with telephones is not exile.) Photography enabled him to reproduce in his *Memoirs* touchingly personal notes to and from the great and the plain. Through impersonal, mass-produced photographic images, he could show hundreds of thousands of readers carefully selected specimens of intimacy, an intimacy authenticated by the old-fashioned irregularity and singularity of handwriting. The White House tape recordings, his own dictated diaries, the twenty thousand pages of handwritten notes he accumulated and saved from 1946 to 1974, supplied him with an unprecedented wealth of artificial memories from which to create his own (selective) representation of his political life.

Of course, the White House tapes also unraveled his presidency. But that is because, unlike these other technologies, they were unfaithful. The published transcriptions, despite their "literal accuracy," nevertheless "completely fail to capture or reflect" the ambiguity and fluidity of conversation. "The written word," Nixon wrote, is "rigid" and "lifeless." This does not prevent him from transcribing selections from such transcripts into his own book: like any good editor, he can provide a contextualization that clarifies the real meaning of the exchange. For Nixon, the only reliable editor is the author himself: the only reliable biography is autobiography. But this very claim is a misrepresentation, since all the autobiographical books Nixon wrote were heavily edited by collaborators who were never represented on the title pages. Nixon was a notorious, lifelong, well-documented liar. The nemesis of misrepresentation was also its master.

A fundamental hostility to representation is incompatible with representative democracy. Nixon extrapolated his righteous indignation at misrepresentation to the point where it endangered the Constitution, to the point where his own secretary of defense told the joint chiefs of staff not to obey any order from Nixon unless he had countersigned it. The president had ceased to represent America; he was representing only himself.

Nixon's threat to the Constitution was unique. But there is nothing unique in his contradictory ambivalences about representation. From the biblical prohibition on graven images to the law of slander, misrepresentation has always been a vilified reality; from Confucian reverence for the past to Alexander Pope's recognition of the "duty" of an editor, accurate reproduction has always been a sanctified ideal. My own distaste for Nixon's lying, for his attack on the press, belongs to the same ethical system. *Representation is always moralized.*

RECOLLECT

Nixon is dead. He survives now only insofar as those who have survived him recollect him.

You remember the story of Nadezhda Mandelstam, who preserved the memory of her dead husband Osip. Nixon was his own Nadezhda. He outlived his prematurely dead presidency, and then spent twenty years trying to transmit to posterity his own memory of its significance. "Resignation," he whined, "is worse than death." The dead cannot say what death is worse than; the dead do not get interviewed by David Frost, do not bank lucrative advances on their next book, do not attend other people's funerals. But the self-pitying falseness of Nixon's metaphor should not obscure the fact that he believed it, and acted the part of his own widow.

In his political afterlife, Nixon became a writer, the author of nine books totaling almost thirty-five hundred pages (not to mention a steady stream of journalism and speeches). Like other cultural memorials, his books are bereaved, retrospective, at war with the present. All are essentially autobiographical—the *Memoirs* and *In the Arena* explicitly so, the rest defending or extending his political record, parading his familiarity with world leaders, emphasizing his access to privileged information. Gore Vidal had compared Nixon to Uriah Heep, endlessly toadying to those he manipulated, but in his own books Nixon was cast more heroically as a spunky David taking on yet another Goliath, or as Old Iron-Butt, a hardworking Atlas supporting the burdens of the world on his shoulders.

Though several were best-sellers, the books—repetitive, rambling, erratic, unreliable, shrill, almost never original—are not very good. All are written in Nixon's trademark pedestrian style, which Robert Lowell described as "servile mush." It is possible, thought Norman Mailer, "that no politician in the history of America employed so dependably mediocre a language in his speeches as Nixon, nor had a public mind ever chased so resolutely after the wholly uninteresting expression of every idea." Who in the future is likely to read any of these books, recite any of these speeches? If recollections of

Nixon depended upon the memorability of his own prose, he would already be well on his way to Oblivion City.

But the cultural memory of Nixon does not depend on Nixon's memory of himself. Nixon may not be quotable, but Robert Coover's novel *The Public Burning* is full of quotable passages; for instance, its description of Nixon "backing bareass out onto the stage" with "his pants in a tangled puddle at his feet, a crumpled homburg down around his ears, 'I AM A SCAMP' lipsticked on his butt . . . hopping on one foot." Nixon's own narrative of his trip to China may anesthetize the most determined intelligence, but *Nixon in China* gives us the clash of cultures, the overlay of public and private, the emotional chest-swell of the historic and the sharp little tang of the ironic, even that twist of ensemble by which Nixon's and Mao's wives become more sympathetic than all the more famous males who surround them. Nixon does not need to be a great artist as long as he is a great *subject*, as long as poets as talented as Mary Campbell and actors as talented as Anthony Hopkins relish representing him.

Nixon's writing, accordingly, was not designed for future admiration, but to secure and direct the attention of the present. If he had wanted to ponder what life had taught him and offer to the future some concentrated wisdom, if he had wanted to create a memoir as memorable as General Julius Caesar's *Commentaries on the Gallic Wars* or Bishop Augustine of Hippo's *Confessions* or Ambassador Benjamin Franklin's *Autobiography* or Admiral Richard Byrd's *Alone*, the retired public servant could have stayed in San Clemente, isolated from the world, distilling a masterpiece. He didn't. He moved back to New York City. The Big Apple did not tempt him with a taste of eternity; it just gave him more opportunities to rivet the present. His determined socializing, like his writing, had the single goal of changing, in his lifetime, the perception of his past.

It takes plenty to purchase the past. Nixon acquired the resources he needed by astutely cashing in on his own notoriety and on the contacts with influential people he had developed during three decades of international prominence. He deployed those resources in three strategic memorial maneuvers. First, he minimized Watergate by making it one unremarkable exhibit in an anthology of political nastiness. Second, he almost entirely ignored his domestic agenda, concentrating instead upon his achievements in foreign policy. Third, he made the resurrection more interesting than the fall.

These maneuvers worked because they satisfied the demands of the niche. Nixon's political campaigns had always been driven by denigration. His retirement gave him twenty years to denigrate incumbents without ever having to become one; indeed, because everyone knew he could never again run for office, no one bothered to campaign against *him*, while he busily campaigned against *everyone*. The public, cynicized by his actions during the nineteen months of Watergate, was easy to persuade that what Nixon had done was no worse than what every other politician did. He emphasized foreign policy partly because it turned attention away from his domestic behavior (which included Watergate); partly because he wanted to establish his independence from his erstwhile chief collaborator Henry Kissinger (who had become an incumbent, easily placed on the defensive); partly because he was more admired abroad than at home; partly because, as always, he could drape himself in the dignity accorded him by state occasions in other countries; partly because his domestic policies would be more divisive among Republicans, the base of his support. His growing reputation as a master statesman depended upon the selectivity of media memory. He reminded people of his accurate prophecies, and let his inaccurate ones die of the neglect accorded all old news. "Old news" also included the story of his fall; everyone was sick to death of that. The story of his resurrection, by contrast, was new news, with an infinitely renewable newness. Every additional sign of the slowly escalating official or unofficial acceptance could prompt a new story. His resurrection was announced over and over again, and on each occasion it was placed (where he placed it) in the larger narrative of the amazing lifelong resilience of Richard Nixon.

Selection always requires ejection; here, as elsewhere, the injunction "Remember this!" implies the injunction "Forget that!"

Indeed, Nixon's presidency is likely to be best remembered for an epidemic of forgetting.

You can say I don't remember
You can say I can't recall

I can't give any answer
  To that
    That I can recall.

The Poetry of Richard Nixon, from which I have lifted this little jingle, consists of a wholly unauthorized collage of phrases culled from Nixon transcripts. For most people I know who watched the Watergate hearings, they can be summed up by the phrase "I can't recollect that point in time." This reiterated amnesia was a tactic explicitly recommended by Nixon—"Just be damn sure you say I don't remember"—for avoiding perjury without telling the truth. After all, who could ever prove that you were lying when you said you forgot something? Forgetfulness is not indictable.

But forgetfulness, like lying, may become pathological. Every act of recollection presupposes and creates separations; putting a memory in one collection often means leaving out another memory, or ignoring another collection, and either choice disconnects an alternative set of possibilities. That is as true of the Declaration of Independence as of *The Presidential Transcripts*. But the programmatic, defensive forgetfulness associated with Watergate characterizes Nixon's entire career. He lived through the Great Depression, America's most severe economic crisis, but he almost never referred to it. His political philosophy and his party loyalties could not comfortably accommodate such a memory.

Nixon's political success, both before and after his presidency, was founded on denial. Any one of his campaigns, from the congressional election of 1946 to the long autobiographical guerrilla war of 1974–94, offers textbook examples of the defense mechanisms of resistance to repressed social memories. Such recollections are linked to vilified minorities—Communists above all, but also (in his own list) "women, blacks, homosexuals, welfare mothers, migrant farm workers." Opposition is evidence of a conspiracy; the powers of the opposition are consistently exaggerated. Revisionists are "arrogant young men" (like those on the special prosecution force). The institutions of authority have lost their authority. (The State Department has been infiltrated by Communists.) The revisionists—"all the nutheads in the nasty crowd"—are insane. The new evidence—the fruits of all those months of judicial and congressional investigations—may appear to give us a better recollection of the past but actually it takes us further from the truth. The "real" truth, the preferred memory, will be justified by the future; the "historic achievements . . . will loom ever larger in history books." In the meantime, though, the resentful traditionalist finds himself hating or despising more and more of the society he is allegedly dedicated to defending. "In politics, academics, and the arts, and even in the business community and the churches, there was a successful and fashionable negativism which, in my judgment, reflects an underlying loss of will, an estrangement from traditional American outlooks and attitudes."

Where others saw, after the Allied victory in World War II, or in the economic and cultural boom of the 1960s, a revolutionary explosion of possibility, Nixon saw only "an underlying loss." That sense of loss underlay what Garry Wills, in *Nixon Agonistes*, long ago identified as "the politics of resentment."

Much of that resentment—which has continued to fuel the political careers of Nixon's successors—is built upon memories of the future. The continually promised golden tomorrow continues, maddeningly, not to materialize. As a result, the shadow of who we should already be mocks and embitters who we actually are. Identity, personal and social, always depends upon memories, including memories of prophecies and fictions, memories of the self—and memories of others. America's identity therefore depends, in part, on what we recollect about Nixon. And because who we think we are can easily affect what we in fact become, America's future depends, in part, upon how we recollect Nixon.

I may seem to be exaggerating the political importance of memory. But politics is simply a game, a genre, like symphonies or epic poetry. Every maker is a survivor whose behavior is stimulated and channeled by the memory of past failures and achievements in the genre. The Gulf War was designed, by people who remembered Vietnam, to prevent a repetition of that bloody mess and to help us forget it. The Iran-contra scandal did not sink Reagan, as Watergate had sunk Nixon, because everyone involved remembered Watergate as Nixon wanted it to be remembered; the latter-day crooks were more sophisticated (they remembered Nixon's "mistakes" and systematically destroyed the evidence), and the public was more cynical (they remembered that politicians routinely lie and break the law). George Bush's midnight pardon of Caspar Weinberger, Elliot Abrams, and others recalled and normalized Gerald Ford's pardon of Nixon. If we continue to recollect Nixon on Nixon's terms, we will become a nation of self-righteous bullies and resentful liars.

Such is the future engendered by reading Nixon's autobiographies. Of course, now that Nixon has fallen out of the news, fewer and fewer people will pick up his books. "Democracy," Alexis de Tocqueville observed, "gives men a sort of instinctive distaste for what is ancient." The bulimic American appetite for novelty, once the new Nixon's ally, is now the dead Nixon's enemy. His lifetime virtually coincided with that of the Soviet Union, and an obsession with the Communists in the Kremlin dominated his political career; with the death of the Soviet Union, most of that career has become irrelevant, almost incomprehensible, to the preoccupied present. Historians can debate among themselves the merits of his domestic agenda, but outside the academy no one cares about the administrative debates of another era.

What do we care about? What is still worth recollecting about Nixon? The Vietnam War and Watergate.

Nixon inherited the war, of course, but he did not win it or end it; he simply and unforgivably extended the bloodshed for six more years. He could not let go. He held on, so brutally and fruitlessly, because of the very conditions of the niche that brought him to power. "Who lost China?" he had asked, as though Truman were personally responsible for the Communist victory there in 1949. "Who lost Russia?" he would ask in 1992, as though Bush were personally responsible for a looming relapse into totalitarianism. The technologies and institutions of the electronic editorial media, by creating a new global simultaneity, increased the visibility of foreign policy. That visibility could, if properly manipulated, increase presidential authority at home, but it could also encourage an electorate to blame the president if the world refused to behave as America recommended. Nixon did not want anyone asking him, "Who lost Vietnam?" The screaming futility of Nixon's war is worth remembering because the conditions of the niche, which caused it, have not changed. Americans still can see the whole delinquent world; presidents still cannot discipline it to their liking. If we forget that there are and should be limits to *American* power, we will not be able to resist the temptation to expand *presidential* power. That is why we should remember the war.

That leaves Watergate. "What was Watergate?" Nixon asked. "A little bugging!" But what is bugging? As he said on another occasion, the men who attempted to bug Democratic Party headquarters were simply "doing their best to get information." Bugging, then, is the pursuit of information. "Who who who are our enemies?" *Nixon in China* sings. "Who who who are our friends?" To answer such questions, you need information. In particular, you need information about who has been leaking information. The 1971 publication of *The Pentagon Papers*—a collection of secret documents about the Vietnam War passed to the media by a disillusioned civil servant, Daniel Ellsberg—had infuriated Nixon, prompting formation of the policies and operations that led directly the next year to Watergate. "Ellsberg, who had leaked top-secret documents, had gone free," Nixon later bitterly recalled; "Ehrlichman, who was trying to prevent such leaks, had been convicted." Nixon's aide John Ehrlichman was convicted because pursuing information by means of burglary and wiretapping is illegal. That illegality created "a public relations problem," Nixon believed, "that only needed a public relations solution." The solution involved covering up White House involvement in the illegal pursuit of information. Was that obstruction of justice? No, said Attorney General John Mitchell. "We were," he testified at the Watergate hearings, simply "not volunteering information." But that is precisely why Americans were riveted by the hearings. "The country," Mary McCarthy wrote, "wanted information." The country, that is, wanted exactly what Nixon wanted. And it got what it wanted, in the end, because of the White House tapes. "Nixon," as McCarthy put it, "had been bugging himself." Watergate is the story of a bugger bugged.

Unlike Andrew Johnson, the only other president to face impeachment, Richard Nixon was arraigned for information crimes: bugging and the attempt to cover up bugging, an illegal pursuit of information and an illegal attempt to conceal information. Nixon was guilty of those crimes and deserved to be evicted from the White House. But those crimes were not a freak occurrence, not just an isolated, personal aberration that can be attributed to what Allen Ginsberg called

> *Nixon's brain Presidential cranium case spying thru binoculars from the Paranoia Smog Factory's East Wing.*

Nixon's Watergate, like Nixon's war, was a symptom of a more general problem with the niche itself, a problem that has still not been solved but has instead intensified.

Watergate was what Haldeman christened at one point "a problem of knowledge," and the nature of that problem is indicated by the contrast between Louis Mitelberg's cartoon (figure 6) and Ranan Lurie's (figure 8). Lurie's journalists heroically fight for the public's "right to know," but Mitelberg's president villainously listens to what he has no right to know. In fact, what America demanded, in the end what it was given by the unanimous Supreme Court decision in *United States v. Nixon*, was the right to listen in on what Nixon himself said when he thought no one outside the room could hear him; it is as though the direction of the signal, in Mitelberg's cartoon, had been reversed, enabling the entire country to listen to the private contents of Nixon's mind.

That is, of course, exactly what the readers of autobiographies and biographies want: they want to get into someone's mind, to see the naked body hiding behind the official seal. In Carl Bernstein and Bob Woodward's account of the end of Nixon's presidency, *The*

Final Days, readers are treated to an account of Nixon's sex life—or rather, lack of a sex life—with his wife. (Would you want *your* sex life discussed in a nationwide best-seller? Would you like the president to know what *you* do in bed?)

The problem of biography is a problem of knowledge. People as different as T. S. Eliot and J. D. Salinger have tried to prevent the future from writing their biographies, and Nixon for the last twenty years of his life fought in the courts—for the most part successfully—to deny public access to his presidential papers. The public wanted to know everything about Nixon precisely because he was notorious; in that, he was no different from any other celebrity hounded by the media. But what made Nixon notorious was his own desire to know everything about others.

The very technologies and institutions that enable us to preserve artificial memory to an unprecedented and still accelerating degree also make it more and more impossible to preserve privacy. In the old Soviet Union, the state apparatus systematically invaded the privacy of its citizens (to the limited extent that an incompetent monopoly could). In the new United States, the assault on privacy has been decentralized, making it impossible to control the proliferation of efficient information predators. Far too many people and organizations find information on our personal lives too valuable to forgo. Targeted marketing—the new tool of successful capitalism and campaigning—depends upon getting a message to the consumers/constituents most susceptible to it. And the information on our personal lives that helps others identify us as targets is relentlessly and continuously accumulated by artificial memory systems: telephones, voice mail, e-mail, credit cards, automated financial transactions, the computers of libraries, hospitals, pharmacies, video stores, cable television networks. Any determined hacker could find out almost anything about any one of us.

Total recall gives us total access to the past. But when does the past begin? In "The Dead Past," Isaac Asimov imagines the future development of a science of chronoscopy, which enables historians and archaeologists to "see" into a targeted moment in the past. But such idle academic curiosity does not exhaust the potential of the device. "What happens if you focus the chronoscope in the past of one-hundredth of a second ago? Aren't you watching the present?" What happens when you develop home chronoscopes as cheap and portable as personal computers? Asimov's character warns, "There will be no such thing as privacy." As Frankenstein Sr. discovers, a life without privacy, a totally accessible life, is totally vulnerable. In David Brin's *Earth*, a future only fifty years away has not invented chronoscopes; it has simply miniaturized video equipment to the point where people can automatically videotape everything they see. Crimes like the Los Angeles police beating of Rodney King are not videotaped by chance; everybody, everywhere, everytime, is recorded. The human world becomes totally visible to itself, and the last world war is an attack on corporate secrecy, epitomized by the bank vaults of Switzerland.

Nixon is worth remembering because in Watergate and in the subsequent biographical pursuit of Nixon himself, the right to know fought the right to privacy. That war, unlike the cold war, is not over; it has only begun. Our futures depend upon its outcome.

What we need to remember about Nixon is the Vietnam War and Watergate. In both cases, his actions exposed a fundamental danger in the political niche we inhabit. The American political environment made his crimes possible, but it did not make them inevitable. In both cases, Nixon refused to let go when he should have: of the war, of members of his staff who had broken the law, of information that the public and the courts had a right to know. The resilience of which he so often bragged, the engine that powered his rehabilitations, was also a refusal to let go—to reconsider, confess, and ask for forgiveness. He prided himself on his willingness to take risks, but he refused to risk the personal vulnerability of ever letting go.

This refusal was not just a personal failure; it destroyed lives and threatened to destroy a democracy that had lasted two hundred years. Bob Dole, who now weeps for Nixon and berates "the debasement of culture," once described a newspaper photograph of Presidents Carter, Ford, and Nixon as "See No Evil, Hear No Evil, and

Evil." You must remember this: Nixon was evil. If we forget that, his crimes will cease to be crimes; evil will become instead the way of the world. Our sense of right and wrong, after all, is not innate. Moses had to bring the Ten Commandments down from the mountain; they were written on tablets because God had not hardwired them into our souls. Children know right from wrong only because adults tell them which is which, and different adults define the terms differently, and some adults impress their definitions upon children more successfully than others. *Morality is a recollection.*

Nixon is dead. But in Philip Roth's satire *Our Gang*, published in 1971, even death does not put an end to Nixon's political career. In hell, Nixon campaigns to unseat the incumbent Satan, appealing for the votes of "My fellow Fallen" and citing "the Job case" as evidence of "secret meetings" between Satan and God.

Hell is, of course, a memory of the future. That future has been remembered in many ways. In Thomas Middleton's 1624 masterpiece *A Game at Chess*—which features, prophetically, both "the White House" and "Watergate"—hell is just an overcrowded bag into which the damned, like captured chess pieces, are tossed and chaotically keep tumbling, scratching, farting, struggling for advantage. Middleton's shapeless clutter is the opposite of Dante's superstructured hierarchical *Inferno*, but for both writers—as for Roth—the kingdom of darkness is where your political enemies spend eternity.

Politics is always moralized, and hell materializes morality. Morality becomes, in our memories of hell, a physical stimulus, as substantial as the electric shock administered to a rat who has chosen the wrong path in a maze constructed by an intelligence it cannot comprehend or overpower. God is a mechanism for translating culture into biology. His hell and heaven turn a recollection of what should be into the palpability of what is.

I promised that this book would be a collection of stories that we tell each other about the past. The story of Richard Nixon reminds us that culture cannot be divorced from morality. Culture could, in fact, be summarized as an effort to reconcile the physical and the ethical. Stimulus—the jolt of the outside world upon us—is amoral; it is biological; it is not uniquely human; it measures the great. Morality, by contrast, measures the good. Greatness and goodness do not, alas, always coincide. Undeniably, Nixon powerfully impacted upon his world, but his most memorable actions were selfish, corrupting, destructive. This discrepancy is not confined to Nixon. Mark Twain observed that "wit and indecency" are "often better literature-preservers than holiness." Buddhists believed that Murasaki Shikibu, the author of the great *Tale of Genji*, belonged in hell; Darwin, too, has often been nominated for damnation. The whole debate over the "political correctness" of the traditional curriculum boils down to a single question: are the "Great Books" also *good* books? Do we want to endorse and perpetuate the particular values they recollect?

Perhaps the most sophisticated and admired academic analysis of "the problem of literary canon formation," John Guillory's prizewinning *Cultural Capital*, dismisses much of the contemporary debate as a regrettable "fall into moralism." Guillory's attempt to talk about culture without talking about ethics is typical of the academic world in particular, and of the political left generally. It cannot be done. The building blocks of culture—all those individual stories of a death, a survivor, a struggle—are inextricably ethical, bound up with memories of duty to the dead, of duty to the future, of moral obligations to tell the truth, defeat lies, and give people what they deserve. Culture is selective, and selection involves choice, and choices are the subject matter of ethics. Literary criticism, after all, is a form of *criticism*.

Nixon is dead, but Nixonism—the attack on democracy in the name of morality—flourishes. To act as though culture were morally neutral is to surrender to others the arsenal of ethics. If we do not define the good, someone else will define it for us, and impose the memory of their definition upon our future. If we let Nixonism define value, then that future will indeed be hell.

Stone Memories.

We are a psychic process which we do not control, or only partly direct. Consequently, we cannot have any final judgment about ourselves or our lives.

CARL JUNG

Rebecca and I visited Florence in September 1975. We were moving from Kansas to England, we had no children to complicate our itinerary, and since the academic year at Cambridge would not start until October, Rebecca suggested that we spend a month in Europe. Our parents couldn't help us organize the trip, so I called up my high school French teacher, Mrs. Grauman (a former fighter in the Resistance, who chaperoned me on my first antiwar rally) and asked her advice. She said, "Don't try to see everything. Pick three cities, and spend at least a week in each." We selected Amsterdam, Paris, and Florence. We visited the usual collections and collected the usual memorabilia. In Florence, I expected to be stimulated by Michelangelo's *David*, and I was. The photographs I had seen of the little killer of giant aliens had not conveyed the polished poise, the larger-than-life power, of the marble original.

In one of the most famous German poems of the twentieth century, Rainer Maria Rilke evocatively describes an "Archaic Torso of Apollo." The sonnet ends with an abrupt, simple, seeming non sequitur: "You must change your life." Michelangelo's *David* stirred me, but it did not change my life. Instead, what I remember most from Florence—indeed, from that whole month in Europe—is another sculpture by Michelangelo, one I did not expect to see, one I had never even heard of. The placard in the Galleria dell'Accademia di Belle Arti described it as *Atlas*; I have since learned that this identification is disputed and that the work belongs to a group of four statues of "slaves." These figures belong to Michelangelo's work, never completed, on a magnificent tomb for Pope Julius II, the man who had commissioned the frescoes for the Sistine Chapel ceiling and the plans for a new church to commemorate the martyrdom of St. Peter.

In 1975 I knew nothing about the history of the statue; my ignorance simply ran up against the rock of Michelangelo's genius. *Atlas* made *David* seem, by comparison, a glib half-truth. What filled me with wonder, what I remember, is the way half of a muscled figure seems to be emerging from, or trapped within, dead rock— twisting out of the marble's immobility, or bent down by its weight, but in either case, embodying terrifically compressed energies. I kept walking around and around the statue, following its unwinding striving. Flesh and rock, organism and environment, work and niche, stability and instability interpenetrate. Is this a slave or a god? Alien or human? Fossil or embryo? Past or future?

Culture is unfinished.

Acknowledgments

I remember

Rebecca Germonprez, who is everywhere in this book, as she is everywhere in my life

Loretta Chasse, my mother, who taught me to read and to feel

Isaac, Josh, Jessie, and Michael, my children, who saturate my present and into whose future I bequeath my past

Paul Golob, my editor at Basic Books, who has confirmed all my theories about the cultural importance of invisible editors

Gabriele Pantucci, my agent, who negotiated the complicated institutional transactions that enabled me to put my thoughts into your hands

John Burt, Mary Campbell, Eugene Goodheart, Karen Klein, Alan Levitan, and Susan Staves, my former faculty colleagues at Brandeis University, for stimuli particular and general

Celia Daileader, John Lavagnino, Brandie Siegfried, and Claudia Wazkis, former graduate students at Brandeis, who all taught me things that have found their way here

Marcie Hess, my administrative assistant at the University of Alabama, who made several emergency contributions to this book before I had even met her; Wayne Chandler, my research assistant, who has checked scores of references for me; and Philip Beidler, my colleague, who reminded me of some Nixon memories I had mislaid

Randy McLeod, who commissioned the work that eventually became chapter 9

Deniz Sengel and Barbara Smith, friends, who incidentally taught me something about Turkey and *Fantasia*

Sarah Stickle, Randall Pink, John Roberts, Cindy Buck, Michael Wilde, Liz Cunningham, Elliott Beard, and Roberto de Vicq de Cumptich, through whose capable and careful hands this text successively passed, on its way from my memory to yours

Ralph Galen, our Unitarian minister, who keeps reminding me of the big questions inextricably connected to the little ones

I remember

Index of
Works Cited

Index of Persons
and Subjects